FOUNDATION PRESS

ENVIRO[N]

LA[W]

RCRA, CERCLA, AND THE MANAGEMENT OF HAZARDOUS WASTE

by

JOHN S. APPLEGATE
Walter W. Foskett Professor of Law
Indiana University School of Law–Bloomington

JAN G. LAITOS
John A. Carver, Jr., Professor of Law
University of Denver Sturm College of Law

TURNING POINT SERIES®

FOUNDATION PRESS
2006

Turning Point Series is a registered trademark used herein under license.

© 2006 By FOUNDATION PRESS
        395 Hudson Street
        New York, NY 10014
        Phone Toll Free 1–877–888–1330
        Fax (212) 367–6799
        foundation-press.com
Printed in the United States of America

ISBN–13: 978–1–58778–718–8
ISBN–10: 1–58778–718–0

TEXT IS PRINTED ON 10% POST CONSUMER RECYCLED PAPER

TURNING POINT SERIES

CIVIL PROCEDURE

Civil Procedure: Class Actions by Linda S. Mullenix, University of Texas (Available 2006)

Civil Procedure: Economics of Civil Procedure by Robert G. Bone, Boston University (2003)

Civil Procedure: Preclusion in Civil Actions by David L. Shapiro, Harvard University (2001)

Civil Procedure: Territorial Jurisdiction and Venue by Kevin M. Clermont, Cornell (1999)

CONSTITUTIONAL LAW

Constitutional Law: The Commerce Clause by Dan T. Coenen, University of Georgia (2004)

Constitutional Law: Equal Protection by Louis M. Seidman, Georgetown University (2003)

Constitutional Law: The Religion Clauses by Daniel O. Conkle, Indiana University, Bloomington (2003)

CRIMINAL LAW

Criminal Law: Model Penal Code by Markus D. Dubber, State University of New York, Buffalo (2002)

FEDERAL COURTS

Federal Courts: Habeas Corpus by Larry W. Yackle, Boston University (2003)

INTERNATIONAL LAW

International Law: United States Foreign Relations Law by Phillip R. Trimble, UCLA (2002)

JURY AND TRIAL PRACTICE

The Jury Process by Nancy S. Marder, Chicago-Kent College of Law (2005)

LEGISLATION

Legislation: Statutory Interpretation: Twenty Questions by Kent R. Greenawalt, Columbia University (1999)

PROPERTY

Property: Takings by David Dana, Northwestern University and Thomas Merrill, Northwestern University (2002)

CORPORATE/SECURITIES

Securities Law: Insider Trading by Stephen Bainbridge, UCLA (1999)

TORTS

Torts: Proximate Cause by Joseph A. Page, Georgetown University (2003)

For Jesse, Jamey, and Gillian
J.S.A.

For Erik and Vicki
J.G.L.

*

PREFACE

Environmental law can be divided into a number of major areas of regulation and study: pollution control, environmental impact assessment, natural resources, wildlife protection, dangerous chemicals and other toxic substances, and hazardous wastes. Our present concern is with the last of these areas, which is defined by the human and ecological toxicity of waste materials and the environmental fate of such materials when deposited in or on the land. Two complex and heavily litigated federal statutes—the Resource Conservation and Recovery Act (RCRA) and the Comprehensive Environmental Response, Compensation, and Liability Act (CERCLA, or Superfund)—dominate the management of hazardous waste, and they reflect the two major management activities—disposal and remediation, respectively—that environmental law addresses.

RCRA creates a comprehensive, complex, and occasionally mystifying regulatory scheme for the handling of hazardous waste from its creation until its eventual disposal, as well as for the clean-up of unsuccessful disposal at RCRA-regulated facilities. The goal of the statute is to minimize human exposure to hazardous waste by reducing the amount of waste created and by assuring the long-term isolation of the waste that is generated. CERCLA, on the other hand, creates a regulatory scheme for remediating sites at which hazardous wastes have been released into the environment, deploying federal response authorities and a tort-like legal framework for liability for the costs of remediation. While CERCLA's remediation standards have largely escaped judicial review (because the statute precludes pre-enforcement review), the relatively terse liability provisions have necessitated, as Congress intended, the creation of a large and complex federal common law of hazardous waste liability. Together, these statutes create the potential for federal regulation of hazardous waste from its generation, to its initial disposition, to its subsequent emergence into the environment. Such "cradle-to-grave" coverage is surely the intention of the statutes, but the reality has not always matched the intention, as we will see.

The management of hazardous waste has special significance for both law students and environmental law practitioners. The amount of regulatory and enforcement effort that has gone into RCRA and CERCLA far exceeds that of many environmental statutes. This is both the cause and consequence of the sheer number of individuals and businesses that are affected or potentially affected by RCRA and CERCLA, which is much greater those affected by other, relatively specialized environmental statutes. Not coincidentally, the volume of litigation and judicial interpretation of RCRA and CERCLA dominates the field, and a lawyer who specializes in environmental law is often in effect practicing RCRA and CERCLA law.

We begin with a chapter on the physical, toxicological, economic, and political characteristics of the hazardous waste problem. These are the problems that the statutes seek to remedy, and they are the constraints within which both statutes must operate. The remainder of the text is divided into two main parts, reflecting the difference between the disposal and remediation problems and the two key statutes. While there is some conceptual overlap between the two, RCRA and CERCLA establish distinct, internally coherent regulatory schemes that are largely understood and administered as separate entities.

The regulation of hazardous waste, as used in this book, refers to the management of dangerous substances in or on the land. This definition includes two important limitations, which act to constrain the scope of our concern and also constrain the effectiveness of the existing regulatory regime. First, the law regulates waste, as opposed to useful products. In RCRA, we see this limitation mainly in the need to distinguish between waste and recycled materials. However, more fundamentally, the focus on the disposal of waste and the post-disposal contamination of land commits us to end-of-the-pipe solutions to waste generation and management. That is, the statutes address waste issues at the end of the process that generates the waste, rather than at the beginning—a strategy which has obvious drawbacks. Second, the RCRA-CERCLA regulatory regime is, with a few exceptions, limited by its terms to discharges to the land, as opposed to the air or water. Obviously, the form of waste, and hence the medium into which it is discharged, is highly mutable; the same waste materials can be burned to generate air discharges, or they can be dumped into a body of water, or they can leak into groundwater. The regulatory structure will need to assure, to the extent possible, that restrictions on one medium do not simply result in shifting pollution to another.

Finally, your authors want to emphasize that the purpose of this volume is not comprehensive coverage of RCRA and CERCLA. For one thing, it would take far more space than this book allows.[1] Nor yet is it a brief outline of the structure and highlights of these statutes, as these are available in other formats. Rather, our goal is to introduce the key legal and policy issues that these statutes raise, with an eye to helping the reader to understand the problems that the drafters of the statutes and regulations, and the courts interpreting them, faced. Many of these problems are essentially open-ended, that is, there is no single way to address them that satisfies all of the statutory goals. They remain, therefore, important points for the continuing development of the law through legislation, regulation, and judicial review.

---

[1] RCRA and CERCLA are covered in far more detail in JOHN S. APPLEGATE, JAN G. LAITOS & CELIA M. CAMPBELL–MOHN, THE REGULATION OF TOXIC SUBSTANCES AND HAZARDOUS WASTES (2000), ch. 9–14 (hereinafter CASEBOOK). The leading treatise is DONALD W. STEVER, LAW OF CHEMICAL REGULATION AND HAZARDOUS WASTE (4 vols., 1986–1995).

ABOUT THE AUTHORS

John S. Applegate is the Executive Associate Dean for Academic Affairs and Walter W. Foskett Professor of Law at Indiana University School of Law–Bloomington. His scholarship and teaching in environmental law have focused on the regulation of toxic and radioactive chemicals, and he is co-author of *The Regulation of Toxic Substances and Hazardous Wastes* (Foundation 2000). Since 1993, he has served in several capacities as an advisor to the U.S. Department of Energy on the environmental consequences of nuclear weapons production, including chairing a citizens advisory board at the Fernald site in Ohio and membership on DOE advisory and National Academy of Sciences committees. He is a scholar-member of the Center for Progressive Reform. Before joining the Indiana faculty, Professor Applegate taught at the University of Cincinnati College of Law, was an associate with Covington & Burling in Washington, D.C., and a law clerk to Hon. Edward S. Smith of the U.S. Court of Appeals for the Federal Circuit. He holds a B.A. from Haverford College and a J.D. from Harvard Law School. Professor Applegate thanks Professor Robert Lee, the Centre for Business Relationships, Accountability, Sustainability, and Society, and the ESRC–SSRC for an extremely congenial month at

Cardiff University, Wales, in which to complete his
portion of this book.

Jan G. Laitos holds the John A. Carver, Jr.,
Chair, and is the Director of the nationally ranked
Environmental and Natural Resources Law Pro-
gram at the University of Denver Sturm College of
Law. He is a Reporter for the Planning and Environ-
mental Law Review, published by the American
Planning Association, a regional board member of
the Rocky Mountain Land Use Institute, the Legal
Analyst for KUSA 9 News, and Trustee of the Rocky
Mountain Mineral Law Foundation. He was Vice
Chair of the Colorado Water Quality Control Com-
mission. In 1996, Professor Laitos was given the
University of Denver's Distinguished Teaching
Award, and in 2005, he was selected a "DU Law
Star." Prior to joining the faculty at the law school,
he was the law clerk to the Chief Justice of the Colorado Supreme Court, and an attorney with the Office of Legal Counsel within the U.S. Department of
Justice. He has written and had published nearly 40
law review articles on natural resources, environmental law, and protection of private property, and
he is the author of nine books, published by West,
Foundation Press, and Aspen. Professor Laitos received his B.A. from Yale University, J.D. from the
University of Colorado, and S.J.D. from the University of Wisconsin. Professor Laitos would like to acknowledge the support and financial assistance provided by the Rocky Mountain Mineral Law
Foundation. The Foundation has supported several

of his books on natural resources and environmental law. Professor Laitos would also like to thank Rachael Reiss, a 2004 graduate of the University of Denver Sturm College of Law, who helped him to edit and update the chapter on CERCLA. Prof. Laitos would also like to acknowledge the support provided this book by Steve Errick, who early on saw a need for a textual and analytical summary of RCRA and CERCLA.

*

TABLE OF CONTENTS

FOUNDATION PRESS

ENVIRONMENTAL LAW:

RCRA, CERCLA, AND THE MANAGEMENT OF HAZARDOUS WASTE

*

CHAPTER I

THE HAZARDOUS WASTE PROBLEM

1. A Cautionary Tale

There is no better way to understand the hazardous waste disposal problem than to examine what can go wrong when the waste is mismanaged. At Love Canal, in the city of Niagara Falls, New York, much did go wrong.[1] Declared a state and federal health emergency in 1978, this dumpsite was a witch's brew of toxic chemicals, including pesticides, produced between 1942 and 1954 by the Hooker Chemical Company and dumped into an abandoned canal on the outskirts of the city. Hooker itself was an apt representative of the rise of the hazardous waste problem. It was a creature of the Twentieth Century, beginning its existence with traditional chemical products, then moving after the Second World War to manufacturing highly hazardous chemicals in vast quantities:

> Hooker was formed in 1905, and its Niagara Falls plant began operating the following year. By 1910, the Niagara Falls plant was producing 20

1. *See* U.S. v. Hooker Chemicals & Plastics Corp., 850 F.Supp. 993 (W.D.N.Y. 1994).

1

tons of caustic soda and 42 tons of bleach per day....

* * *

The Company grew substantially during World War II because of the demands of the United States government and defense contractors. From 1940 until 1953, its sales grew from $7.1 million to $38.7 million. This dramatic growth continued, and by 1970 its annual sales reached $450 million.

Until Hooker began its wartime production, it was able to sewer and dispose of chemicals on-site. Increased volume of chemical waste, combined with growing opposition to open dumping in streams, forced Hooker to consider alternative means of waste disposal. Incineration could not handle the anticipated heavy waste disposal demands. In-ground disposal developed as a viable alternative.[2]

Love Canal became the repository for these waste products. As the city of Niagara Falls grew, however, the area around Love Canal became residential. Hooker was not oblivious to the dangers of its wastes. It created several cells within the canal ditch, and the canal itself had been dug in relatively nonporous clay. Nevertheless, the nature of the material disposed and the various dumping practices resulted in exposure of the local population to the waste or waste products throughout its operations. Even during the period of its active use and

2. *Id.* at 1004.

relative isolation from residential areas, there were frequent fires and explosions. Distinct chemical odors were emitted from it. Two chemicals disposed there were known to mix to create the infamous World War I poison gas, phosgene. Only a fence separated this material from the public, and the fence was apparently only incompletely effective, especially when material was ejected in an explosion. Much of the waste, moreover, was liquid. While Hooker took some precautions to keep the liquid from overflowing the canal itself, it did nothing to keep it from leaching through the lining.

As use of the dumpsite wound down, Hooker sold the property to the local school district. The deed of transfer expressly noted the existence of the landfill and purported to hold Hooker harmless for any liability arising therefrom. However, this qualification was apparently quickly forgotten, because the school district promptly built an elementary school on the site for the growing local population. Worse, after the dump was closed and covered, subsidence of the surface was a constant problem (because the underlying material was heterogeneous and had not been compacted), revealing liquids, solid waste, and drums. Moreover, the water table brought disposed material to the surface and contaminated the soil above the site. Finally, the construction of a nearby highway disrupted the hydrology of the area, and waste products not only surfaced but seeped into neighboring basements.

The resulting outcry in 1978 and 1979 encouraged passage of the remedial CERCLA legislation in

1980, but the story of Love Canal has lessons for initial waste disposal, as well. There was little or no examination of the physical and hydrological features of the site, only minimal preparation of the site for the long-term isolation of wastes, no assessment of the appropriateness of the waste for in-ground disposal, no long-term maintenance of the site, and only the most rudimentary notification to subsequent buyers or neighbors of the existence and nature of the hazard. The waste materials themselves were not recorded in any systematic fashion, they were disposed irrespective of their compatibility with land disposal techniques or with each other, and there was no effort to pretreat the wastes to reduce their inherent toxicity, volume, or mobility in the environment. Nothing was known of the toxic effects (other than obvious acute effects) of the chemicals. These were all fundamental problems with the disposal of the Hooker wastes, and RCRA seeks to address them all. Following disposal, there was no assurance that Hooker or its successor would be in a financial position to clean up the mess it created—or, indeed, that it would be responsible for cleaning it up—or that the state and federal government would have the funds or even the authority to undertake remediation if private action was not forthcoming. This became the impetus behind the enactment of CERCLA.

2. *The Hazardous Waste Problem*

Unfortunately, Love Canal was by no means unique. Enterprises and individuals in the United States dispose of more than 10 billion tons of solid waste each year from households, industries, mining, and other activities.[3] The vast majority (about 90%) is "solid waste," that is, waste material without especially dangerous characteristics. In a recent report, EPA found that 236 million tons of municipal solid waste (that is, general solid waste, not including industrial, construction, or hazardous waste) were generated in 2003. The amount disposed in landfills has decreased since 1990, to 131 million tons (recycling, composting, and incineration account for the remainder), and the number of landfills has dropped precipitously.[4] However, the remaining 10% or so that is formally classified as "hazardous waste" amounts to an enormous volume of potentially very dangerous material. The waste problem therefore includes both non-hazardous ("solid") and hazardous waste. Both must be managed in some way, and there is often no absolute distinction between hazardous and non-hazardous waste. It is a difficult problem to solve because our industrial and consumer society is truly built on the production of large amounts of waste. Thus, the economic impact of waste management, or of reori-

3. *See generally* Marcia E. Williams & Jonathan Z. Cannon, *Rethinking the Resource Conservation and Recovery Act of the 1990s*, 21 ENVTL. L. REP. 10063 (1991); William F. Pedersen, Jr., *The Future of Federal Solid Waste Regulation*, 16 COLUM. J. ENVTL. L. 109 (1991).

4. EPA, Municipal Solid Waste Generation, Recycling, and Disposal in the United States: Facts and Figures for 2003, available at http://www.epa.gov/msw/pubs/msw05rpt.pdf (last visited Aug. 6, 2005). *See also* John C. Dernbach, *The Unfocused Regulation of Toxic and Hazardous Pollutants*, 21 HARV. ENVTL. L. REV. 1, 10 (1997).

enting production and consumption patterns to reduce waste generation, are exceptionally high.

Moreover, because it is so heterogeneous, even solid waste presents a wide variety of hazards. The hazards we most associate with garbage deposited in "sanitary landfills" (*i.e.*, the local dump) are biological: pathogens associated with decomposing organic matter and with the animals and birds that are attracted to such sites. The enormous growth of industrial waste raised the new specter of chemical hazards, though chemical hazards are by no means limited to industrial waste. Household waste includes things like batteries, used oil, household chemicals, and computer parts, all of which contain significant amounts of heavy metals and other toxic compounds. Nevertheless, the bulk of hazardous materials are generated by industries like chemical manufacturing, petroleum and coal products, waste treatment and disposal (ironically), and metal manufacturing and metalworking.

The most prominent danger from such materials is the induction of cancer. Cancer has been the focal concern of the environmental regulation of chemicals and chemical waste for nearly three decades. It is actually a suite of many diseases that have in common the uncontrolled growth of dysfunctional cells which interfere with the normal operation of organs and metabolism. Cancerous cells can also metastasize, spreading from one body system to another. Not all cancers are equally fatal, in that some are more readily curable than others, but it is nevertheless an extremely serious—indeed, a dreaded—disease. Not only is the public justifiably concerned about cancer, but cancer is also a very sensitive marker of exposure to toxic substances. The exact mechanisms of chemical induction of cancers are not fully understood, but most cancer-causing agents (carcinogens) are thought to have no threshold below which they pose no risk. In other words, even at extremely low doses there is a risk, albeit a low risk, that cancer will result from exposure. It is impossible to say with carcinogens, then, that there is a "safe" level of exposure.

3. Risk and Waste Management

Cancer is the most important *hazard* posed by toxic chemicals. The *risk* posed by a given chemical is a function of its toxicity (how potent a carcinogen it is) and the level of exposure to the chemical. A higher level of toxic potency or a higher level of exposure will result in a higher risk.[5] Conversely, to

5. This concept of environmental risk was "codified" by a National Academy of Sciences report (known as the Red Book), and it and has been widely if not universally followed. NATIONAL RESEARCH COUNCIL, RISK ASSESSMENT IN THE FEDERAL GOVERNMENT: MANAGING THE PROCESS (1983). To be more specific, the Red Book divided the risk regulation process into two large parts, a descriptive "risk assessment" and a prescriptive "risk management." Risk assessment, a largely scientific process, is comprised of hazard identification, which examines the inherent qualities of a substance (*e.g.*, does it cause cancer?), its potency or dose-response profile (how much of the substance causes what level of cancer risk?), the exposure assessment (how much of the substance reaches human or ecological receptors?), and finally risk characterization, which is the product of dose-response and exposure. Risk management combines the results of risk assessment with considerations of policy, cost, social and economic factors,

reduce risk, one must either reduce the toxic potency of the chemical in some way or reduce the amount of it to which people are exposed. Risk is an important measure of environmental compliance under both RCRA and CERCLA. Because it is often difficult or impossible to reduce toxicity (since toxicity is an inherent characteristic of a chemical), we will find that these statutes focus on means of controlling exposure. And this is a considerable challenge, because hazardous wastes come in both solid and liquid forms (and contained gases) and they have different properties as they move through the environment from their source to a human or ecological receptor. Moreover, unlike biological wastes, chemical wastes retain their hazardous character indefinitely—they are "persistent"—and so a strategy of isolation must be prepared for the long haul.

The single most important thing to remember about hazardous waste management is that it involves the deliberate introduction or retention of toxic material in the environment. While some hazardous wastes can be destroyed, many cannot (elements like lead and mercury, for example) and the destruction of other materials poses its own threats (for example, incineration of dioxins and PCBs). There are, in fact, only a few things that can be done to manage waste. As we see in Figure I–1, the first level of options is isolation in the environment, for instance, in a landfill; doing nothing with it, and anything else that the decisionmaker is permitted or required to take into account.

that is, simply releasing it into the environment; or treating it in some way. Putting time, effort, and money into treatment only makes sense, of course, if it gains something in terms of the three possible end states: destruction, isolation, or release. Thus, treatment that reduces the volume of the waste or its mobility in the environment—both of which aid in isolation—or which reduces its hazardous characteristics—makes it safer to release—may well be worth the effort. Treatment, however, often results in multiple fractions of the waste, some of which may have been destroyed, some still dangerous and requiring isolation, and some "clean" and appropriate for release into the environment. Finally, it is important to remember that isolation (and certainly isolation on a less heroic scale than the deep geologic repositories for highly radioactive waste) is exceedingly unlikely to be permanent over the very long term. Indeed, ironically, the better we isolate the waste from the environment, the better we assure its ability to outlive its repository.

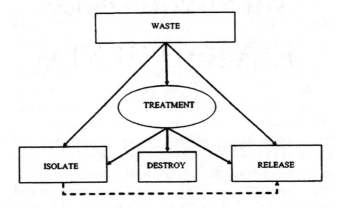

Fig. I–1. Waste Management Options

The goals, strategies, and specific provisions of RCRA and CERCLA are best understood against the physical reality that very little hazardous waste can be destroyed and that the remainder must go somewhere in the environment; moreover, that "somewhere" may in the long run be the equivalent of release into the environment.

CHAPTER II

DISPOSAL: THE RESOURCE CONSERVATION AND RECOVERY ACT

RCRA and CERCLA represent a time line of waste management. Working backwards, CERCLA deals with unsuccessful waste disposal that has resulted in the uncontrolled release of hazardous substances into the environment. RCRA seeks to avoid that eventuality by aggressively regulating the handling of waste from its generation through to its disposal. RCRA concentrates on a particular type of waste—hazardous waste—despite the fact that it represents a small portion of the total waste disposal problem, and the disposal restrictions are particularly strict. These restrictions contribute not only to the statutory effort to avoid future Love Canals, but also to the other ostensible goal of the statute, pollution prevention. However, while RCRA attempts to discourage the generation of waste in the first place, it does not do so directly, through control of manufacturing processes. Rather, it operates indirectly through strict waste management. Accordingly, our consideration of RCRA will, like the statute itself, focus primarily on the handling and disposal of hazardous waste.[1]

1. Convenient quick-reference guides to RCRA include JOHN W. TEETS *ET AL.*, RCRA: RESOURCE CONSERVATION AND RECOVERY ACT

A. Introduction to RCRA

Statutes, like nations and individuals, are the products and the captives of their histories. RCRA is no exception. Its goals, coverage, strategies, and structure cannot be understood without knowing where the statute came from and what Congress was trying to accomplish. Therefore, we begin with a brief history of the statute and consideration of its goals. We then turn to the structure of the regulatory regime established by the statute. This is unusually important in RCRA, because the structure accounts for one of the most distinctive features of RCRA: an all-or-nothing regulatory scheme in which waste products are either regulated extremely intensively or almost not at all. The all-or-nothing quality goes far to explaining the areas of legal contention in RCRA and to identifying the aspects of RCRA that are most ripe for reform.[2]

(ABA Best Practice Series) (2003), and THEODORE L. GARRETT, ED., THE RCRA PRACTICE MANUAL (2d ed. 2004). EPA, RCRA Orientation Manual (2003) (hereinafter RCRA Orientation Manual) is a detailed but quite accessible guide to the operation of the statute. It can be viewed on or downloaded from the web, http://www.epa.gov/epaoswer/general/orientat/ (last visited May 16, 2005). Useful overview articles include Randolph L. Hill, *An Overview of RCRA: The "Mind–Numbing" Provisions of the Most Complicated Environmental Statute*, 21 ENVTL. L. REP. 10254 (1991); Pedersen, *supra*; John C. Chambers & Mary S. McCullough, *From Cradle to Grave: An Historical Perspective of RCRA*, 10 NATURAL RES. & ENVT. 21 (Fall 1995).

2. Valuable policy analyses of RCRA include Pedersen, *supra*; Office of Technology Assessment, Technologies and Management Strategies for Hazardous Waste Control (1983); EPA, The Na-

1. History

Congress first addressed the problem of land-disposed waste in the Solid Waste Disposal Act (SWDA) of 1965.[3] The SWDA reflected the movement, led by First Lady Lady Bird Johnson, for beautification of an increasingly polluted America. The "Keep America Beautiful" campaign was characterized by anti-littering and anti-billboard laws, and the SWDA was firmly in that genre. It concentrated on the obvious aesthetic and pathogenic problems associated with trash sent to landfills. To that end, it mandated minimum safety requirements for landfills and addressed issues like incinerating waste. The federal government played a largely advisory role, as was typical of early anti-pollution legislation, and it relied entirely on the states to impose actual regulatory measures. Not surprisingly, this structure resulted in extremely uneven regulation of waste disposal.

By 1976, however, the nature of environmental legislation had changed significantly, and concerns for obvious aesthetic harm had been joined (replaced, even) by concern with environmentally induced disease and cancer in particular. The most intensely debated legislation of that year, the Toxic Substances Control Act (TSCA), focused on the carcinogenic properties of industrial chemicals.

tion's Hazardous Waste Management Program at a Crossroads: The RCRA Implementation Study (1990); EPA, RCRA Implementation Study Update: The Definition of Solid Waste (1992).

3. Chambers & McCullough, *supra*; Hill, *supra*; Williams & Cannon, *supra*.

Likewise, beautification was far from the minds of the drafters of the Resource Conservation and Recovery Act (RCRA), also enacted in 1976. Technically, RCRA is simply a set of amendments to the SWDA, but it is such a thoroughgoing revision that the hazardous waste law is universally referred to as RCRA. Together with the National Environmental Policy Act and its requirement for environmental impact statements, RCRA was one of the great sleepers of the Environmental Decade (1970–1980). It was regarded at the time of its enactment as far less significant than TSCA; in fact, TSCA has been a notable underachiever among environmental laws, and RCRA has become one of the most complex and burdensome—and necessary—elements of toxics regulation.

The movement away from concern for aesthetics and pathogenic disease was completed by the Hazardous and Solid Waste Amendments (HSWA) in 1984.[4] (The statute as a whole is still referred to as RCRA.) Between 1976 and 1984, the Love Canal episode had unfolded and major federal clean-up legislation (CERCLA) had been enacted. EPA had only begun to get busy implementing RCRA after 1980, and Congressional impatience and a series of scandals in the Reagan EPA led to the imposition of stringent and extremely detailed provisions in HSWA. The factual situation and policy choices before Congress were thoroughly laid out in a 1983

4. *See generally* RICHARD C. FORTUNA & DAVID J. LENNETT, HAZARDOUS WASTE REGULATION—THE NEW ERA: AN ANALYSIS AND GUIDE TO RCRA AND THE 1984 AMENDMENTS (1987).

report by the Office of Technology Assessment (OTA), Congress' highly respected and now-defunct policy "think tank." OTA emphasized that continued land disposal was simply putting off the present costs of properly managing hazardous waste to the future, when they would have to be dealt with— much more expensively—as clean-up under CERCLA.[5] Therefore, in addition to the permitting and tracking system, identification of solid and hazardous wastes, and design and performance standards for treatment, storage, and disposal facilities that RCRA had created, HSWA imposed stringent disposal standards and prohibitions (the land disposal restrictions (LDRs), otherwise known as the "land ban"), which required intensive treatment of virtually all hazardous wastes, as well as strict deadlines on EPA's regulation of hazardous wastes. Mindful of CERCLA, Congress wanted HSWA to *prevent* future Love Canals and Superfund sites. In fact, HSWA included specific provisions for CERCLA-like clean-up (called "corrective action") of active waste disposal sites with uncontrolled contamination.

Congress has made other, relatively minor changes to RCRA over the years. For example, it added a subtitle on medical waste,[6] enacted the related and almost entirely hortatory Pollution Prevention Act,[7] and clarified the application of RCRA to radioactive waste and to the federal govern-

5. OTA, Technologies, *supra.*

6. 42 U.S.C. §§ 6992–6992k.

7. 42 U.S.C. § 13101–13109. For more detailed discussion, *see* CASEBOOK, *supra,* ch. 14(B)(3).

ment's activities in the Federal Facilities Compliance Act.[8] A major addition in 1986 regulates underground storage tanks (USTs),[9] of which the United States has thousands upon thousands for all kinds of non-waste substances, mostly gasoline.

2. *Statutory Objectives*

The key statutory objectives of RCRA flow from its history and from the nature of hazardous waste and the hazardous waste problem. The first goal of the statute is the management of solid and especially hazardous waste to achieve *protection of human health and the environment*. If one takes Love Canal as the model of poor management, then the protectiveness goal suggests that RCRA must tackle a wide range of activities, using a range of regulatory techniques. Love Canal demonstrated the failure to locate a disposal area properly (either in terms of hydrogeology or neighboring uses), to select appropriate and compatible waste for land disposal, to stabilize or detoxify the wastes,[10] to prepare the site for short- or (especially) long-term stability, to provide for long-term maintenance, to record the nature and amounts of materials disposed, or to make any kind of financial or other provision for responsibility for harm from or clean-up of the wastes. In one way or another, RCRA tackles all of these

8.   42 U.S.C. §§ 6903(15), 6961. For discussion, *see* CASEBOOK, *supra*, ch. 12.

9.   RCRA §§ 9001–9010, 42 U.S.C. §§ 6991–6991i.

10.   The Love Canal wastes, it has to be observed, exhibited every one of the RCRA hazard categories. They were corrosive, reactive, flammable, and toxic.

problems, seeking to assure that, to the extent possible, hazardous wastes are safety placed into the environment.

The second principal statutory objective is *pollution prevention and waste minimization,* originally couched as "resource recovery" (in the sense of avoiding running out of scarce resources and the energy required to produce them). In the years since RCRA's enactment, however, this goal came to focus more on recycling as a means of minimizing the amount of solid waste going into landfills and of hazardous waste that needs to be isolated from the environment. It also came to be recognized that by far the most effective way to avoid the uncontrolled release of hazardous waste into the environment is to avoid producing the waste in the first place, by altering production processes or other industrial and commercial practices. However, while RCRA takes the pollution prevention goal seriously, it is extremely limited in its tools. Apart from requirements that waste minimization plans be in place,[11] it does not regulate industrial production processes directly, because this would have been regarded as a major incursion into private industrial policy.[12] (Recall that TSCA, which does regulate useful chemi-

11. RCRA §§ 3002(a)(6) (generator permits), 3005(h) (TSDF permits), 42 U.S.C. §§ 6922(a)(6), 6925(h).

12. For an excellent discussion of the difficulties of "management-based regulation," *see* Cary Coglianese & David Lazer, *Management-Based Regulation: Prescribing Private Management to Achieve Public Goals,* 37 L. & SOCIETY REV. 691 (2003); Manik Roy, *Pollution Prevention, Organizational Culture, and Social Learning,* 2 ENVTL. L. 203 (1992). *See also* Office of Technology Assessment, From Pollution to Prevention (1987).

cals, was the controversial enactment of 1976, while RCRA was regarded as innocuous. Even today, the Pollution Prevention Act, which addresses production processes directly, is essentially advisory.) Thus, despite some contemporary rhetoric about RCRA not being just an end-of-the-pipe statute, that is precisely what it is: it seeks to achieve pollution prevention and waste minimization by increasing enormously the cost and difficulty of disposing of hazardous waste. And, in fairness, it has not been ineffective. If the numbers of generators and handlers of hazardous waste are an indication, in 1980 there were 50,000 generators and 30,000 handlers of 3 million tons of hazardous wastes, including 1000 disposal impoundments. By 1999, there were only 20,000 generators, 2,000 handling facilities, 1.2 million tons of hazardous waste, and only 50 impoundments.[13]

To accomplish this objective through largely end-of-the-pipe controls, RCRA adopts a strategy of *cradle-to-grave waste management*. From the moment that hazardous waste is generated, the generator, all subsequent handlers, and the eventual disposer must keep careful records of its source, content, volume, disposition, and other relevant information through a system of manifests that accompany the waste. (*See* Fig. II–1.) Otherwise, RCRA has relatively little to say about generators and less about transporters (transportation safety is left to the

13. EPA, The National Biennial RCRA Hazardous Waste Report (Based on 2001 Data), National Analysis (2003), available at http://www.epa.gov/epaoswer/hazwaste/data/brs01/index.htm (last visited, July 18, 2005).

Department of Transportation), though they must keep records and, depending on the amount of hazardous waste involved, identify themselves, and make reports to EPA. RCRA's main focus is treatment, storage, and disposal (TSD) and the TSD facilities (TSDFs) that undertake these activities.

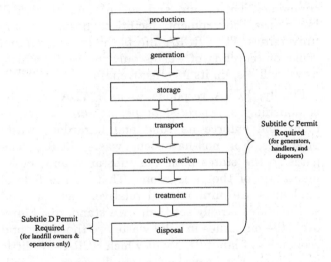

Fig. II–1. RCRA's Life Cycle Terminology

Not only must they track the waste, but they must also obtain permits to operate, and the application process is quite onerous. As one observer trenchantly puts it, RCRA is less cradle to grave than "deathbed to grave," since it begins with waste generation rather than the production processes that create the wastes.[14] Nevertheless, RCRA is

14. Jeffrey M. Gaba, *Recycled Materials Under RCRA: Separating the Chaff from the Wheat*, 16 ECOLOGY L.Q. 623, 651 (1989).

quite rigorous in regulating the funeral arrangements. The statute imposes substantive standards for storage and disposal, including the conditions of disposal, what can be disposed, and treatment before disposal. The regulated entities include heavy industry of the kind one would expect—chemical companies, petroleum, and so on—and also small businesses, government facilities, hospitals, and universities. Thus RCRA affects the generation and reuse or recycling of wastes only *indirectly*, which, as we will see, limits its effectiveness.

Finally, RCRA responds to its SWDA roots by establishing a *federal-state partnership* to implement and enforce its solid and hazardous waste programs. For non-hazardous waste, RCRA delegates to the states both the substance and implementation of the restrictions. That is, the federal guidelines are minimal and relatively general, and so the states largely set their own standards. Moreover, the big issues in solid waste are the siting and economics of landfills, about which RCRA says little or nothing. For hazardous waste, however, the federal direction is pervasive, especially for those aspects covered by HSWA. While in fact forty-eight states and the District of Columbia have been authorized to manage at least some part of their own RCRA programs, the patchwork of delegations and timing of subsidiary state regulation means that many aspects of the hazardous waste programs, and even of permits, are subject to EPA authority and others to the relevant state. In addition, EPA retains authority to inspect and enforce directly, especially when it believes that the state has done an inadequate job, which gives the federal government the final word on many issues. The state role in RCRA is important and, on a day to day basis, primary; however, from 1965 to 1976 to 1984, the federal role, especially for hazardous waste, has only expanded.

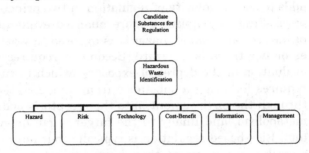

Fig. II–2. Regulatory Criteria

3. Regulatory Criteria

Having identified the substances that are subject to regulation as hazardous waste (a topic on which there will be much more to say), RCRA deploys several legal techniques to accomplish its goals, using different kinds of criteria to determine the substance of the regulatory requirements. The simplest can be called *hazard-based* regulation. These regulations look only to the inherent characteristics of the material under consideration. If it is ignitable or toxic, for example, classification as hazardous waste follows, with its attendant requirements, no matter the other circumstances of the generation or handling of the material.

A more complex strategy is *risk-based* regulation. We saw in Chapter I that risk, as understood in environmental regulation, means the product of toxicity (one type of hazard) and exposure, that is, toxicity × exposure = risk. Thus, the greater the toxic potency or the level of exposure, the higher the risk; the less of either, the lower the risk. Risk adds to the complexity of regulation in two principal ways. First, it requires a more nuanced evaluation of hazard—*how much* hazard, as opposed to whether or not there is a hazard. Second, it requires an evaluation of the degree of exposure, which in turn requires following a substance from its generation, through the environment, into the receptor's bodily metabolism, and finally to the target organ or system. Risk-based regulation is typically (but not necessarily) less stringent than hazard-based, because risk discounts hazard by level of exposure. Risk is the basis for several proposed reforms of RCRA.

Technology-based regulation takes a very different approach. Instead of concerning itself with hazard or risk, it asks what are the most effective technologies for managing a particular substance and demands that those technologies be applied or that an equivalent level of performance be met. (Another name for this criterion is feasibility-based regulation.) Technology-based regulation is usually thought of as less stringent than risk-based, but that is not necessarily the case, and RCRA's land disposal restrictions are an example of the latter.

Cost-benefit-based regulation considers both the benefits (*i.e.*, the harm avoided) and the costs of

achieving the benefit. The required relationship between cost and benefit can vary from simply taking
cost into account to requiring that the benefits
outweigh the costs. Interestingly, this is not a basis
for regulation that appears explicitly in RCRA,
though we shall that it works its way into some
statutory and regulatory exemptions.

RCRA also deploys *information-based* regulation.
Information-based regulation requires that information about a regulated entity or activity be made
available to the public and gives the public an
opportunity to object. Information was the basis of
the National Environmental Policy Act (NEPA), the
first major environmental legislation of the Environmental Decade (which, incidentally, closed with
the passage of CERCLA in 1980). NEPA requires
the preparation of environmental impact statements for major federal or federally approved or
financed projects, and it has proven to be a major
obstacle to environmentally harmful activities.
More recent information-based regulation includes
the Toxic Release Inventory, which requires industries to disclose publicly all releases to any environmental medium of a list of dangerous chemicals.[15]
RCRA's contribution to information-based regulation is the permitting process.

Last, *management-based* regulation, a term
coined by Professors Coglianese and Lazer, would
involve the regulatory agency in the inner workings
of an enterprise in order to improve environmental

15. 42 U.S.C. § 11023.

performance.[16] Pollution prevention is often cited as an example of this, and RCRA distinctly chooses *not* to adopt this strategy, even though pollution prevention is a statutory goal.

B. RCRA's Waste Management Programs

EPA has established three major regulatory programs under RCRA, which are named for the relevant parts of the statute: Subtitle C for hazardous waste, Subtitle D for solid (non-hazardous) waste, and Subtitle I for underground storage tanks. This section outlines the scope and key requirements of each program. For Subtitles D and I, this section will be the extent of our discussion of the programs; for Subtitle C, however, it will be the springboard to the rest of the chapter, which is devoted to the hazardous waste program. The relationships among the subtitles is shown in the following diagram.

1. *Subtitle C: Hazardous Waste*

The most distinctive feature of RCRA's regulatory structure is the enormous significance it places on the distinction between ordinary waste—"solid waste," even though it can include non-solid material—and "hazardous waste." Solid waste, which includes municipal waste and non-hazardous industrial waste of all kinds, is regulated by RCRA in the most minimal way, whereas hazardous waste is

16. Coglianese & Lazer, *supra.*

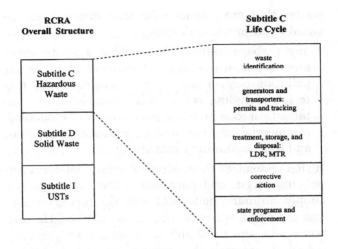

**RCRA
Overall Structure**

- Subtitle C
  Hazardous
  Waste
- Subtitle D
  Solid Waste
- Subtitle I
  USTs

**Subtitle C
Life Cycle**

- waste identification
- generators and transporters: permits and tracking
- treatment, storage, and disposal: LDR, MTR
- corrective action
- state programs and enforcement

Fig. II–3. RCRA's Subtitle Structure

regulated extremely intensively. And some material, most notably certain recycled material, is not considered a waste at all. Consequently, the legal definitions of solid and hazardous waste have huge consequences for the entities that generate, handle, and dispose of waste materials. RCRA's management of solid waste (Subtitle D) is so minimal and its regulation of hazardous waste is so intensive, that one simply cannot appreciate the intensity of the legal battles over waste classification without an appreciation of the gulf between the consequences of one or the other.

Because of its history as an amendment to the SWDA, RCRA covers both traditional (landfills) and new (toxic) waste management concerns. "Solid waste," in RCRA parlance, refers generally to wastes that are intended for land disposal (as opposed to air or water discharge)[17]:

> any garbage, refuse, sludge from a waste treatment plant, water supply treatment plant, or air pollution control facility and other discarded material, including solid, liquid, semisolid, or contained gaseous material resulting from industrial, commercial, mining, and agricultural operations, and from community activities. . . .[18]

RCRA recognizes three kinds of solid waste: municipal, industrial, and hazardous. Municipal waste is simply ordinary household and commercial trash, and industrial waste is what it sounds like. Hazardous waste, the third subset of solid waste, is comprised of materials that exhibit any of four dangerous properties: ignitability, corrosivity, reactivity, and toxicity.[19] In statutory terms, these are characteristics that—

> (A) cause, or significantly contribute to an increase in mortality or an increase in serious irreversible, or incapacitating reversible, illness; or

> (B) pose a substantial present or potential hazard to human health or the environment when

17. RCRA technically includes disposal into water, RCRA § 1004(3); 42 U.S.C. § 6903(3) (definition of "disposal"), but it also excludes point source discharges regulated under the Clean Water Act. RCRA § 1004(27); 42 U.S.C. § 6903(27).

18. RCRA § 1004(27); 42 U.S.C. § 6903(27).

19. Note that this list does not include radioactivity, which is regulated primarily under the Atomic Energy Act, and infectiousness, for which RCRA has a modest medical waste tracking program under Subtitle J, RCRA §§ 11001–11012, 42 U.S.C. §§ 6992–6992k.

improperly treated, stored, transported, or disposed of, or otherwise managed.[20]

Solid wastes that meet this description are regulated in Subtitle C; otherwise, they are regulated, if at all, in Subtitle D.

Subtitle C seeks to track and control hazardous waste from the moment of its generation to its eventual disposition. It therefore requires EPA to establish rules for identifying hazardous wastes; establishes a manifest system for following hazardous waste through its life cycle; and sets standards for treatment, storage, and disposal facilities, applied through a detailed permit system. Generators and transporters are also covered, but much less intensively. The life cycle is covered by Subtitle C as follows:

§ 3001 Identification and Listing of Solid and Hazardous Waste

§ 3002 Standards for Generators

§ 3003 Standards for Transporters

§ 3004 Standards for Treatment, Storage, and Disposal; Land Disposal Restrictions; Facility Design Standards; Corrective Action

§ 3005 Permit System for TSD Facilities

§ 3006 Authorization of State Programs

Finally, EPA can authorize states to carry out the Subtitle C program if the state program is at least as stringent as federal requirements. Both EPA and

20. RCRA § 1004(5); 42 U.S.C. § 6903(5).

the states are given substantial enforcement authorities.

One of the most important aspects of Subtitle C is the land disposal restrictions (LDRs), which were enacted in HSWA. The LDRs essentially constitute a parallel, cumulative system of regulation, establishing treatment requirements or outright disposal bans for any waste that at any point in its life cycle is classified as hazardous. Corrective action, the remediation of contaminated facilities that have (or should have) a RCRA permit, can be seen as a separate part of Subtitle C. The statute itself refers to corrective action only very briefly (the relevant subsections were added by HSWA) and it gives EPA almost no guidance in carrying it out.[21] However, EPA's *regulatory* scheme for corrective action is detailed, and corrective action has grown increasingly like the CERCLA clean-up program.

2. *Subtitle D: Solid Waste*

Subtitle D covers solid waste that is not hazardous, and so it includes garbage, refuse, municipal solid waste, sludges and slags from waste treatment and pollution control, and non-hazardous industrial wastes.[22] Municipal solid waste accounts for 236 million tons per year, and non-hazardous industrial wastes for 7.6 *billion* tons per year, more than thirty times as much as municipal solid waste.[23]

21.   RCRA § 3004(u), (v); 42 U.S.C. § 6924(u), (v).

22.   RCRA § 1004(27), 42 U.S.C. 6903(27).

23.   EPA, Municipal Solid Waste: Basic Facts, available at http://www.epa.gov/epaoswer/non-hw/muncpl/facts.htm (last visited May 24, 2005); EPA, Industrial Waste Management, avail-

(Hazardous waste, by contrast, amounts to about 28 million tons/year.[24]) RCRA has relatively little to say about these wastes, even though they are great in volume. Moreover, they are not necessarily benign, since they include hazardous products, household hazardous waste, and small-quantity generators' wastes, all of which may be exactly the same substances as hazardous waste.[25] The first Subtitle D criteria were published in 1979, and they were thoroughly revised in 1991.[26]

Subtitle D focuses on the design and operation of landfills, and it sets national goals and good practices standards to assist states and localities in designing their own regulatory programs. For example, EPA recommends a hierarchical, integrated approach to solid waste, including (from most to least favored) source reduction, recycling, combustion, and landfilling.[27] To implement its actual requirements, Subtitle D distinguishes between open dumps and sanitary landfills (or municipal solid waste landfills (MSWLFs), as they are known). Open dumps must be closed or upgraded to the standards of sanitary landfills. The federal regulations for sanitary landfills ban open dumping and open burning of solid waste, and they require con-

able at http://www.epa.gov/industrialwaste/ (last visited May 24, 2005).

    24. EPA, RCRA: Reducing Risk from Waste 13–14 (1997).

    25. Barry Breen, *Environmental Law from Resource to Recovery*, in SUSTAINABLE ENVIRONMENTAL LAW (Celia Campbell–Mohn *et al.*, eds. 1993), pp. 85–86.

    26. 40 C.F.R. parts 257 & 258.

    27. RCRA Orientation Manual, *supra*, at II–3 to II–5.

trol of basic disease vectors, like mosquitoes (pooled water) and birds (uncovered garbage). New landfills must be properly located, outside of flood zones, wetlands, and unstable geology. The regulations set design standards for new landfills, including a compacted soil base, a synthetic liner, and a leachate collection system at the bottom; impervious covers on the top[28]; and a collection system for explosive gases that collect in the waste cells. Landfill operators must establish operations rules, such as daily covering of the waste, controlling access to the site, and controlling run-off. They must operate a local groundwater monitoring system and undertake corrective action if problems are discovered. The regulations require safe closure of landfills, post-closure care, and financial assurance for maintenance of safe closure for thirty years.[29] Finally, sanitary landfills are required to institute procedures to avoid the acceptance of hazardous wastes. However, both household hazardous waste and hazardous waste from "conditionally exempt small-quantity generators" (CESQGs) are exempted from the definition of hazardous waste, so they can go into a Subtitle D landfill.[30] All of the Subtitle D requirements are intended to be self-implementing by the

28. It is worth noting that neither covers nor liners are perfect. Liners, in particular, are susceptible to the hazardous chemicals that are permitted in Subtitle D landfills.

29. This is, of course, a trivial amount of time. In a landfill, hot dogs have been shown to survive intact for decades, to say nothing about persistent toxic chemicals and heavy metals.

30. HSWA required that facilities accepting CESQG waste also had to meet certain location, monitoring, and corrective action requirements. 40 C.F.R. §§ 257.5.

regulated entities, and enforcement is left almost entirely to the states.

In sum, the Subtitle D program is notable for what it does *not* do in terms of RCRA's statutory goals. First, it provides only basic protection of health and the environment. Very little retrofitting of old landfills is required, and in any event the operating standards address only the most egregious problems. EPA is invited by the statute to limit its health-based standards by "practical capability,"[31] a major loophole as far as existing facilities are concerned. Subtitle D requires no treatment of waste to reduce toxicity, mobility, or volume. Second, despite the fact that solid waste is the overwhelming majority of waste volume, Subtitle D's pollution prevention and waste minimization efforts are limited to encouragement and advice to states and municipalities. The difficulty of finding a place for new landfills places more pressure on waste generation than RCRA itself. Third, cradle-to-grave regulation is neither practiced nor feasible, since there are no tracking requirements. Fourth, the federal-state partnership in Subtitle D gives the federal government a minor role, indeed. Its state authorization program is not robust, and there is considerable variation among states in the strictness of their controls. Finally, Subtitle D is notable for whom it does *not* regulate. While the requirements for owners and operators of landfills are not insignificant, they are negligible for generators, interim handlers, and even disposers who use

31. RCRA § 4010(c), 42 U.S.C. § 6949a(c).

MSWLFs. Overall, the contrast with Subtitle C could not be greater: Subtitle C regulates almost everything about hazardous waste, and Subtitle D regulates almost nothing about solid waste.[32]

It will probably have occurred to you that there must be a third category in addition to solid and hazardous waste: not waste at all. (*See* Fig. II–4.) Interestingly, the regulatory significance of this category lies almost wholly in the ability of a generator of waste to avoid the consequences of classification as a hazardous waste, and not in any serious regulatory difference between being a solid waste and not a regulated waste at all.

32. In many ways, the biggest solid waste problem is something that RCRA says nothing about. The federal standards have in fact reduced the number of MSWLFs for solid waste, and it is more and more difficult to site new landfills over local opposition. This has encouraged many states and localities to adopt "flow control" legislation to protect their dwindling landfill capacity. *See* Paula C. Murray & David B. Spence, *Fair Weather Federalism and America's Waste Disposal Crisis*, 27 HARV. ENVTL. L. REV. 71 (2003); John H. Turner, *Solid Waste Flow Control: The Commerce Clause and Beyond*, 19 MISS. C.L. REV. 53 (1998); Bruce J. Parker & John H. Turner, *Overcoming Obstacles to the Siting of Solid Waste Management Facilities*, 21 NEW MEXICO L. REV. 91 (1990). The Supreme Court, however, in *City of Philadelphia v. New Jersey*, 437 U.S. 617 (1978), declared that solid waste is an article of commerce subject to the Dormant Commerce Clause, which bans discrimination against out-of-state articles. Later, more sophisticated legislation and ordinances have fared little better. *E.g.*, C & A Carbone, Inc. v. Town of Clarkstown, 511 U.S. 383 (1994). This is not necessarily a bad thing, because flow control can be a way of keeping old, substandard landfills in business. However, Congress could resolve this issue with its plenary commerce power, but it has not done so, and so the RCRA adds nothing to this area.

Fig. II–4. RCRA's Waste Categories.

The key structural feature of RCRA, therefore, is that there is a far larger gap in stringency between Subtitles C and D, than between D and unregulated materials. Therefore, the legal objective of regulated entities is to avoid the application of Subtitle C, and there is little to be gained from avoiding Subtitle D. But—and this is the peculiar aspect of RCRA that flows from hazardous waste being a subset of solid waste—in many cases, it is possible to escape from Subtitle C by arguing that the material is not a solid waste at all, *even though* it is not possible to argue that the material is not hazardous. Thus, handlers of hazardous materials and EPA are placed in the position of arguing between no-regulation (because the material is not a solid waste at all) and onerous Subtitle C regulation; there is no meaningful middle ground. As we will see, major reform efforts under RCRA are, for this reason, aimed at creating a meaningful middle ground—a C-/D+ solution, to use Professor Jeffrey Gaba's descriptive phrase[33]—either in the context of Subtitle D or otherwise. RCRA's all-or-nothing structure

33. Jeffrey M. Gaba, *Regulation by Bootstrap: Contingent Management of Hazardous Wastes Under the Resource Conservation and Recovery Act*, 18 YALE J. ON REG. 85 (2001).

puts a great deal of pressure on the classification decision, and as a result, it is worth it for the regulated community to expend an extraordinary amount of legal effort to press for a lower classification.

3. *Subtitle I: Underground Storage Tanks*

RCRA's third major program regulates underground storage tanks (USTs). USTs pose a particular threat to the environment from leaks that have a direct impact on groundwater, and groundwater protection was an overriding concern of Congress in HSWA. Congress addressed tanks for *waste* in Subtitle C, and so Subtitle I was needed to cover storage containers for non-wastes, that is, for useful products. The great majority of the tanks of concern are the gasoline tanks at service stations, but they also include fuel and other chemical storage tanks at any facility. To give an idea of the magnitude of the problem, EPA reports that there are 660,274 USTs in the United States. Since 1984, 1.6 million tanks have been closed, there have been 448,807 confirmed releases, and 416,246 clean-ups have been initiated.[34] The core concern of Subtitle I is old tanks that were poorly designed or have simply outlived their useful lives; however, the statute is also concerned to ensure, on an ongoing basis, that new tank systems are designed to prevent leaks and spills and to ensure early detection and remediation of leaks. Subtitle I thus casts a wide net covering

34. Storage Tanks: EPA Says 6,181 Cleanups Completed During First Half of Fiscal Year 2005, 36 Envt. Rep. (BNA) 1177 (June 10, 2005).

any tank or system of tanks and piping that has 10% of its total volume underground. There are two groups of regulated substances: petroleum and petroleum products, and "hazardous substances" as defined by CERCLA.[35] There are, however, extensive statutory—for example, small household (*e.g.*, heating oil) and farm tanks receive exemptions[36]—and regulatory exemptions.

The centerpiece of Subtitle I is a detailed set of performance standards for new tanks.[37] EPA's regulations cover design and construction of the tanks themselves, overfill protection systems, systems to detect and check for leaks, secondary containment (that is, a double-shelled tank) for some particularly hazardous substances, and detection monitoring systems for tanks and pipes. Subtitle I also requires owners and operators to put in place financial mechanisms to ensure clean-up, and it establishes a Leaking Underground Storage Tank[38] Fund, analogous to the Superfund created by CERCLA, for "orphan" clean-ups. In establishing these standards, however, EPA relied heavily on existing industry practices, including primary reliance on single-walled tanks, to establish its performance standards, and it permitted a ten-year period for upgrading old systems. In effect, as Pro-

35. RCRA § 9001(2), (8), 42 U.S.C. § 6991(2), (8). "Hazardous substances" under CERCLA is a wider category than "hazardous waste" under RCRA. *See* 42 U.S.C. § 9601(14).

36. RCRA § 9001(1); 42 U.S.C. § 6991(1).

37. RCRA § 9003, 42 U.S.C. § 6991b.

38. The acronym, LUST, is about as risqué as hazardous waste law gets.

fessor Thomas McGarity has observed, EPA relied less on tank design than on clean-up technology to deal with the leaks that were sure to follow from single-walled and old tanks. The consequences of this choice became apparent when MTBE, a gasoline additive required by EPA to replace lead, was discovered to move quickly to groundwater, leading to a crisis in MTBE contamination in some areas of the country.[39]

The system for identifying and remediating leaks in USTs begins with an inventory. States are required to establish an office that creates and monitors an inventory of USTs, and it must be notified of all existing and new tanks.[40] UST owners and operators must report the closure of USTs, and the regulations specify approved methods of closure, such as cleaning and filling or removing the empty tank. To address leaks effectively, owners and operators must report actual leaks and also—because of the difficulty of confirming underground leaks—suspicions of leaks. Suspicions must subsequently be confirmed, typically through testing of the tank for tightness.[41] Actual releases are followed by corrective action—short-term abatement to limit the size of the release and to remove acute dangers like fire and vapors, and long-term actions, like excava-

39. Thomas O. McGarity, *MTBE: A Precautionary Tale*, 28 HARV. ENVTL. L. REV. 281 (2004).

40. RCRA § 9002, 42 U.S.C. § 6991a.

41. RCRA Orientation Manual, *supra*, at IV–9.

tion, replacement or repair of the tank, and soil clean-up.[42]

The requirements of Subtitle I are enforced by broad powers of inspection, monitoring, reporting, and enforcement.[43] Finally, the UST program is delegated to individual states that adopt their own regulations which are at least as stringent as federal requirements and have full powers of inspection and enforcement.[44]

C. The Identification of Hazardous Waste

The remainder of this chapter concentrates on hazardous waste and Subtitle C. As the previous section suggests, the first and overwhelmingly important issue in our consideration of Subtitle C is the distinction between solid and hazardous waste,[45] and that is the subject of this section. Subsequent sections (D, E, and F) will consider in detail the consequences of classification as hazardous waste.

1. *Identification of Solid Waste*

RCRA makes hazardous wastes a subset of solid wastes, and so a substance cannot be a hazardous waste if it is not first determined to be a solid waste. Consequently, identification of hazardous wastes must begin with the identification of solid wastes. A great deal of the legal complexity of

42. RCRA § 9003(h), 42 U.S.C. § 6991b(h).

43. RCRA §§ 9005–9006, 42 U.S.C. §§ 6991d–6991e.

44. RCRA §§ 9004, 9008, 42 U.S.C. §§ 6991c, 6991g.

45. *See generally* Williams & Cannon, *supra.*

RCRA arises from waste owners' efforts to exclude a given material from the ambit of "solid waste," because that will necessarily excuse it from the rigors of Subtitle C. A material whose characteristics seem in all respects to be hazardous, or which even appears on EPA's list of hazardous wastes, is not a hazardous waste if it is first determined not to be a solid waste. This section is devoted to unraveling this apparent paradox.

a. The Statutory Definition and the Problem of Recycling. Recall that the statutory definition of solid waste is "any garbage, refuse, sludge from a waste treatment plant, water supply treatment plant, or air pollution control facility *and other discarded material*" (emphasis added), from which the courts and EPA have uniformly drawn the conclusion that the essence of waste is that something is "discarded."[46] The difficult problem arises when a material that is the waste product of one process is not simply thrown away, destroyed, or otherwise abandoned, but rather is reused or kept for possible reuse in the same or another process. Where does one draw the line, in other words, between discarding and recycling?[47] The high cost of handling and disposing of hazardous waste puts great pressure on generators to create sham recycling techniques, such as road filling, burning, or

46. "Solid" obviously has no literal meaning here, since by definition it includes liquid and contained gaseous materials. RCRA § 1004(27), 42 U.S.C. § 6903(27).

47. For an overview of the recycling problem, *see* Stephen Johnson, *Recyclable Materials and RCRA's Complicated, Conflicting, and Costly Definition*, 21 ENVTL. L. REP. 10357 (1991).

backfilling, that are really disposal methods, or to claim to be accumulating materials for future recycling that may never occur. At the other end of the spectrum is the direct and immediate reuse of materials inside a so-called closed-loop production process.[48] The latter is unquestionably bona fide recycling, and it is environmentally and economically far more desirable to recover end-of-process residual materials and return them to the front of the process, than to discard them as waste. The difficulties arise, of course, between the easy cases. For example, it is common and worthwhile for end-of-process residues not to be fed directly back into the manufacturing process, but to require additional processing before they can be reintroduced into the original or another process. The additional processing might be done by the original generator or by someone else, at the site of original generation or elsewhere, and the next process might be the original generator's, the processor's, or someone else's, taking place and back at the original site, at the reprocessing site, or at a third location.[49] How should this be handled?

Importantly, recycling is not necessarily a benign process. At worst, there is the possibility of collecting and storing waste materials that have no reuse potential and/or with no intention of reusing them. It is also entirely possible—and it not infrequently

48. *See, e.g.,* American Mining Congress v. EPA (*AMC I*), 824 F.2d 1177 (D.C. Cir. 1987).

49. *See, e.g.,* American Petroleum Institute v. EPA, 906 F.2d 729 (D.C. Cir. 1990).

happens—that good intentions are either neglected or frustrated, and what begins as a bona fide attempt to recycle ends with abandoned material, or at least material that is left lying about. The obvious danger from these scenarios is that the material remains in an uncontrolled condition or location, exposed to the environment, or is altered or handled in ways that actually increase toxicity or exposure. Batteries awaiting recycling for their lead, for example, could be sitting on the ground and leaching their lead and acid contents into the soil and groundwater. Unconsummated recycling, in other words, is the same or worse than disposal. And even if the recycling is carried forward, the period of storage or transport to another person or other location raises the possibility of loss of control and exposure to humans or the environment. The possibility of lack of control is attested by the disproportionately large number of so-called recycling facilities that have made their way onto CERCLA's National Priorities List for clean-up sites.

b. EPA Regulations. One might imagine that it would be relatively easy to resolve the problem of distinguishing waste from recycled material by simply applying the protective goals of the statute to err on the side of finding such reuse or storage for reuse to be discarding. In general, this is how EPA approached the issue. However, a central objective of RCRA is to *encourage* recycling, and the over-eager declaration that recycling is waste—triggering burdensome consequences—would be a serious disincentive to recycle. Therefore, EPA's central problem in crafting its definition of solid waste was to be inclusive enough to cover any activities that pose a risk to human health or the environment, while at the same time leaving enough room for genuine recycling to flourish. We will look first at EPA's regulatory definition of solid waste, which has remained structurally unchanged since its promulgation in the early 1980s, and we will then examine a series of cases that have imposed limitations on EPA's inclusiveness as a matter of statutory interpretation.

Because it is trying to balance a number of concerns, EPA's regulatory structure is relatively simple in overall structure but complex in details. It is organized as follows:

1) Discarded (40 C.F.R. § 261.2).

   a) Abandoned

   b) Inherently waste-like

   c) Military munitions

   d) Recycled

      i) Types of recycling

      ii) Types of non-recycling

      iii) Types of materials

2) Separately excluded from being a solid waste (40 C.F.R. § 261.4(a)).

The regulations first ask whether the material has been "discarded," which it goes on to define as four categories: abandoned, inherently waste-like, military munitions, and recycled. "Abandoned" is relatively self-explanatory: it means disposed of or thrown away in the ordinary sense of the term, as well as burned or incinerated. This does not include use as fuel, which is a form of recycling, though it raises the possibility of sham recycling (that is, material that is *said* to have energy value, but in fact does not). "Inherently waste-like" is a marvelously suggestive term, but actually refers to a short list of fairly specific and unusually hazardous materials, which is an apt description for military munitions, as well. The presumption that recycled materials are solid waste reflects the strategy of erring on the side of inclusion.

Turning to recycling, while it is not clear from the regulations themselves, EPA divides recycled materials into two groups. Exempt recycled materials *are*:

- used as an ingredient in a process,
- used as a substitute for a useful product, or
- returned to the production process directly and without further treatment,

and they *are not*:

- reclaimed (that is, processed to recover a useful product or regenerated to remove contaminants),
- used in manner constituting disposal, which essentially means placing in or on the land,
- burned for energy recovery, *i.e.*, as a fuel,
- accumulated speculatively for reuse in the indefinite future, or
- certain dioxin wastes.

If the material meets these two groups of tests, then it is not a solid waste. If, however, they are not described by the first list or are described by the second list, then they are considered solid waste, and the regulatory consequence is determined by a third part of the analysis based on the type of material. If the material is—

- spent material,
- sludge,
- by-product,
- commercial chemical product, or
- scrap metal—

then it is a solid waste; however, if it fits into *none* of these categories, then it is not solid waste.[50]

For example, in *United States v. Self*,[51] the court considered the surreptitious use as a gasoline additive of the highly flammable condensate that forms in natural gas pipelines. Clearly this material is hazardous due to its ignitability, and this kind of uncontrolled use of a hazardous material is exactly what RCRA is supposed to control—automobile engines are not authorized hazardous waste destruction devices, to say the least. The court found that the condensate met recycling tests because it was used as a substitute for fuel and was burned for energy recovery. However, the condensate did not meet the third test. It was not one of the listed

50. It is slightly more complicated than this, depending on a matrix of type of material with manner of recycling; however, for present purposes this will suffice.

51. 2 F.3d 1071 (10th Cir. 1993).

types of material because, in another proceeding, EPA had ruled that natural gas condensate is not a "by-product." The consequence was that this environmentally uncontrolled use of natural gas condensate could continue unregulated.

Finally, one must examine the regulation's list of specific exemptions to determine whether, regardless of the above analysis, the material is not deemed a solid waste. These exemptions are quite significant for individual generators and handlers, especially when one remembers that exclusion at this point in the analysis means entire freedom from regulation under either Subtitle C *or* D. It is, in fact, a fairly miscellaneous group, and many are derived directly from statutory exclusions. Some have a reasonably firm basis in the purposes of the statute or of environmental law. For example, laboratory samples of waste and closed-loop recycling pose low risks to human health and the environment. Others are designed to avoid duplicative regulation, such as domestic sewage and point source discharges which are regulated under the Clean Water Act. Still others are quite specific to particular industrial processes ("splash condenser dross residue"), and finally, some, it must be said, are redolent of the wishes of special interests, for example, certain high-volume mining wastes, irrigation returns, and coke by-product waste. All of the latter are potentially highly toxic, but the cost of managing them to RCRA standards would be very high, indeed.

c. The Case Law. Litigation was the predictable reaction to EPA's expansiveness in bringing recyclable material into the ambit of solid waste, and several judicial decisions have set out the statutory boundaries within which the agency's regulations must operate. As noted, the courts also take "discarded" is the starting point for the definition of solid waste. Regulated industries scored an early victory in *American Mining Congress I*, which held that "materials that are recycled and reused in an *ongoing* manufacturing or industrial process" are not discarded, because they "have not yet become part of the waste disposal problem; rather, *they are destined for beneficial reuse or recycling in a continuous process by the generating industry itself.*"[52] The court applied this reasoning broadly to cover reuse in other parts of the same production process, as well as reuse in different production processes in the same industry.

Subsequent cases trimmed *AMC I*'s sails somewhat. For example, *American Mining Congress II* held that sludges held in surface impoundments could indeed be considered solid waste, because impoundments (*i.e.*, ponds or lagoons) pose threats to the environment from leaking, overflowing, breach, and human contact.[53] In the words of *AMC I*, materials in impoundments are still "part of the waste disposal problem." (Impoundments are not a

52. *AMC I, supra*, 824 F.2d at 1186 (emphasis in original).

53. American Mining Congress v. EPA (*AMC II*), 907 F.2d 1179 (D.C. Cir. 1990); *see also* American Petroleum Institute, *supra*, 906 F.2d 729.

favored way of handling dangerous wastes, but they are a common way of handling industrial waste, a direct consequence of industrial waste not being classified as hazardous waste.) In *Association of Battery Recyclers*, the D.C. Circuit again restricted EPA's flexibility by holding that the agency could not adopt an absolute rule that *any* storage time, between generation and reuse using an unapproved storage method, rendered the material solid waste.[54] The test is whether the material is used in a continuous process, not the immediacy of the reuse.

From these and other cases, one can derive a number of factors that are relevant to the statutory analysis:

- certainty of reuse (there was a suggestion in *AMC II* that the reuse was speculative),

- duration of storage or accumulation (*i.e.*, immediacy of reuse),

- identity of reuser (generator or another enterprise),

- conditions of storage (exposure to the environment),

- location of reuse (same process/same facility, different process/same facility, different process/different facility).

A recent Ninth Circuit case, addressing the rather creative claim that the burning of cut grass on grass farms was an unpermitted burning of a solid waste (the smoke caused the plaintiffs' respiratory prob-

54. Association of Battery Recyclers, Inc. v. EPA, 208 F.3d 1047 (D.C. Cir. 2000).

lems), held that the grass was not a waste because burning added important nutrients to the farmland. The court identified three tests that must be met for a material *not* to be considered solid waste under the statute[55]:

(1) "whether the material is 'destined for beneficial reuse or recycling in a continuous process by the generating industry itself,' "

(2) "whether the materials are being actively reused, or whether they merely have the *potential* of being reused," and

(3) "whether the materials are being reused by its original owner, as opposed to use by a salvager or reclaimer."

The case law, in sum, imposes some statutory constraints on EPA's administrative definition of solid waste, but it does not alter EPA's basic analysis, nor does it simplify the analysis much.

d. Recycling Definition Reform. Is there a better way to distinguish recycling from disposal?[56] One possibility is to focus on intent: what does the generator of the material expect, in good faith, to do with it? This approach, however, garners few adherents for good and obvious reasons. Good intentions

55. Safe Air for Everyone v. Meyer, 373 F.3d 1035 (9th Cir. 2004).

56. For some industry-oriented suggestions, *see* R. Michael Sweeney, *Reengineering RCRA: The Command Control Requirements of the Waste Disposal Paradigm of Subtitle C and the Act's Objective of Fostering Recycling—Rethinking the Definition of Solid Waste, Again*, 6 DUKE ENVTL. L. & POLICY FORUM 1 (1996); J.T. Smith II, *The Solid Waste Definitional Dilemma*, 9 NAT. RESOURCES & ENVT. 3 (Fall 1994).

do nothing to protect the environment during the period during which hazardous secondary material awaits reuse. Moreover, proving intention and good faith are often difficult and are in any event a distraction from the true issues of environmental protection.

Instead, EPA has seriously considered replacing its current "functional" approach with an economic approach that would focus on whether economic value actually attaches to the secondary material. In its simplest (not to say, simplistic) form, one would ask whether the generator can get money from some third party for its waste material. If so, then it is recycled; if not, then it is waste. A more realistic approach would ask whether there is a genuine market (bona fide third-party buyers, for example) for the material, whether the generator or others treat it as they would a useful product or ingredient, or whether it substitutes for a material that would otherwise be purchased. EPA, however, has rejected this approach for several reasons. Sold-for-value is actually quite hard to determine except in money transactions. Secondary material may quite legitimately be traded ("take this off my hands, and I'll let you have it"), for example, so it would be difficult to determine whether it was a bona fide transaction without returning to the intention test. Indeed, requiring a cash transaction to validate recycling status would discourage perfectly legitimate recycling transactions that only make sense as barter or that involve individually small, uneconomic amounts of material. And, also like the intention test, purchase for value really has nothing to do with environmental protection; a third-party purchaser could pay good money and still store the material unsafely.[57]

EPA has not, however, entirely rejected the economic approach. In a case arising out of a recent rulemaking, the agency had created a special exemption from classification as solid waste for secondary material used to make zinc-based fertilizers. The secondary material would otherwise be a solid (and hazardous) waste, and the petitioners challenged EPA's authority to treat it as exempt recycling. EPA justified its action on the basis of what it called the "identity principle": market participants treated the material more like a valuable product than like a waste, it was not managed as if it was being thrown away, and the final fertilizer product was in fact chemically indistinguishable from fertilizer products not made from secondary material. The D.C. Circuit ratified EPA's approach, at least in theory.[58]

A third possibility, which has not been widely explored, is an environmental harm test that would look at the environmental consequences of certain management practices. If the practices do not result in the dangers anticipated by RCRA—*e.g.*, failure to isolate dangerous material from the environment— then they could be considered recycled. Alternative-

57. EPA, Proposed Rule, Hazardous Waste Management System, 48 Fed. Reg. 14472 (1983).

58. Safe Food & Fertilizer v. EPA, 350 F.3d 1263 (D.C. Cir. 2003), *amended on rehearing*, 365 F.3d 46 (D.C. Cir. 2004).

ly, a risk assessment might be performed on the waste stream. This test tends to collapse the question of proper waste management into the classification question, however.

In 2003, EPA proposed to overhaul its recycling definition in response to the *Association of Battery Recyclers* case, discussed above.[59] This proposal, still under review in the agency, has two parts. First, it recrafts the meaning of "reclaimed" to include secondary material "generated and reclaimed in a continuous process within the same industry." Typical materials covered are sludges and byproducts, scrap metal, or spent materials. The new rule would not apply to the recycling categories of burned and inherently waste-like, to materials that require further reclamation, to speculatively accumulated material, or to material passed through brokers or middlemen. However, as written, the rule's coverage is much more expansive than it might appear, because it does not require that the reuser be the same entity as the generator or in the same location—just in the same industry—and EPA anticipated that it would ease recycling of 1 million tons of hazardous waste. The proposal is, in other words, an expansive reading of the case law on "discarded." In addition, as a safety net for the first part, the second part of the proposal sets out criteria for identifying sham recycling:

- the secondary material is not managed as a valuable commodity, consistently with the han-

59. EPA, Proposed Rule, Revisions of the Definition of Solid Waste, 68 Fed. Reg. 61558 (2003).

dling of analogous non-secondary products and ingredients;

- the material does not provide a useful contribution to the next product or process of which it becomes a part;

- the material fails to yield a valuable product or intermediate that is sold to a third party or that is used by generator as an effective substitute for a product or ingredient;

- the material contains significantly greater amounts of hazardous constituents than analogous products (the toxics are, the saying goes, just "along for the ride").

This is in many ways the economic or commodity test that EPA had previously rejected, though it wisely steers clear of intent questions.

All of these alternatives have some merit, though none offers the kind of bright-line simplicity that is so signally lacking in the current definition. The important point to remember here and throughout this section is that an exemption, or a finding that a substance is not a solid waste, means that it is no longer monitored or regulated or kept track of *at all*, at least under RCRA. We shall return to this problem of all-or-nothing regulation in Section D of this chapter.

2. *Hazardous Waste*

Compared to the difficulty of determining whether something is a solid waste, determining whether it is a hazardous waste is relatively simple. This is the second part of the explanation for the oddity that most of the litigation and regulatory effort under RCRA goes into the solid waste part of the analysis. In fact, virtually all of the solid waste cases are ones in which it is understood that the material at issue, if it is a solid waste, will be a hazardous waste. RCRA is, to continue a theme from Section B, very much an all-or-nothing scheme: as a practical matter, the kinds of materials that are litigated are either not a solid waste at all, in which case there is no regulation at all, or they are solid *and* hazardous, in which case the full weight of Subtitle C comes down upon it. There are, however, some important issues in identifying hazardous waste, to which we now turn.

    a. Tests for Hazardous Characteristics. EPA, following Congress' mandate, established four characteristics that make a solid waste a hazardous waste: ignitability, corrosivity, reactivity, and toxicity. The regulations set out fairly straightforward tests for each hazardous characteristic[60]:

- *ignitability* is determined by the flashpoint of liquids and the ability of solids to combust spontaneously;

- *corrosivity* is determined by the acidity or alkalinity (as measured by pH) of the material, or by its ability to corrode a certain amount of steel in a certain time;

- *reactivity* means materials that explode or violently react, or that produce toxic fumes under ordinary conditions; and

60. 40 C.F.R. §§ 261.21–261.24.

- *toxicity* refers to specific concentrations of a list of chemicals of concern.

Toxicity is measured by the characteristics of the solution created when mildly acidic water passes through a sample of the waste. This is called the Toxicity Characteristic Leaching Procedure (TCLP), and it is meant to simulate the fate of waste disposed in a Subtitle D landfill. EPA tests the leachate for the presence and concentration of only forty toxic constituents (the "D" list of chemicals), mainly heavy metals and organic chemicals.[61]

All of these tests are meant to be applied to individual waste streams or waste forms. If the numerical values are exceeded, the waste is deemed to be hazardous and so subject to Subtitle C restrictions on generators, transporters, and handlers. Wastes that come to be classified as hazardous through this process are known as "characteristic" hazardous wastes.

  b. The Concept of Listing. RCRA authorizes EPA to identify hazardous wastes not only on the basis of a case-by-case analysis of characteristics, but also by creating lists of secondary materials that typically have the characteristics of hazardous waste.[62] Because of the vast number of individual waste streams, listing is essential to the practical operability of the regulatory scheme. EPA has developed four lists of hazardous wastes: F (generic industrial processes), K (certain sectors of industry), and P

  61. 40 C.F.R. § 261.24.

  62. RCRA § 3001(b)(1), 42 U.S.C. § 6921(b)(1).

and U (unused pure chemical products).[63] Each listed substance or mixture of substances (*e.g.*, wastewaters or sludge resulting from a particular process) also receives a hazard code that gives the primary basis for its listing (ignitability, etc.). In addition, the codes distinguish between wastes that simply meet the toxicity characteristic, those that include chemicals that could pose a threat if improperly managed (recall the definition in section 1004(5)(B)), and those ("acutely hazardous") that could pose a threat even if properly managed.

Listing is a surprisingly subjective process. It begins, of course, with the four characteristics of hazardousness and asks whether, considered on a generic, nationwide basis, the described wastes typically meet the characteristics or contain the forty chemicals on the D list.[64] More importantly, EPA considers several other factors, such as the persistence of the chemical in the environment and its capacity for bioaccumulation, and it is not limited to the D-list chemicals. RCRA was in a sense ahead of its time in this respect. Internationally and domestically, environmental agencies are becoming more and more interested in focusing on PBT (persistent, bioaccumulative, and toxic) and vPvB (very persistent, very bioaccumulative) chemicals as priorities for research and restriction. These chemicals have in common a degree of irreversibility—once released to the environment, they will stay there, available to human and ecological receptors, for a long time—

63. 40 C.F.R. §§ 261.31–261.33.

64. 40 C.F.R. § 261.11(a).

and thus are in special need of control.[65] The flexibility of the listing process makes RCRA potentially very responsive to these concerns. Moreover, EPA includes management concerns in making the listing decision. Some waste streams are more commonly mismanaged than others, or the consequences of their mismanagement are typically more dire. The statutory definition is broad enough to permit, and even require, EPA to take a broad look at these potential dangers of waste materials. Wastes that are classified as hazardous as a result of being on one of EPA's lists are known as "listed" hazardous wastes. It makes a surprisingly big difference whether a waste is a listed or a characteristic waste.

c. *The Mixture, Derived From, and Contained In Rules.* While the use of listing has significant advantages in certainty for both the regulator and the regulated, it also has a very significant drawback: deviation from the description on the list results in

65. The concern for persistent chemicals is reflected in two treaties, the Stockholm Convention on Persistent Organic Pollutants (entered into force May 17, 2004), reprinted in 40 I.L.M. 532 (2001), available at http://www.pops.int (last visited Aug. 6, 2005), and the Rotterdam Convention on the Prior Informed Consent Procedure for Certain Hazardous Chemicals and Pesticides in International Trade (entered into force Feb. 24, 2004), reprinted in 38 I.L.M. 1 (1999), available at http://www.pic.int (last visited Aug. 6, 2005), and in a proposed regulation of the European Union, Commission of the European Communities, *Proposal for a Regulation of the European Parliament and of the Council Concerning the Registration, Evaluation, Authorisation and Restriction of Chemicals (REACH)*, COM 2003 0644 (03) (October 29, 2003), available at http://europa.eu.int/comm/environment/chemicals/reach.htm (last visited Aug. 6, 2005).

the waste material no longer being included on the list, and so individualized testing is required. Changes in the described waste can happen in a number of ways and for a number of reasons. Some changes are entirely legitimate, like convenience of storage or attempted treatment of the waste, but others are designed to circumvent regulation without any corresponding environmental benefit—and, given the onerousness of compliance with Subtitle C restrictions, attempts at circumvention are entirely predictable. To remedy this problem, EPA developed three policies to close this potentially huge loophole in the listing system: the mixture rule, the derived-from rule, and the contained-in policy.[66] The effect of each is to expand greatly the material potentially covered by each listed waste.

The basic principle underlying each of these rules is that "a hazardous waste does not lose its hazardous character simply because it changes form or is combined with other substances."[67] While this is treated as an article of faith by EPA, it also has a firm factual foundation, especially as it relates to toxicity. Recall that Congress' and EPA's approach to toxic chemicals is largely defined by the non-threshold nature of carcinogens (*i.e.*, there is no completely safe level of exposure above zero). From this perspective, toxic chemicals are little time bombs in hazardous waste, just waiting to go off, regardless of the form or concentration of the

66.   40 C.F.R. § 261.3(a)(2)(iv).

67.   Chemical Waste Management, Inc. v. EPA, 869 F.2d 1526, 1539 (D.C. Cir. 1989).

waste. The degree of risk that they pose can be decreased, but the risk cannot be entirely eliminated as long as the chemical is present. Furthermore, listing is the result of the multi-attribute analysis described above, so changing one characteristic of the resultant waste by adding something or changing its form does not necessarily alter the determination of hazard on which the listing is based. Finally, a cradle-to-grave regulatory scheme needs to assure that the waste is really dead, so to speak, and not going anywhere. If waste generators could readily avoid designation as hazardous through the simple addition of other materials or treatment to change the form of the waste, the material might well end up being (to extend the analogy too far) un-dead, and the grave just a way-station instead of a permanent resting place.[68]

The *mixture rule* states that a listed waste mixed with *another solid waste* remains the same listed waste. There are various reasons why a generator might mix wastes, but the one of greatest concern is dilution of the waste to below-characteristic levels, a temptation created by the use of concentrations to determine toxicity in the D List. "Dilution is not the solution to pollution" is another EPA article of faith, and by and large it, too, is true. Dilution does not reduce the overall toxicant loading in the environment (those little time bombs are still around, in other words). Dilution also dramatically increases

68. For an excellent description and critique of these rules, *see* Jeffrey M. Gaba, *The Mixture and Derived–From Rules Under RCRA: Once a Hazardous Waste Always a Hazardous Waste?*, 21 ENVTL. L. REP. 10033 (1991).

the volume of material with hazardous constituents, worsening the solid waste disposal problem and potentially leading to wider dispersion of the toxic constituents. And the persistence and bioaccumulative qualities of the toxics mean that the low concentrations will not remain low for long. Merely mixing a listed waste with another solid waste, therefore, should not be a way of avoiding hazardous status. Corrosivity, ignitability, and reactivity (CIR) are legitimate exceptions to the dilution mantra, however. For example, dilution of a corrosive liquid will permanently render it less corrosive; adding an alkaline substance to an acid will accomplish the same thing. Therefore, the mixture rule applies only to toxic characteristic wastes; CIR wastes are exempted from it.

(It is worth noting here that the land disposal restriction (LDR) regulations required by HSWA add a layer of related consequences to the mixture rule. Since LDRs attach at the time of generation of the wastes, rather than at the time of actual disposal, CIR wastes are still subject to the LDRs, even though they are for other purposes (recordkeeping, storage, etc.) not considered hazardous wastes.[69] This effect of the LDRs is really just an extreme application of the anti-dilution-policy, and in that sense it is wholly in keeping with Congress's intent when it enacted HSWA in 1984. The LDRs also contain an explicit general prohibition of dilution.[70])

69. RCRA Orientation Manual, *supra*, at III–91.

70. 40 C.F.R. § 268.3.

The *derived-from rule*[71] applies to solid wastes that are derived from listed wastes. It is typically triggered when the listed waste has been managed in some way that changes its physical form. For example, sludges that precipitate out of a listed liquid waste, leachate consisting of water that has flowed through a listed waste, and ash resulting from the burning of a listed waste are all derived-from wastes—and all remain classified as the original listed waste, regardless of their new characteristics. Again, CIR wastes may be exempted if they fall below characteristic levels. Secondary materials that are recycled in ways that do *not* involve burning or placement in or on the land are also exempted. The common theme here is maintaining cradle-to-grave control over hazardous wastes. The derived-from rule is particularly concerned with efforts to treat, dispose, or recycle listed waste that are ineffective in isolating the waste from the environment (for example, there is no exemption for recycling that leaves the waste in or on the land) or that amounts to little more than dilution. In addition, it is not acceptable to handle waste in a way that simply shifts media, for example, from a liquid to a solid form.

The *contained-in policy*[72] is not a rule *per se*, but rather EPA's policy in cases where a waste has contaminated environmental media such as soil, groundwater, or sediment, typically as the result of leaks and spills. This policy is necessary because the

71. 40 C.F.R. § 261.3(c)(2)(i).
72. 40 C.F.R. § 261.3(d)(2).

mixture and derived-from rules do not by their terms apply to mixtures with non-wastes or to new non-waste forms, respectively. It is only the waste material within the matrix of (say) soil that is the hazardous waste, so the policy only applies to actually contaminated soil.[73] However, the practicalities of removing the waste from the media mean that the contained-in policy also has the effect of expanding greatly the volume of material that needs to be handled. On the other hand, *not* to follow the contained-in position would be to abandon jurisdiction over a very significant setting in which hazardous waste is found, and in which it is, by definition, exposed to the environment and uncontrolled.

The mixture and derived-from rules had a somewhat rocky administrative history, having been overturned on procedural grounds in 1990.[74] Because they were so important to the operation of the listing provisions, EPA issued an emergency rule reinstating them, and Congress, agreeing, legislatively extended the emergency rule pending thorough revision. EPA returned to the rules a decade later, and chose to continue them in all fundamental respects. They received judicial approval in *American Chemistry Council v. EPA.*[75] The court found that EPA was justified in classifying such materials as hazardous waste without individual-

---

73. RCRA Orientation Manual, *supra*, at III–27. The contained-in policy was upheld in Chemical Waste Management, *supra*, 869 F.2d 1526.

74. Shell Oil Co. v. EPA, 950 F.2d 741 (D.C. Cir. 1991).

75. 337 F.3d 1060 (D.C. Cir. 2003).

ized proof of risk, both because its assumption that hazardous waste remains hazardous is generally valid, and because it is reasonable for EPA to want to avoid having to list every possible permutation or combination of wastes. More broadly, the court said that it was entirely permissible for EPA to err on the side of safety in its listing practices and to place the burden on the generator to show the non-hazardousness of a new mixture or waste form.

d. Exclusions. As with solid waste, there are a number of exclusions from hazardous waste, that is, materials that may be solid wastes but cannot be hazardous wastes, regardless of their characteristics.[76] As before, they are a hodge-podge of materials that Congress or EPA has categorically excluded for a variety of reasons, mostly to deal with the all-or-nothing quality of RCRA. Thus, waste streams like household hazardous waste (paints, pesticides, fertilizers, and batteries), agricultural waste, mining wastes, and oil and gas production wastes are materials that occur in very large quantities but are not, arguably, particularly hazardous. Of course, one might also suspect that there are political factors at work, too, such as avoiding aggressive and expensive regulation of individual citizens, of farmers, or of the mining and petroleum industries. Some of the exclusions leave some quite dangerous materials minimally regulated; for example, one individual's disposal of a Ni–Cd computer battery may not be very meaningful, but the cumulative total in ordi-

76.   40 C.F.R. § 261.4(b).

nary landfills is a serious threat to the environment.

e. Exit. The means of exiting from the hazardous waste system (other than by proper destruction or disposal) differs between listed and characteristic wastes. In general, a characteristic waste is no longer a hazardous waste at any point at which it no longer exhibits a hazardous characteristic.[77] However, the land disposal restrictions (LDRs) on hazardous wastes take the position that a hazardousness is determined at the time of generation and, for LDR purposes, it always remains so.[78] The LDRs thus create a parallel, cumulative system to the identification rules, and in this situation it increases the stringency of the regulation.

Listed wastes, in which the hazardous designation is determined by the generic identity of the waste rather than by the character of the individual waste stream, raise the possibility that the generalization does not fit the specific situation. Therefore, RCRA provides for the "delisting" of individual waste streams.[79] This is a burdensome process. The generator of the waste must submit a petition to EPA demonstrating that its particular waste stream does not exhibit the criteria for which it was listed, *and* that it presents no other hazardous characteristics, *and* that it poses no other hazards. Since the original listing is a multi-attribute analysis, carry-

77. 40 C.F.R. § 261.3(d)(1).

78. 40 C.F.R. §§ 261.3(d)(1), 268.9.

79. RCRA § 3001(f), 42 U.S.C. § 6921(f).

ing the delisting burden is difficult. Indeed, for this reason, the characteristic levels required for delisting are lower than for de-characterization. Looking only at the characteristics, it is entirely possible that a listed waste would not be classified as a characteristic waste, but would nevertheless be denied delisting because the listing criteria include factors in addition to ignitability, TCLP toxicity, and so on. The apparent inconsistency, however, has given rise to some calls for reform, as we shall see.

A final word on listed and characteristic wastes: the foregoing description and analysis glosses over numerous qualifications, exceptions, and subdivisions of the various rules. EPA is constantly seeking to develop general rules for the identification (and, for that matter, treatment and disposal) of hazardous waste—to provide predictability for the regulated community and for its own convenience—and it is constantly thwarted by the vast array of processes and permutations of processes that generate hazardous wastes, and by the many ways in which a waste may pose a hazard. The Byzantine structure we have just reviewed, in other words, is not arbitrary or deliberately confusing, as is often charged. Rather, it is the inevitable consequence of multiple goals being applied to a vast and complex industrial economy.

3. C-/D+ Reform

We have seen that the practical significance of classification as solid waste is relatively minor for generators; RCRA imposes no serious limitations on where and how they must dispose of solid wastes, unless they choose to dispose of it themselves as the operator of a dump or landfill. The consequences of classification as hazardous, by contrast, are enormous. Permits are required; waste tracking is required; each stage of the waste's life cycle is subject to significant regulatory control, especially storage and disposal; and the land disposal of certain wastes without pretreatment is prohibited. Since RCRA regulation is largely an all-or-nothing proposition, the generator of a waste material with some hazardous character has every incentive to exploit the complex rules distinguishing solid waste from recycling to avoid the rigors of Subtitle C. In an effort to find a balance between Subtitle D and Subtitle C, and to recognize the wide range of environmental hazards posed by the vast number of different wastes, several efforts have been launched to create in effect middle categories of wastes that are subject to less than C but more than D.[80] Professor Gaba aptly calls this C-minus and D-plus regulation.[81]

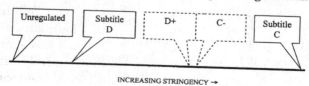

INCREASING STRINGENCY →

Fig. II–5.   C-/D+ Reform

80. These difficulties are explored in Office of Technology Assessment, *Classifying for Hazard Management* (1981).

81. Gaba, *Regulation by Bootstrap, supra.*

Neither Congress nor EPA has enacted C-/D+ reforms in a systematic way, and many of the reforms have at least the suggestion of special pleading behind them. EPA has for years advocated the existence of a general category of "special waste" consisting of hazardous waste that is treated less stringently than Subtitle C because of its low toxicity and high volume.[82] The relevance of low toxicity is obvious; high volume, however, which suggests a high potential for exposure and therefore a *higher* risk, can only signal a concern over cost. Cost is not an unreasonable concern in regulatory systems, especially ones as broad in scope and strict as RCRA, but it is not a factor that the statute expressly recognizes. Until recently, therefore, EPA has not pursued special waste rules aggressively. In addition, HSWA makes it impossible to avoid the most burdensome consequences of classification as hazardous waste, the LDRs, so little would be gained by reclassification. So instead, EPA has approached the issue piecemeal, with some help from Congress.

Congress took the lead in creating a middle-ground system for mining, smelting, and refining operations. These often generate mountain-sized piles of removed overburden and post-processing tailings, and the piles often contain relatively high concentrations of metals and processing chemicals that are regulated under RCRA. The so-called Bevill Amendment, enacted in 1980,[83] told EPA to consid-

82. *Id.* at 97–98.
83. RCRA § 3001(b)(3)(A)(ii), 42 U.S.C. § 6921(b)(3)(A)(ii).

er C-minus regulation of these high-volume mining wastes.[84] Sponsors of the amendment argued that the material has low concentrations of toxic materials; that the volume and constituents of the waste are largely uncontrollable, being dependent on the quality of the rock; and that, moreover, process changes cannot make much of a difference to the volume of waste. These claims were probably overstated, but at least hypothetically they make a case for middle-range treatment. Unfortunately, EPA has never succeeded in developing a real C-minus program for Bevill wastes, because the amendment actually exempts them from Subtitle C altogether, and EPA has no legal authority to create a Subtitle D program for the wastes. The upshot is that Bevill wastes are not regulated at all by EPA.[85] EPA limits the exemption to wastes that are *actually* high in volume and low in toxicity,[86] but it has not made any real progress in figuring out a D-plus arrangement, either.

Used oil, on the other hand, does have its own management system[87] mandated by the Used Oil Recycling Act of 1980.[88] Used oil is not benign, but

84. *See* Steven G. Barringer, *The RCRA Bevill Amendment: A Lasting Relief for Mining Wastes?*, 17 NAT. RES. & ENVT. 155 (Winter 2003) (an industry perspective).

85. Environmental Defense Fund v. EPA (*EDF I*), 852 F.2d 1309 (D.C. Cir. 1988) (extraction and beneficiation wastes); Environmental Defense Fund v. EPA (*EDF II*), 852 F.2d 1316 (D.C. Cir. 1988) (mineral processing wastes).

86. The court had to stiffen EPA's spine in *EDF II*.

87. 40 C.F.R. part 279.

88. RCRA § 3014, 42 U.S.C. § 6935.

it is generated in huge quantities by a vast number of very small entities, including individuals. The regulatory problem, therefore, is not so much a matter of the cost *per se* as of the feasibility of implementing strict regulation. Administrative feasibility, of course, is not a statutory goal, but it is not an unreasonable consideration (for example, it underlies the exclusion of household waste, some of which is cumulatively quite hazardous). Moreover, the benefits of encouraging recycling (by easing compliance) in this setting are unusually high, because recycling used oil is fairly easy, it avoids the need for more petroleum, and it saves the energy needed to produce oil from crude petroleum. Consequently, EPA created a completely separate system for used oil. It establishes considerably less onerous requirements for persons who handle only used oil and not other hazardous wastes. It also recognizes that, due to the large number of small and dispersed generators of used oil, the chain of handlers will be longer than for industrially generated hazardous waste, and that the beginning of the chain (generators and collection centers) are far more easily discouraged by stringent requirements than later members (refiners and marketers).

Most recycled hazardous waste (which is to say, material that does *not* escape the definition of solid waste[89]) is subject to all of the restrictions of Subti-

89. The proposed revisions to the definition of hazardous waste to encourage recycling, discussed above, can be seen in the same light. EPA's goal is to identify low-risk waste streams (specifically, a "continuous" process within the same industry) and to avoid types of recycling (burning or use on land; sham

tle C on generators, transporters, and storers. However, some hazardous wastes, including scrap metal and certain waste-derived fuels, receive more favorable treatment, as long as they meet lesser (C-) standards.[90] If the wastes are to be placed in or on the land, for example, the LDRs must be met, but other Subtitle C requirements (recordkeeping, etc.) need not.

EPA has also established special standards for what is known as "universal waste."[91] This includes discarded batteries, unused pesticides, discarded mercury-containing thermostats, and discarded fluorescent and mercury-vapor light bulbs. They are "universal" in that they are generated by a very large number (millions) of small, primarily non-industrial generators; they are generated in a large number of disparate settings; they present a relatively low hazard; and they are frequently managed in non-hazardous waste management facilities as part of municipal waste. Like the used oil provisions, the universal waste regulations create gradations in management based on the amount of material managed by a given handler, and by its place in the disposal chain. Small-quantity generators and handlers have fewer requirements than larger-quantity ones; TSDFs, on the other hand, are sub-

recycling) that have the highest risk. However, this proposal would exempt such materials from Subtitle C altogether, so it is still essentially an all-or-nothing proposition.

90. 40 C.F.R. part 266.

91. *See generally* Gretchen N. Smith, Note, *The Universal Waste Rule: Modification of the Hazardous Waste Recycling Program*, 2 ENVTL. LWYR. 203 (1995); 40 C.F.R. part 273.

ject to full Subtitle C regulation. Universal waste is, in fact, the logical place for managing the already vast and growing problem of computer and electronic waste, and EPA is exploring this possibility.

Professor Gaba identifies another phenomenon with a similar goal, called "contingent management," in which a particular waste is exempted from Subtitle C *on condition that* certain management and disposal practices are followed.[92] EPA has done this with cement kiln dust, for example, and it proposes to treat certain dye and pigment production wastes, otherwise hazardous, as non-hazardous if both the "mass loadings" of a particular chemical constituent are low enough and the waste is disposed in a Subtitle D or Subtitle C landfill.[93] This exemplifies a middle-ground, risk-based approach, as it moderates the hazardous waste management requirements based on a combination of toxicity (the chemical constituent) and likely exposure scenario (placement in a controlled landfill). The approach, in other words, gives credit for reduced exposure in making the hazard classification, which RCRA otherwise does not do (instead, RCRA usually directs EPA to classify based on the consequences

92. Gaba, *Regulation by Bootstrap, supra.*

93. EPA, Proposed Rule, Hazardous Waste Management System; Identification and Listing of Hazardous Waste; Dyes and/or Pigments Production Wastes, 68 Fed. Reg. 66164 (2003).

Note that it would be advantageous to a waste generator to avoid classification as hazardous *even if* the waste was disposed in a Subtitle C landfill, because Subtitle C imposes many additional restrictions on, for example, storage and treatment before disposal, which would not be triggered if the waste was not classified as hazardous.

of a *failure* to control the waste properly). Likewise, in the *Safe Food* case, *supra*, EPA exempted material used in zinc fertilizers as long as contaminants did not reach certain threshold amounts.[94] This, too, is contingent management, and risk (constituent concentrations and management practices) was the driving factor.

EPA's legal theory in support of these moderated requirements is that it has the discretion *not* to list wastes that would otherwise be listed, based on actual management practices, just as it has discretion to list wastes that would not otherwise be listed, based on concerns with *mis*management. Gaba is critical of this argument, observing that it also considers factors like cost that are not part of RCRA. He also sees this as a D-plus rather than C-minus provision, because EPA has no authority under Subtitle D to ensure that the waste is handled properly in the landfill. This creates the danger—realized in the Bevill Amendment—that piecemeal C-/D+ reform will leave hazardous materials unregulated under Subtitle C, but with no adequate safety net in Subtitle D. In other words, it will go from all to nothing, and not be a middle-ground reform at all.

EPA is also considering a more systematic approach. Up to this point, RCRA's regulatory strategy has been primarily *hazard*-based, and a waste is either hazardous or it is not. The C-/D+ options create some flexibility in that all-or-nothing system, though not in a systematic way. If one looks closely,

94. *Supra*, 350 F.3d 1263.

however, all of the C-/D+ schemes have in common a sense (accurate or not) that some substances deserve less than "all" and more than "nothing," because they pose a level of *risk* that is neither at the top nor at the bottom of the scale. Risk is not the underlying theory of RCRA; RCRA tends to focus on the inherent hazardous characteristics of waste material (ignitability, etc.) with little regard to the exposure side of the risk equation. To the extent that exposure is a factor, it is as the potential for mismanagement of materials with those inherent characteristics. The C-/D+ arrangements we have seen may be groping their way toward risk; in any event, they raise the possibility of a more thorough-going reform of the waste identification rules based explicitly on risk.

In 1999, following several iterations, EPA issued a proposed Hazardous Waste Identification Rule (HWIR)[95] that is designed to ease the regulation of low-risk wastes generally. To ensure adequate coverage of hazardous wastes, EPA would not do this by exempting or conditionally exempting certain wastes, but by providing a simpler *exit* from Subtitle C than the present delisting process. The basic

95. EPA, Proposed Rule, Hazardous Waste Identification Rule: Identification and Listing of Hazardous Wastes, 64 Fed. Reg. 63382 (1999). For discussion of an early version of HWIR, *see* Philip L. Comella, *HWIR: A New Era in Hazardous Waste Management?*, 26 ENVTL. L. REP. 10304 (1996).

Revisions to the mixture and derived-from rules were finalized at EPA, Final Rule, Hazardous Waste Identification Rule: Revisions to the Mixture and Derived–From Rules, 66 Fed. Reg. 27266 (2001). This rule was upheld in *American Chemistry Council, supra.*

idea is to create a three-tier system of hazardous waste management:

- full Subtitle C treatment;
- a "landfill-only" exemption, in which wastes *must* go to a Subtitle D landfill and are tracked to be sure they go there; and
- a "generic exemption," which is a total exemption from Subtitle C.

Assignment to one of these tiers would be determined by risk. HWIR would also be self-implementing, in contrast to the present delisting process, which is anything but self-implementing. EPA hopes that HWIR will encourage innovation and pollution prevention by giving more flexibility in management techniques, though it would also remove some of the pressure to innovate and to prevent pollution to avoid the full rigors of Subtitle C.

The risk-based approach still poses serious challenges, in particular, the complexity of the many routes of exposure to hazardous material. One possible remedy would be the use of a simplified risk assessment based only on groundwater, the key concern in land-based disposal. EPA, however, proposes a *not*-very-simplified risk assessment model for HWIR, requiring more than 700 input parameters. Moreover, as presently proposed, HWIR makes no fundamental changes in the LDR system. They still apply if the waste was at any time a hazardous waste, and so its pretreatment, dilution, and storage restrictions still apply. When EPA is more certain of its ability to assess risk, it plans to propose changes to the LDRs consistent with HWIR exit levels.

All of the above exemptions and proposals have in common an effort to fine-tune regulation to take advantage of the spectrum of hazard and risk, rather than accept an all-or-nothing model. They purport to look for areas of limited risk (low toxicity and/or limited exposure, or the likelihood of careful handling), though it is clear that they also target wastes as to which Subtitle C seems to impose excessive costs (large number of generators or large volumes of material). Establishing a more fine-tuned system has many attractions. Today, RCRA usually errs on the side of over-regulation (Bevill excepted), which was surely Congress's intention, especially after HSWA. The challenge, however, is to find a classification scheme that will correctly distinguish low and high hazard *and* that remains a classification scheme, that is, does not require testing of each and every waste stream each and every time it is altered. Even if one retains the classification part, a great deal of information is required for a fine-tuned approach: a full hazard assessment and analysis of the wide variety of other factors that go into risk assessment, such as genotoxicity, acute toxicity, chronic toxicity, persistence, concentration, bioaccumulation, safety issues, exposure potential, environmental mobility, and sensitive ecosystems or subpopulations. Given the enormity of the task, it may simply not be worth it, or it may be that incremental, step-wise change of the kind we have seen makes more sense. So, for example, it might be better to set out a C-/D+ framework (as in universal wastes) and simply add items (*e.g.*, computer and electronic wastes) as appropriate. Or, perhaps it would be best to establish a C-framework (for universal wastes, say) *and* a D+ one (for mining wastes, possibly). This would argue against an thorough-going change like HWIR, but it would create the need for a complex classification system and equally the need for determining the basis for classification. This is a major challenge for the administration of RCRA in coming years.

D. Disposal Restrictions

We now examine the land disposal restrictions (LDRs) in Subtitle C, which are perhaps the most important regulatory consequence of classification as a hazardous waste. As we saw in Chapter I, the elements of risk tell us that there two things that we want to accomplish—separately or, better, in combination with each other—in managing hazardous waste. First, we would like to make the waste less inherently hazardous, which can be done by treating it to destroy it or somehow to de-toxify it. Second, we would like to isolate it effectively once it has been disposed of in the environment. Isolation can be accomplished by placing the waste in a robust containment facility (a strong liner and cover, for example), by reducing its volume (so there is less to lose control of), and/or by changing its physical characteristics to reduce its mobility (so it will not go far if it escapes). The disposal restrictions of

Subtitle C parallel these techniques. They specify the characteristics of waste that can be land disposed[96] and the design of the disposal facility, and their common objective is to minimize the toxicity of the wastes being disposed and to minimize their movement within the environment. These restrictions are HSWA's main contribution to RCRA, and they contribute decisively to the gap between the burdens imposed by Subtitles C and D. It is important to remember, however, that the LDRs were separately enacted and so they sometimes are parallel, rather than integrated into, the waste identification portion of Subtitle C.

1. *The Land Ban*

HSWA was enacted in a period of extreme Congressional concern for the safety of hazardous waste disposal and extreme frustration with the Reagan EPA's slowness and mendacity in enforcing RCRA and CERCLA. The central provision of the LDRs is the so-called Land Ban.[97] Its policy basis was the 1983 OTA report, discussed above, which emphasized the dangers of land disposed waste, especially to groundwater, and the unlikelihood that any land disposed waste would remain permanently isolated from the environment. With CERCLA undoubtedly on its mind, OTA suggested that one could either pay now to control the waste, or much more later to

96. Subtitle C restrictions cover all kinds of land disposal, including deep injection wells, landfills, surface impoundments, and land treatment.

97. RCRA § 3004(d)–(h), (m); 42 U.S.C. § 6924(d)–(h), (m).

clean it up.[98] The HSWA "land ban" prohibits land disposal of certain hazardous wastes *unless* they are pretreated to reduce their toxicity or mobility in the environment. It also bans dilution and storage as management techniques. Thus, the land ban effectively shifts the presumption from managing hazardous waste in or on land, to treatment to detoxify or immobilize it. The shifted presumption was reified by the "hammer" provisions of HSWA, which foreclosed land disposition of certain wastes entirely unless EPA acted to establish a treatment standard by certain deadlines,[99] thus creating an incentive for waste generators to facilitate rather than oppose treatment standards.

   a. Applicability. The LDRs apply to all wastes (with a few exceptions, of course, most notably small generators) that are hazardous at *any* point in their life cycle.[100] EPA has insisted on this point, because HSWA's concurrent bans on storage and

98. OTA, Technologies and Management Strategies, *supra.*

99. *See, e.g.,* RCRA § 3004(g); 42 U.S.C. § 6924(g). These dates have all passed, and EPA has completed the staged process of setting treatment standards.

100. 40 C.F.R. § 261.3(d)(1). Another requirement of applicability is that EPA issue a treatment standard for the hazardous waste in question. This was a major issue for years, because HSWA required EPA to establish treatment standards according to a rigid schedule, enforced by the aforementioned "hammers," roughly based on risk. These gave rise to various distinctive terms—"California list," "third third list," "Phase III list"— that one occasionally runs into and which can be deployed to demonstrate one's membership in the RCRA cognoscenti. However, EPA has by now issued all of the treatment standards and its current practice is to set an LDR treatment standard at the same time that it lists a new waste.

dilution could otherwise be circumvented. It has significant consequences for hazardous wastes that exit the system before disposal, because it means that they still must meet the LDRs. (This is our first example of LDRs being a parallel and cumulative system.) Accordingly, generators are required to characterize their wastes at the point of generation,[101] and as soon as a waste is identified as hazardous, it is given an LDR waste code and must be disposed of in accordance with the treatment specified by that code.

b. Treatment Standards. The LDRs consist of three distinct prohibitions: land disposal without pretreatment, dilution to achieve LDR treatment standards, and storage for an extended period. Of these, the treatment standards are the most complex and include issues such as variances, technology-based regulation, and the special situation of characteristic wastes. Accordingly, we will discuss treatment standards first, before moving on to the dilution and storage bans.

The statutory language of HSWA describes the nature and purpose of the treatment standards:

those *levels or methods* of treatment, if any, which *substantially diminish the toxicity* of the waste or *substantially reduce the likelihood of migration* of hazardous constituents from the

101. *See* 40 C.F.R. § 262.11.

waste so that short-term and *long-term threats* to human health and the environment are *minimized*.[102]

The five italicized phrases indicate key points about the treatment standards:

Statutory Language	Consequence for Treatment Standards
"levels or methods of treatment"	The standards can be expressed as either concentrations of hazardous constituents or as required treatment techniques.
"substantially diminish the toxicity"	Their purpose is to reduce risk
"substantially reduce the likelihood of migration"	by de-toxifying and/or immobilizing the waste.
"long-term threats"	Congress is concerned with the long-term fate of land-disposed waste, which OTA and EPA assert is, eventually, reintroduction into the environment.
"minimized"	The applicable substantive standard is to "minimize"—and not (for example) to optimize or cost-justify environmental threats.

The treatment standards themselves come in two basic forms: maximum permitted concentrations of hazardous constituents in the waste itself or its leacheate, and the effective application of a designated technology.[103] EPA recognizes numerous treatment technologies which treat waste thermally, biologically, chemically, and/or physically.[104] Con-

102. RCRA § 3004(m)(1), 42 U.S.C. § 6924(m)(1) (emphasis added).

103. 40 C.F.R. §§ 268.40, 268.42.

104. EPA, Reducing Risk from Waste, *supra*, at 16. They include biological treatment, carbon adsorption, dechlorination (reduces toxicity), incineration/combustion, thermal treatment,

centration standards are generally the preferable technique, because they permit the generator to match its waste with any effective technology, and so technology standards are only used when it is clear that only one technology will work or where constituent levels are difficult or impossible to measure.[105]

c. *BDAT: Technology–Based Treatment Standards.* Section 3004(m) makes "minimiz[ation]" of "long-term threats to human health and the environment" the statutory goal of treatment, and EPA chose a technology-based standard—best demonstrated available technology (BDAT)—to accomplish this. The waste manager must either use a certain technology to treat the waste or obtain the same level of hazardous constituents that would be achieved by the application of that technology. In some ways, a technology basis seems an odd choice of regulatory criterion, since technology-based standards are often viewed as *less* stringent than risk-or hazard-based standards. In the RCRA setting, this is frequently not the case, however. In addition, EPA was highly skeptical of the ability of risk assessment to make adequate predictions of the risks associated with these wastes, especially since it would require detailed exposure assessments far into the future. Combining these rationales, the technology-based standard provides a valuable mar-

neutralization (acids, alkalais), oxidation, precipitation (to remove the solid fraction), "soil washing," solidification and stabilization, and solvent extraction.

105. RCRA Orientation Manual, *supra*, at III–91.

gin of safety in a physical environment in which the long-term isolation of the waste is uncertain and the statutory command is to "minimize ... the long-term threats." The D.C. Circuit affirmed EPA's approach in *Hazardous Waste Treatment Council v. EPA,* accepting the possibility of, as the generators put it, "treatment for treatment's sake," that is, treatment below health-based levels of concern.[106]

This fundamental approach was followed and extended in *Chemical Waste Management, Inc. v. EPA,*[107] which permitted EPA to impose technology-based standards that indicated treatment to levels of hazardous constituents *below* EPA's own standards for identifying wastes as characteristic and for delisting. The court also permitted EPA to measure the constituent levels at the point of generation, meaning that waste might be subject to LDRs even though it was below characteristic levels at the time of disposal (*see* Fig. II–6). The court not only relied, as did *HWTC III*, on the term "minimize" in section 3004(m)(1), but it pointed out that otherwise reliance on concentration levels invites dilution. Similar reasoning underlay the same result in a very different setting. In *American Petroleum Institute v. EPA,*[108] petroleum waste generators argued that BDAT for their waste included land treatment, the placement of wastes directly on land to

106. Hazardous Waste Treatment Council v. EPA (*HWTC III*), 886 F.2d 355 (D.C. Cir. 1989).

107. 976 F.2d 2 (D.C. Cir. 1992).

108. *Supra*, 906 F.2d 729.

facilitate biological or sunlight treatment, making the land both the treatment and disposal unit. The court accepted EPA's position that a land disposal facility must fully treat the hazardous waste *before* applying the waste to the land. The court thus enforced Congress' concern in HSWA—in the storage prohibition, as well as in the pretreatment requirement—that hazardous wastes *never* be placed in the environment in an untreated or uncontrolled way, even if it means, in some cases, repetitive treatment.

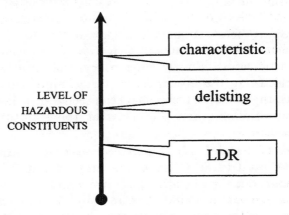

Fig. II–6. RCRA Constituent Levels

The illogic of different constituent levels in different parts of RCRA is more apparent than real. The anomaly arises because, as we have seen before, the LDR system is parallel and cumulative to the rest of RCRA, and each system has a different function. Characteristic levels simply bring wastes into the system and subject them to a range of handling and tracking requirements. It is perfectly logical to be more conservative for delisting, because in doing so the agency is forgoing any meaningful future control over the material (that is, leaving it to Subtitle D). And the whole idea behind the LDRs is that the only way to control wastes over the long term is to alter their inherent characteristics of toxicity and mobility; therefore, LDR levels need to be particularly low so that when (not if) they escape they will cause minimal harm. In other words, LDRs are simply a further extension of the reasoning behind setting delisting levels based on a multi-attribute analysis, considering issues like mismanagement to account for uncertainty and lack of control of the waste, and thus allowing them to be below characteristic levels. Finally, this policy and result are reflected in the all-important term "minimize" in section 3004: if technology can achieve a lower concentration, then that is what the statute requires.

d. *Universal Treatment Standards.* Because EPA set treatment levels separately for different waste streams, including both listed and characteristic wastes, it found that it mandated different levels of the same constituents in different waste streams, even though it was consistently applying a BDAT standard. Because these anomalies were *within* the LDR system, they could not be justified as above, and so EPA created a system of Universal Treatment Standards (UTS) to achieve greater consistency across waste streams in the required reduction of hazardous constituents.[109] The UTS are also

109.   40 C.F.R. § 268.48.

based on BDAT, and EPA uses them primarily as reference points to set individual treatment standards.

The UTS levels are also helpful in dealing with the difference between the management of listed and characteristic wastes. Characteristic wastes are subject to special standards in the LDR system.[110] The usual management for characteristic wastes is, as we have seen above, de-characterization, that is, removing the quality that rendered them characteristic. However, in the LDR system it is also necessary to look for "underlying hazardous constituents," that is, hazardous constituents of the waste *other* than the ones that rendered it characteristic. The latter must *also* be treated to the concentrations in the UTS before the waste can be land disposed.

e. Variances. The requirement to meet LDR treatment standards is not absolute. Generators of non-exempt waste can apply for a "national capacity" variance, which permits a later date for compliance when "adequate alternative treatment, recovery, or disposal capacity that protects public health and the environment" is unavailable.[111] Likewise, case-by-case variances allow a delay in compliance of up to two years.[112] EPA also offers alternative

110. 40 C.F.R. § 268.9.

111. RCRA § 3004(h)(2), 42 U.S.C. § 6924(h)(2); *see also* 40 C.F.R. § 268.5.

112. RCRA § 3004(h)(3), 42 U.S.C. § 6924(h)(3); *see also* 40 C.F.R. § 268.5.

treatment standards for contaminated soil and debris, to account for the huge volumetric increase occasioned by the application of the contained-in interpretation. EPA does not, however, offer any relief from the mixture and derived-from rules, much to the chagrin of hazardous waste generators.

Of particular interest is the so-called no-migration variance, which may be obtained upon demonstrating "to a reasonable degree of certainty, that there will be no migration of hazardous constituents from the disposal unit or injection zone for as long as the wastes remain dangerous."[113] The statute treats this as a genuine alternative to treatment,[114] but EPA treats it as an exceptional situation because it (following the OTA report) is unconvinced of the likelihood of making such a showing. The no-migration variance is applied almost entirely to deep injection wells, a common way of managing hazardous waste. Consequently, EPA limits the no-migration variance to natural conditions, it uses a 10,000–year modeling horizon, and engineered barriers will not contribute to a no-migration showing. It does, however, interpret migration to mean waste movement in amounts above health-based levels; the disposer need not show, for example, that not even a single molecule of a hazardous constituent will leave the disposal area.[115]

113. RCRA § 3004(d)(1), 42 U.S.C. § 6924(d)(1); *see also* 40 C.F.R. § 268.6.

114. *See HWTC III*, *supra*, 886 F.2d 355.

115. *See* Natural Resources Defense Council v. EPA, 907 F.2d 1146 (D.C. Cir. 1990) (upholding these standards for injection wells).

f. The Dilution and Storage Prohibitions. Recall that the LDR land ban has three major components: the pretreatment requirement that we have been discussing, a dilution prohibition, and a storage prohibition. Dilution is of course a tempting reaction to treatment standards that are expressed in terms of concentration levels. One simply adds more material, and the concentration of the hazardous constituents drops. EPA prohibited dilution as a means of meeting LDR treatment standards,[116] in part for the substantive reasons we have already seen, and in part as a technical "fix" for a loophole in the regulatory technique it had chosen (just as it had to adopt the mixture rule for listed wastes). EPA does accept dilution for CIR wastes; however, it will only do so if it can be demonstrated that—in light of its concerns about dilution in other settings—the waste still meets the "minimized threat" standard of section 3004.[117]

The storage prohibition encourages waste generators to adopt what is known as a treat-as-you-go approach.[118] The regulations provide that if the waste is stored for more than a year, then the generator must rebut the presumption that it is being disposed; if less than a year, then EPA must rebut the presumption that it is only being stored.[119] The storage prohibition expresses Con-

116. 40 C.F.R. § 268.3. Dilution is permitted to occur in the course of legitimate accumulation of material for treatment.

117. Chemical Waste Management v. EPA, *supra,* 976 F.2d 2.

118. RCRA § 3004(j), 42 U.S.C. § 6924(j).

119. 40 C.F.R. § 268.50.

gress' concern that hazardous waste not be left lying about for long periods in unsuitable facilities. Moreover, the problem of sham storage (*i.e.*, storage that is really disposal) is addressed by prohibiting storage altogether, or at least drastically limiting it. As with the land ban itself, the storage prohibition is not absolute.

g. HWIR and LDRs. Despite having good reasons for using technology-based standards in the LDR program and for having a range of permissible hazardous constituent levels within RCRA, EPA is under pressure (much of it self-generated) to adopt unitary, risk-based identification and treatment standards. The proposed Hazardous Waste Identification Rule, discussed above, would adopt risk-based standards for waste identification, and it looked forward to establishing a single risk level that would serve as an exit level for identification as well as a treatment level for LDRs. This enterprise, while theoretically attractive, suffers from both legal and practical problems. The legal problem is that the LDRs remain a parallel and cumulative requirement, and so bringing them into the identification system would require a thorough rethinking of the entire system by EPA, if not by Congress. The practical problem is that EPA adopted technology-based standards designed to minimize hazard for good reasons. It was uncertain about the ability of risk assessment techniques to characterize and, especially, to predict the dangers of hazardous wastes. More importantly, risk assessment would necessarily be based on assumptions about the ability to control hazardous wastes "for as long as they remain hazardous." These are extremely dicey assumptions over long periods of time (EPA uses 10,000 years) because the ability to predict and prescribe the future is so limited.[120] In other words, there is much to be said for the essential wisdom of the HSWA policy that recognized that long-term future is uncertain, and so the inherent toxic and mobility characteristics of land-disposed waste ought to be the first and best defense against escape into the environment.

2. *Design Standards*

HSWA also required EPA to improve the capacity of land disposal units to isolate the (pretreated) hazardous wastes disposed in them. This is strictly a secondary measure, because neither Congress, nor OTA, nor EPA had much confidence in disposal units over the very long term. It is nevertheless a logical and important element of waste management.

Within the general rubric of establishing design standards for TSD facilities, HSWA specifically provides for "minimum technological requirements" (MTRs) for land disposal units.[121] RCRA's goal is total isolation of the waste. Therefore, while there is particular attention to the bottom lining of the unit to prevent groundwater contamination, the objective is to contain the waste on all sides with

120. John S. Applegate & Stephen Dycus, *Institutional Controls or Emperor's Clothes? Long–Term Stewardship of the Nuclear Weapons Complex*, 28 ENVTL. L. REP. 10631 (1998).

121. RCRA § 3004(*o*), 42 U.S.C. § 6924(*o*).

robust, long lasting, and redundant physical structures. These structures must receive frequent attention in the form of leachate collection systems, leak detection systems, and groundwater monitoring systems (reflecting the special concern in HSWA for groundwater protection).[122] There are cognate provisions for Subtitle D landfills,[123] but Subtitle C is, as one would expect, far more prescriptive, detailed, and stringent.

Land disposal facilities encompass a wide variety of structures, including land treatment units, landfills, surface impoundments (ponds, pits, or lagoons), and injection wells. Based on its authority under section 3004, EPA sets technological standards for design, operation, inspection, release prevention and response, specially prohibited wastes, and closure and post-closure monitoring.[124] It should be evident that Subtitle C facilities are not only very expensive to construct, they are also very expensive to maintain before and after their closure. The MTRs are thus another reason why it is worth a great deal of effort to avoid the application of Subtitle C, and—coming full circle—this drives the waste identification disputes.

E.   The Permitting System

On a day-to-day basis, the major consequence of classification of wastes as hazardous is the permit

122.   RCRA § 3004(p), 42 U.S.C. § 6924(p).

123.   RCRA §§ 4004, 4010, 42 U.S.C. §§ 6944, 6949a.

124.   40 C.F.R. part 264.

requirement of Subtitle C. The permit requirement goes beyond extensive procedural demands (obtaining the permit, recordkeeping, etc.), because RCRA and its regulations aggressively use the permit system—as regulatory schemes frequently do—to impose detailed substantive requirements on permittees.[125] In the case of RCRA, the permittees include those who generate, store, treat, and dispose of hazardous wastes, and they are required by their permits to have facilities that meet certain design and operational standards, to plan for the facility's closure and post-closure management (including financial responsibility), and to remedy any contamination at the facility (*i.e.*, corrective action). Permits are, in this sense, the operational extension of the MTRs. In addition, because the permitting process is open to public involvement, it presents an opportunity for the public to object to the siting of a facility in a particular location.

1. The Manifest System and Exportation of Hazardous Waste

Even though it is the foundation of RCRA's cradle-to-grave approach, the hazardous waste manifest system can be dealt with summarily because it is conceptually very simple. EPA requires everyone who handles a hazardous waste to obtain an EPA identification number, and it is illegal to transfer

125. For a description of the RCRA permitting process from an unhappy customer, *see* Miriam Feder, *The Permit Application Process Under RCRA—A Lament*, 18 ENVTL. L. 671 (1988).

hazardous waste to or obtain it from someone who does not have a number. A manifest must follow the waste from generator to final disposition. The manifest contains basic who, what, when, and where information; it is signed at each step along the way; and it certifies compliance with applicable legal requirements. The manifest not only tracks the waste, but also forms the basis for the recordkeeping requirements of RCRA. The brunt of this tracking and recordkeeping falls on generators and TSDFs; apart from the manifest, transporters are mainly governed by Department of Transportation regulations for hazardous materials.[126]

Transfer of hazardous waste out of the United States is a serious concern in international environmental law, because industries in the industrialized world have a strong economic incentive to dispose of hazardous waste in the developing world, where regulation is often lax or non-existent.[127] RCRA extends the domestic manifest system to exportation in a limited way.[128] Before shipping hazardous waste out of the country, the exporter must provide EPA with certification that the exporter has notified and obtained the written consent of the importing country (unless this requirement is superseded

126. RCRA § 3003, 42 U.S.C. § 6923.

127. *See* Theodore Waugh, *Where Do We Go From Here: Legal Controls and Future Strategies for Addressing the Transportation of Hazardous Wastes Across International Borders,* 11 FORDHAM ENVTL. L.J. 477 (2000); D. KOFI ASANTE-DUAH & IMRE V. NAGY, INTERNATIONAL TRADE IN HAZARDOUS WASTE (1998).

128. RCRA § 3017, 42 U.S.C. § 6938; 40 C.F.R. §§ 262.50–262.58.

by an international agreement). However, EPA has virtually no resources to police the legitimacy of the documentation and none to determine if the conditions of disposal elsewhere are at all appropriate to the waste—and even if it could discover this, EPA has no authority to deny export permission on this ground.

The Basel Convention on the transboundary movement of hazardous waste,[129] would require stronger controls on export based on the concept of *prior informed consent* by the importing country. The convention also requires appropriate disposal in the importing country and, most importantly, reimportation of waste material that was not properly managed in the importing country. These are much more onerous requirements than RCRA; nevertheless, Basel is widely regarded among developing nations as weak and in effect an invitation to exploitative disposal.[130] Many developing countries have declined to join Basel, and the countries that have ratified it subsequently adopted a complete ban on export from industrialized to developing countries. The U.S. has signed and ratified the treaty, but it has not yet taken the necessary steps to implement it by making conforming changes in

129. Basel Convention on the Control of Transboundary Movements of Hazardous Wastes and Their Disposal (entered into force May 5, 1992), reprinted in 28 I.L.M. 649 (1989), available at http://www.basel.int (last visited Mar. 30, 2005).

130. Ibrahim J. Wani, *Poverty, Governance, the Rule of Law, and International Environmentalism: A Critique of the Basel Convention on Hazardous Wastes*, 1 KANSAS J.L. & POLICY 37 (1991).

RCRA.[131] Since many other nations have ratified the Basel Convention, they are precluded by the convention from accepting U.S. hazardous waste. As a practical matter, therefore, U.S. firms are limited to exports to the countries with which the U.S. has bilateral waste treaties, Canada and Mexico.

2. Generator Permits

Generators of hazardous waste are broadly defined to include those whose activities result in the creation of materials that are classified as hazardous wastes and those who import hazardous wastes. The kinds of requirements that flow from generation of hazardous waste include, among others, determining whether waste materials are hazardous, notifying authorities and obtaining an identification number (to begin the manifest system), keeping records on the quantity and identity of wastes, following proper labeling, containment, and worker training standards, designating an appropriate TSD facility for the wastes, *not* accumulating waste beyond 90 days, and submitting biennial reports.

One requirement deserves special mention, since it goes to the heart of RCRA's goals. Section 3002(b)(1) of the statute requires generators to certify in the manifest that it has a program in place to reduce the volume or the quantity and toxicity of its hazardous waste "to the degree determined by the generator to be economically practica-

131. EPA, International Waste Activities, Basel Convention, available at http://www.epa.gov/epaoswer/osw/internat/basel.htm (last visited July 18, 2005).

ble.''[132] This is a nod toward direct pollution prevention, but unfortunately little more. Not only is this patently a requirement for a plan, as opposed to actual waste reduction, but the goals of the plan are entirely within the judgment of the generator itself. Moreover, the generator does not even need to commit to following or meeting the goals of its own plan. If Congress were serious about pollution prevention and waste minimization by any means other than the indirect one of making waste management difficult and expensive, this would be the place to do it. Clearly, however, it has chosen to go nowhere near the internal operations of a waste generator, exercising its influence only externally.

The extent of the requirements differs substantially according to the class of generator. EPA divides generators into three classes, and an individual's status may change from month to month. Generators who produce over 1000 kg/month of hazardous waste (or smaller amounts of acutely hazardous waste) are required to obtain permits and meet all of the requirements. Small quantity generators, who produce between 100 and 1000 kg/month, have less recordkeeping and may store hazardous waste longer. Conditionally exempt small quantity generators (CESQGs), who produce less than 100 kg/month, are exempted from most of the procedural requirements—permit, identification number, recordkeeping, and even manifests—but

132. RCRA § 3002(b)(1), 42 U.S.C. § 6922(b)(1). A virtually identical provision applies to permits for TSD facilities on the generator's premises. RCRA § 3005(h), 42 U.S.C. § 6925(h).

must comply with the substantive requirements for identifying hazardous waste and for proper storage and disposition for transportation, treatment, and disposal.

The exemption for CESQGs makes sense for many of the same reasons that the reduced burdens for used oil make sense. It is simply not administratively feasible to regulate a huge number of small operators; furthermore, heavy burdens on small operators will encourage evasion which will be difficult to monitor and enforce. Nevertheless, permits do perform several important functions that are lost with respect to exempted generators. First, a permit identifies the individuals handling hazardous waste and allows tracking of hazardous waste. This is clearly a fundamental part of RCRA. Second, it allows participants in the chain of custody of hazardous waste to protect themselves (as well as the environment) by knowing whether they are dealing with an operation that is qualified, for example, to treat or dispose of hazardous waste properly.[133] Third, permits act as a "barrier to entry" for generators (or TSDFs) of hazardous wastes, discouraging small, unprepared firms from engaging in the activity. Permits are a crude instrument, to be sure, but they presumably discourage unfit entities from op-

133. The courts have held that RCRA § 3008(d)(1), 42 U.S.C. § 6928(d)(1), requires scienter (actual knowledge, which may be inferred, of course) of the permit status of the receiver of hazardous waste. U.S. v. Hayes International Corp., 786 F.2d 1499 (11th Cir. 1986); U.S. v. Speach, 968 F.2d 795 (9th Cir. 1992) ("knowingly" in § 3008(d)(1) modifies both the transportation of the waste and also the lack of a permit by the recipient).

erating and encourage all entities to reduce the amounts of hazardous waste generated. Fourth, permits generate important information for EPA to use in understanding the general nature of the waste disposal problem, and in exercising continuing control over and monitoring compliance by individual actors. Fifth, permits allow for individual requirements tailored to site-specific issues, and they can serve as the compilation in one place of the many RCRA requirements, variances, and other legal limitations (*e.g.*, zoning) that apply to the site. Sixth, permits can act as a shield for their holders, not only setting out in clear terms all that is required of them, but providing legal cover if they are followed. Finally, permits are a useful focal point for public participation in hazardous waste management, as they offer an opportunity for the public to know who is generating and handling these wastes and to raise objections.

3. TSDF Permits

Permits for TSD facilities are more complex and demanding.[134] Indeed, RCRA is mostly about regulation of TSDFs: what they may dispose of, how they may operate, how they must close operations, and what they must clean-up. Treatment means any method that changes the physical, chemical, or biological character of a hazardous waste; storage means any containment of hazardous waste, which is not disposal; and disposal means the intentional or unintentional placement of the waste into or on

134. 40 C.F.R. parts 264 (generally), 265 (interim status facilities).

land or in the water so that it can enter the environment. A permit is required for all of these activities. As an initial matter, note that these terms do not require *intent* to treat, store, or dispose; the permit requirement can attach unexpectedly to anyone who takes these actions.

The regulations identify a number of general types of TSD facilities, each suitable for particular purposes:

- *treatment and storage only*: containers (*e.g.*, 55-gallon drums), containment buildings, drip pads, tanks, waste piles, incinerators;
- *disposal only*: landfills and injection wells;
- *treatment, storage,* and *disposal*: surface impoundments and land treatment units.

The basic requirements for TSD permits are familiar: a facility must notify EPA that it is managing hazardous waste, obtain an identification number, and participate in the manifest system. The permit requirements go on to include detailed specifications for location, design, and construction of each type of facility, based on the MTRs discussed above; contingency plans for containment failures; groundwater monitoring; assurances of the facility's financial responsibility, that is, its ability to build, operate, and close the facility within the requirements of the law; and, where indicated, corrective action to clean up contamination at the site.[135] The recur-

135. An issue of great significance early in the history of the statute was so-called interim status permits, which were designed to transition existing, operating facilities into the RCRA regulatory scheme. RCRA § 3005(e), 42 U.S.C. § 6925(e). The

ring themes in TSDF permits are groundwater monitoring and financial responsibility, reflecting the overriding concerns in HSWA for, respectively, groundwater protection and prevention of contaminated sites that the public will need to remediate through the Superfund program.

These themes return in the provisions for the closure of TSDFs. All permits require submission of a detailed closure plan from the outset, and the plans focus not only on the closure as such, but also on the post-closure period. Upon closure, the facility must either remove all waste and contamination, or else maintain the containment of the waste so that it does not pose a risk to human health or the environment.[136] The great divide here is between "clean closure"—which is to say complete removal of all hazardous waste and clean-up of any environmental media to background levels of hazardous material—and the creation of, in effect, a hazardous waste landfill, which requires a post-closure permit. Protection of groundwater is the primary statutory driver,[137] and the regulatory goal (reflecting the statutory standard for LDRs) is to "minimize" the escape of hazardous waste or constituents into the

application process for these permits was not itself very burdensome, but it came with major substantive requirements, especially groundwater monitoring and financial responsibility. All interim permits needed to be made permanent or the facility closed by 1992, so these requirements now apply only to facilities that handle newly listed wastes.

136. 40 C.F.R. §§ 264.110–264.120.

137. HSWA specifically requires it. RCRA § 3004(p), 42 U.S.C. § 6924(p).

environment.[138] This goal is severely undercut, however, by the remarkably short post-closure monitoring and maintenance period of thirty years.[139] Hazardous wastes are frequently persistent—indeed, that is a basis for listing—and will certainly still be around in thirty years.[140] Moreover, isolating hazardous waste from the environment is also *protecting* hazardous waste from the environment, so the more successful we are in isolating the waste, the more we can be assured that the hazardous waste will remain hazardous. It is hard to imagine that, as these closure periods begin to expire, Superfund obligations will not escalate.

4. *Corrective Action*

"Corrective action" means cleaning up RCRA facilities at which hazardous waste has been released into the environment, typically in soil or groundwater. Prior to HSWA, EPA's only authority for ordering clean-up was the "imminent and substantial endangerment" provision of section 7003 (discussed below). HSWA made corrective action a condition of obtaining and holding a new or interim status permit, and it gave EPA broad authority to require corrective action. RCRA now authorizes corrective action for releases from waste management units within permitted sites and offsite contamination, in addition to the existing section 7003 authority.[141]

138. 40 C.F.R. § 264.111.

139. 40 C.F.R. § 264.117(a)(1).

140. *See* Applegate & Dycus, *supra*, at 10633–34.

141. RCRA §§ 3004(u), (v), 3008(h), 42 U.S.C. §§ 6924(u), (v), 6928(h). EPA also claims the power to require corrective

The trigger for corrective action is the release of a hazardous waste or a constituent of a hazardous waste at a facility which after November 19, 1980, stored, treated, or disposed of hazardous waste and which failed to obtain certified closure before January 26, 1983. Each of these elements is more expansive—sometimes much more so—than might at first appear:

- *Permit.* The touchstone for the application of corrective action requirements is a facility's need for a RCRA permit of some kind. This includes any site where treatment, storage, or disposal of hazardous waste occurs, as well as post-closure activities at a site that has not been "clean closed." Facilities that *should,* but do not, have a permit are equally subject to corrective action.

- *Timing.* Corrective action may be required regardless of the time at which the waste was placed at the facility, if the facility otherwise meets the above timing requirements.

- *Facility.* A facility includes all "solid waste management units" (SWMUs) within the fences of the facility, including contiguous property held by the same owner. "Solid," not "hazardous"—a release at any disposal area of the facility gives rise to liability. Moreover, EPA uses the concept

action under its general authority craft permits to protect public health, RCRA § 3005(c)(3), 42 U.S.C. § 6925(c)(3). For a useful overview, *see* Richard G. Stoll, *Corrective Action in RCRA Permits: An Emerging Rival to Superfund as the Hot Area for Environmental Lawyers and Consultants,* 21 ENVTL. L. REP. 10666 (1991).

of "areas of concern" to include parts of the facility that involve no waste handling at all. EPA can also require clean-up of areas outside the facility under section 3004(v).

• *Constituent.* A triggering release is not limited to hazardous wastes; it includes hazardous constituents, referring to the D List discussed above. The release of a constituent triggers corrective action even if the release is below characteristic or listing levels of the constituent or the waste that generated it (and thus is not itself a hazardous waste).

• *Solid waste management unit.* Section 3004(u) speaks of releases from "solid [—not hazardous—] waste management units." Combined with the inclusion of constituents, this confirms that the source of the release need not be a characteristic or listed waste. Moreover, EPA can require corrective action at SWMUs that are not themselves leaking if the facility is otherwise subject to corrective action.

• *Scope of clean-up.* HSWA requires the clean-up of *all* environmental media, not just soil.

Since a person can unintentionally store or dispose of hazardous waste, it is relatively easy to find oneself in the position of needing a permit—and then needing to clean up, to clean close the site, or to become the post-closure owner of a hazardous waste landfill. The overall effect is to make permits a very powerful tool for cleaning up contaminated land.

Given its breadth of application and coverage, RCRA itself has surprisingly little to say about the process for undertaking corrective action, who should pay for it, or the clean-up goals—subjects that occupy an entire, complex statute in CERCLA. Nor has EPA issued formal, comprehensive regulations like the National Contingency Plan adopted for CERCLA. Instead, EPA relies primarily on guidance documents[142] and on individual judgments in individual permits, and it has used this legal informality to develop a variety of ways to make the corrective action process more flexible and less onerous than it would otherwise be (or than CERCLA is).

The main target of flexibility is the LDRs. Their burdens are particularly noticeable in the corrective action setting, where the burden is in a sense retroactive. Corrective action, unlike the usual TSD restrictions, is not about prevention of future harm but remediation of past harm. The first technique for creating flexibility is remedial action plans (RAPs), which are in effect permits for treatment, storage, and disposal at a corrective action site, but which are far easier to obtain than a regular permit.

Another technique for flexibility is special waste management units that allow for alternative treatment standards for wastes, like contaminated soil,

142. EPA has collected this guidance in a handbook for corrective action. *See* EPA, Handbook of Groundwater Protection and Cleanup Policies for RCRA Corrective Action (Updated Version) (2004), available at http://www.epa.gov/correctiveaction/resource/guidance/gw/gwhandbk/hwhndbk.htm (last visited Aug. 6, 2005).

which are generated by remediation. "Staging piles" permit the temporary accumulation of non-liquid wastes without triggering either the LDR or MTR requirements. "Temporary units" allow for treatment and storage of wastes during remediation to avoid the storage limitations in the LDRs. And "corrective action management units" (CAMUs) allow for disposal of remediation waste at less than LDR and MTR standards, but at least at the standards of a new Subtitle D landfill. EPA further simplifies clean-up by focusing on current human exposure and groundwater migration as program indicators for priorities and progress. While these are not the only standards for actual remediation, their importance in evaluating the overall program suggests that they will have substantive significance, as well.

Finally, EPA is being strongly encouraged to consider "risk-based corrective action" (RBCA, or Rebecca) for clean-up. The basic standards under RCRA are technology-based and aimed at "minimizing" hazard. Since EPA assumes that all wastes will eventually escape, its standards focus on the intrinsic qualities of the material to reduce the danger to the public, rather than lack of exposure to the material in a given physical location. As a result, the LDR standards tend to be very stringent. While CAMUs and other forms of flexibility pull back from the LDRs to some extent, they do not adopt a fully risk-based approach. RBCA would replace generic clean-up standards based on intrinsic qualities with a particularized evaluation of the risks posed by a particular site, specifically taking limited future exposure into account.[143] (Recall that risk is toxicity × exposure, and reduction of either reduces risk.) Thus, unlike the current approach to corrective action, which focuses on reducing contamination levels below prescribed numerical standards, the RBCA approach concentrates on a site's present and potential risks, seeking to reduce contamination to an acceptable level of risk based on exposure pathways determined by expected future land use. EPA currently advocates this approach under the name "results-based" corrective action,[144] and in nonbinding guidance it has urged states and regional offices to focus on a "holistic" risk approach to the site in setting clean-up goals.

The risk-based approach can be criticized from two directions. First, the use of numerical risk point estimates as the basis for regulation is limited by inadequate data and incomplete understanding of underlying toxicity and exposure processes. As a consequence, point estimates are the result of a process riddled with uncertainties and subjective

143. For enthusiastic discussions of RBCA, *see* James R. Rocco & Lesley Hay Wilson, *The Risk Based Corrective Action Process*, in BROWNFIELDS: A COMPREHENSIVE GUIDE TO REDEVELOPING CONTAMINATED PROPERTY 15 40 (Todd S. Davis & Kevin D. Margolis eds., 1997), at 250–67; James P. O'Brien, *The Tiered Approach to Corrective Action Objectives and the Site Remediation Program in Illinois*, 27 ENVTL. L. REP. 10611 (1997).

144. EPA, Results–Based Approaches and Tailored Oversight Guidance for Facilities Subject to Corrective Action Under Subtitle C of the Resource Conservation and Recovery Act (2003), available at http://www.epa.gov/epaoswer/hazwaste/ca/resource/guidance/gen_ca/reslt-bse.pdf (last visited July 6, 2005).

judgments.[145] Second, to the extent that exposure estimates are based on assumed future land uses— will it be a factory? an undeveloped park? a home? a school? a farm?—it depends on the ability to predict and to prescribe future land uses, which is a notably inexact science.[146]

While RBCA is not yet firmly entrenched, the other forms of flexibility are well established in the corrective action program, and it is fair to say that they reflect the same kind of "C-/D +" impulse that we saw previously in the definitional section of this chapter. Both situations throw into sharp relief the all-or-nothing quality of RCRA. Congress and EPA have extremely good reasons for imposing highly protective standards under Subtitle C, most importantly the conviction that containment is not forever and the related goal of preventing of future Superfund sites. These stringent standards are (arguably) nevertheless ill-suited to certain types of waste (*e.g.*, "universal" waste), just as they are to certain settings like corrective action and its remediation waste. It is not coincidental that the CAMU rule permits land disposal of material that is pro-

145. There is an entire literature on the strengths and limitations of risk assessment. They are applied to RBCA in Victor B. Flatt, *"[H]e Should at His Peril Keep It There . . .": How the Common Law Tells Us that Risk–Based Corrective Action is Wrong*, 76 NOTRE DAME L. REV. 341 (2001); *see also* Alex Geisinger, *Rethinking Risk–Based Environmental Cleanup*, 76 IND. L.J. 367 (2001).

146. John S. Applegate, *Risk Assessment, Redevelopment, and Environmental Justice: Evaluating the Brownfields Bargain*, 13 J. NAT. RESOURCES & ENVTL. L. 243 (1997–1998); Applegate & Dycus, *supra.*

scribed by the land ban in Subtitle C *as long as* it is disposed in a Subtitle D qualified landfill. This is another C-/D+ standard.

Much more could be said about the corrective action program, but its basic purpose is very much the same as that of CERCLA, and it raises similar legal and policy issues. We will therefore defer further discussion of clean-up issues to the CERCLA chapter. It is worth noting, however, a number of important differences between the RCRA and CERCLA programs. First, while RCRA is limited to wastes (CERCLA covers "hazardous substances" from many sources), it does cover petroleum and petroleum products which are excluded from CERC-LA. EPA can, and often does, use its ability to proceed concurrently under RCRA and CERCLA to expand the reach of its clean-up authority. Second, unlike CERCLA, RCRA programs, including corrective action, can be delegated to and carried out by the states. Thirty-eight states and territories have corrective action authority.[147] This gives rise to complications where both RCRA and CERCLA apply, because regulatory authority is shared between EPA and states, and it is not always a happy coexistence for either the regulators or the regulatee. Third, there are many more RCRA corrective action sites—about 5000—than Superfund clean-up sites, though they tend to be much smaller than Superfund sites. Finally, the most fundamental difference between them is that RCRA corrective action does not have the liability aspect that is central

147. EPA, Handbook of Groundwater Protection, *supra*, at v (number as of 2001).

to CERCLA; rather, being a prerequisite for a TSD permit, its burdens fall entirely on the owner or operator of the TSD facility itself.[148]

5. *Environmental Justice*

At the beginning of this chapter, we saw that RCRA deploys regulations based on different kinds of criteria: risk, feasibility, cost-benefit, and so on. The principal way in which RCRA uses *information*-based regulation is the public participation aspect of the permitting process. To obtain a permit for a TSD facility, the owner or operator must not only provide EPA with the detailed information discussed above, but the public gains access to this information. Moreover, the statute specifically requires notification of the public of permit applications and requires a public hearing in any case where an objection to the permit is submitted.[149] EPA's regulations go beyond these requirements and provide for public information and/or participation from the pre-application phase through modifications, closure, and corrective action.[150] These information requirements are a form of regulation in the sense that they give members of the public an opportunity to raise objections based on the application. Members of the public frequently object to the location of the facility.[151] This is sometimes described as the NIMBY (not in my backyard) Syndrome, in which residents oppose what they

148. TSD owners and operators can sometimes use CERCLA to recover from other responsible parties.

149. RCRA § 7004(b)(2), 42 U.S.C. § 6972(b)(2).

150. RCRA Orientation Manual, *supra*, at VII–3.

151. For a detailed discussion of facility siting and environmental justice, *see* CASEBOOK, *supra*, ch. 13.

perceive as an environmental disamenity—a highway, a landfill, a factory, a large building or shopping center, or even a halfway house. These are collectively known as locally undesirable land uses (LULUs). While the term NIMBY conjures up a selfish desire to maintain the existing character of the area against the intrusions of industrial or social necessity[152]—and sometimes that is the case—location objections often involve bona fide concerns about threats to human health. Objections to TSD facilities (which, after all, handle *hazardous* waste) need to be taken seriously, and public participation in the permitting process allows that to happen.

An important species of objection to the location of a TSD facility is not to the individual facility *per se*, but rather to the distribution of that facility and others like it. It should be obvious, given a few moments' thought, that environmental amenities (like parks) and disamenities (like landfills) are not evenly distributed among persons and places. This is true for all environmental goods and bads—from forests to air pollution—but nowhere are the distributive effects more noticeable or well documented than with hazardous waste facilities.[153] "Environmental justice" refers to the

152. For an interesting perspective on NIMBY as a human instinct, *see* Michael B. Gerrard, *Territoriality, Risk Perception, and Counterproductive Legal Structures: The Case of Waste Facility Siting*, 27 ENVTL. L. 1017 (1997).

153. *See generally* Richard J. Lazarus, *Pursuing "Environmental Justice": The Distributional Effects of Environmental Protection*, 87 Nw. U.L. REV. 787 (1993).

unequal distribution of environmental bads (and goods), primarily along the lines of political and social empowerment, that is, the poor and racial and ethnic minorities.

The environmental justice movement had its origins in the siting of hazardous waste facilities. A 1982 protest against a PCB landfill by the African-American community of Warren County, North Carolina, was followed by studies by the General Accounting Office[154] and the United Church of Christ Commission on Racial Justice,[155] both of which suggested that hazardous waste landfills are disproportionately located in minority communities. Robert Bullard's 1990 book, *Dumping in Dixie*,[156] catalyzed the movement by bringing together these, his own, and other studies and stories of injustice in the siting of environmentally undesirable facilities into a powerful indictment of siting practices.[157]

154. General Accounting Office, Siting Hazardous Waste Landfills and Their Correlation with Racial and Economic Status of Surrounding Communities (June 1983).

155. UNITED CHURCH OF CHRIST, COMMISSION ON RACIAL JUSTICE, TOXIC WASTES AND RACE IN THE UNITED STATES: A NATIONAL REPORT ON THE RACIAL AND SOCIOECONOMIC CHARACTERISTICS OF COMMUNITIES WITH HAZARDOUS WASTE SITES (1987).

156. ROBERT D. BULLARD, DUMPING IN DIXIE: RACE, CLASS AND ENVIRONMENTAL QUALITY (1990).

157. For a brief summary of the movement, *see* U.S. Commission on Civil Rights, Not in My Backyard: Executive Order 12,898 and Title VI as Tools for Achieving Environmental Justice (2003), available at http://www.usccr.gov/pubs/envjust/main.htm (last visited Aug. 6, 2005). A longer treatment is LUKE W. COLE & SHEILA R. FOSTER, FROM THE GROUND UP: ENVIRONMENTAL RACISM AND THE RISE OF THE ENVIRONMENTAL JUSTICE MOVEMENT (2001).

The evidence for a general pattern of discriminatory siting has not gone unchallenged,[158] and there are a number of significant methodological difficulties in demonstrating both national and local instances of disproportion.[159] Perhaps the most significant difficulty has been disaggregating the effects of race, economic status, and the market for land. The question, to paraphrase Professor Vicki Been, is whether it is a matter of "coming to the nuisance or going to the barrios"?[160] Been's careful empirical and theoretical studies come to few firm conclusions on these questions,[161] in large part because, as she emphasizes, it is very difficult to define the terms of disproportion or environmental justice, especially over time—how are the neighborhoods defined? how is fairness defined? what are the relevant percentages? compared to what? how are confounding factors handled?

158. Douglas L. Anderton *et al.*, *Environmental Equity: The Demographics of Dumping*, 31 DEMOGRAPHY 229 (1994); Civil Rights Commission, *supra* at 182–83 (dissenting views).

159. *See, e.g.*, Paul Mohai, *The Demographics of Dumping Revisited: Examining the Impact of Alternate Methodologies in Environmental Justice Research*, 14 VA. ENVTL. L.J. 615 (1995); General Accounting Office, Demographics of People Living Near Waste Facilities (1995) (surveying ten other studies).

160. Vicki Been, *Coming to the Nuisance or Going to the Barrios? A Longitudinal Analysis of Environmental Justice Claims*, 24 ECOLOGY L.Q. 1 (1997).

161. Vicki Been, *Locally Undesirable Land Uses in Minority Neighborhoods: Disproportionate Siting or Market Dynamics?* 103 YALE L.J. 1383 (1994); Vicki Been, *What's Fairness Got to Do with It? Environmental Justice and the Siting of Locally Undesirable Land Uses*, 78 CORNELL L. REV. 1001 (1993).

These difficulties notwithstanding, many share an intuitive sense that environmental disamenities are concentrated in poor and minority areas, and so environmental justice has become a significant basis for objecting to the siting of individual TSDFs. Conversely, the TSDF permitting process has become a significant tool for those seeking to achieve environmental justice.[162] Efforts to block the siting of TSDFs through judicial remedies for discrimination under the Fourteenth Amendment and Title VI of the Civil Rights Act of 1964 (prohibiting discrimination in federal programs)[163] have been generally unavailing, however. The requirement to prove discriminatory intent in addition to disproportionate impact has been a major obstacle to such claims, especially since land use decisions usually involve many factors that can be used to justify the choice of location in nondiscriminatory terms.[164] While section 602 of the Act permits federal agencies to adopt regulations that do not require intent to discriminate (that is, permit an administrative remedy

162. *See generally* THE LAW OF ENVIRONMENTAL JUSTICE: THEORIES AND PROCEDURES TO ADDRESS DISPROPORTIONATE RISKS (Michael B. Gerrard ed. 1999); CLIFFORD RECHTSCHAFFEN & EILEEN GAUNA, ENVIRONMENTAL JUSTICE: LAW, POLICY & REGULATION (2002); Richard J. Lazarus & Stephanie Tai, *Integrating Environmental Justice into EPA Permitting Authority*, 26 ECOLOGY L.Q. 617 (1999).

163. 42 U.S.C. §§ 2000d–2000d–7.

164. *See* Village of Arlington Heights v. Metropolitan Housing Devel. Corp., 429 U.S. 252 (1977) (Amend. XIV); *see also* Bean v. Southwestern Waste Management Corp., 482 F.Supp. 673 (S.D. Tex. 1979), aff'd without opinion, 782 F.2d 1038 (5th Cir. 1986) (challenge to landfill siting brought under 42 U.S.C. § 1983).

based on disproportionate impact alone),[165] the federal courts have recently held that this does not create an implied private cause of action, either directly under section 602 or under section 1983.[166] These cases may not be the last word on the use of Title VI for these purposes[167]; however, they make proceeding under the general discrimination statutes an uphill climb.

Administrative remedies remain, however. In 1994, President Clinton issued Executive Order No. 12,898, "Federal Actions to Address Environmental Justice in Minority Populations and Low–Income Populations."[168] The executive order requires relevant federal agencies to make environmental justice part of their missions, to develop strategies and policies to achieve environmental justice, to ensure that recipients of federal funding comply with Title VI, and to collect data on the environmental effects of their programs and activities.[169] Spurred by the executive order, EPA has issued guidance for handling Title VI. It first issued an "interim" guidance[170] that proved highly unpopular with busi-

165. 42 U.S.C. § 2000d–1.

166. 42 U.S.C. § 1983. *See* Alexander v. Sandoval, 532 U.S. 275 (2001); Gonzaga University v. Doe, 536 U.S. 273 (2002); South Camden Citizens in Action v. New Jersey Dept. of Envtl. Protection, 274 F.3d 771 (3d Cir. 2001).

167. The Title VI case law is traced in Civil Rights Commission, *supra*, at 79–97.

168. 59 Fed. Reg. 7629 (1994).

169. Executive orders, however, does not amend existing laws, nor do they create judicially enforceable rights or obligations.

170. EPA, Interim Guidance for Investigating Title VI Administrative Complaints Challenging Permits (Feb. 5, 1998),

nesses and state and local governments. It then issued two revised "draft" guidance documents that focus less on proving disproportionate impact than on inclusive decisionmaking processes.[171] Indeed, EPA has come to treat environmental justice largely as a matter of procedural fairness rather than substantive proportionality.[172] Administrative challenges to RCRA permits using Executive Order 12898 and EPA guidance have been notably unsuccessful.[173] Nevertheless, opportunities remain in in-

available at http://www.epa.gov/civilrights/polguid.htm (last visited Aug. 6, 2005). The controversy surrounding this guidance is described in June M. Lyle, Note, *Reactions to EPA's Interim Guidance: The Growing Battle over Environmental Justice Decisionmaking*, 75 IND. L.J. 687 (2000); Civil Rights Commission, *supra*, at 32–34.

171. EPA, Draft Title VI Guidance for EPA Assistance Recipients Administering Environmental Permitting Programs (June 27, 2000); Draft Revised Guidance for Investigating Title VI Administrative Complaints Challenging Permits (June 27, 2000), available at http://www.epa.gov/civilrights/polguid.htm (last visited Aug. 6, 2005).

172. *See, e.g.*, Memorandum from EPA Administrator Whitman, EPA's Commitment to Environmental Justice (Aug. 9, 2001), available at http://www.epa.gov/compliance/resources/policies/ej/admin_ej_commit_letter_081401.pdf (last visited Aug. 6, 2005) (characterizing environmental justice as "fair treatment" and "meaningful involvement"). *See also* Alice Kaswan, *Environmental Justice: Bridging the Gap Between Environmental Laws and "Justice,"* 47 AM. U. L. REV. 221 (1997) (distinguishing types of environmental justice).

173. *See, e.g.*, In re Ash Grove Cement Co., 7 Envtl. App. Dec. 387, available at 1997 WL 732000 (EPA EAB 1997); In re Chemical Waste Management of Indiana, Inc., 6 Envtl. App. Dec. 66, available at 1995 WL 395962 (EPA EAB 1995). EPA's general performance under Title VI is critically reviewed in Civil Rights Commission, *supra*, at 34–62.

dividual permit decisions to assert cumulative or unique risks to the recipient community, to require special monitoring or inspection requirements suited to the particular community, and to establish special public participation procedures.[174] Such a "retail" approach to environmental justice, if pursued aggressively, could have a significant impact on the TSD permitting process.

F. Enforcement and State Hazardous Waste Programs

RCRA provides a veritable menu of enforcement procedures to enable regulators to compel compliance with the statute and regulations. The statute also provides mechanisms for the law to be enforced by the states as the primary regulators, and by individual citizens.

1. *Actions Available to the Government*

There is an implicit hierarchy of enforcement tools under RCRA, as with most environmental statutes. The starting point is information gathering. RCRA gives broad powers to EPA to enter, inspect, and collect samples, documents, and other information from hazardous waste facilities of all

174. EPA General Counsel Memorandum (Gary S. Guzy), EPA Statutory and Regulatory Authorities Under Which Environmental Justice Issues May Be Addressed in Permitting (Dec. 1, 2000), available at http://www.epa.gov/compliance/resources/policies/ej/ej_permitting_authorities_memo_120100.pdf (last visited Aug. 6, 2005); Lazarus & Tai, *supra.*

kinds, in addition to mandatory periodic inspections of TSD facilities.[175] The courts have consistently upheld a broad interpretation of EPA's information-gathering powers.[176] In addition, EPA is empowered to order a facility (including past owners in appropriate cases) to conduct its own testing, monitoring, or analysis, upon a formal finding that the presence of the waste at the facility may present a substantial hazard to human health and the environment.[177] The penalties for noncompliance with either a judicial or an administrative order to provide such information are substantial.

Following the information gathering phase, EPA can move through a series of increasingly serious remedies for violations, beginning with informal administrative action and moving to formal administrative action, civil judicial remedies, and criminal prosecution. Additionally, under section 7003, EPA can seek a judicial injunction to abate an "imminent and substantial endangerment to human health and the environment."[178]

Section 3008(a) authorizes EPA to issue compliance orders and to assess civil penalties for their violation. EPA can also revoke or suspend individual permits. Most enforcement action is administrative, and most of that is informal, such as warning

175. RCRA § 3007(a), (e), 42 U.S.C. § 6973(a), (e).

176. *See, e.g.,* National–Standard Co. v. Adamkus, 881 F.2d 352 (7th Cir. 1989).

177. RCRA § 3013, 42 U.S.C. § 6934.

178. RCRA § 7003, 42 U.S.C. § 6973.

letters and notices of violation. EPA's preference for administrative action is mainly pragmatic, as it can stretch its limited resources when matters can be resolved relatively informally and it maintains a cooperative relationship with regulated entities. Administrative action also permits the agency to control the management of the dispute, since it need not involve the Justice Department. This in turn allows EPA to develop flexible and creative remedies for violations. For example, EPA often allows violators to undertake "supplemental environmental projects" in lieu of all or part of a monetary penalty.[179] It is debatable whether such flexibility— that is, encouraging cooperation over deterrence—is a more effective strategy for achieving greater compliance, but it is the direction that EPA distinctly prefers.[180]

Judicial remedies, by contrast, are generally reserved for serious or chronic violations and for cases of noncompliance with administrative orders. Section 3008(a) also authorizes EPA to "commence a civil action ... for appropriate relief, including a temporary or permanent injunction," and section 3008(g) provides for penalties of up to $25,000 for each day in violation. Good faith efforts to comply with RCRA do not excuse violations, but they can affect the penalty.

179. Supplemental environmental projects may also be part of judicial settlements.

180. *See* Clifford Rechtschaffen, *Competing Visions: EPA and the States Battle for the Future of Environmental Enforcement*, 30 ENVTL. L. REP. 10803 (2000).

The most serious violations are subject to criminal prosecution if the defendant "knowingly" violated various aspects of the RCRA regulatory scheme. Actual knowledge must be proven for most elements of these crimes, though courts have generally rejected the argument that the defendant must be proven to have known that a dangerous material is the subject of regulation, on the ground that "the probability of regulation [of hazardous materials] is so great that anyone who is aware that he is in possession of them or dealing with them must be presumed to be aware of the regulation."[181] RCRA creates a separate crime of "knowing endangerment" for cases in which the violation "places another person in imminent danger of death or serious bodily injury."[182]

RCRA's most important civil enforcement power is a civil action under section 7003 for an injunction to abate "past or present handling, storage, treatment, transportation or disposal of any solid waste or hazardous waste [that] may present an imminent and substantial endangerment to health or the environment."[183] Section 7003 has a wider application than the above actions in three important ways: violation of RCRA is not a prerequisite to the action, it is not limited to hazardous wastes (section 3008 is in Subtitle C and section 7003 is not), and EPA can seek relief from *any* person who has "con-

181. U.S. v. International Minerals & Chemical Corp., 402 U.S. 558, 565 (1971).

182. RCRA § 3008(e), 42 U.S.C. § 6928(e).

183. RCRA § 7003, 42 U.S.C. § 6973

tributed or who is contributing to" the improper handling, etc., that is, the potential defendants are not limited to persons who are or should be RCRA permittees.

Moreover, the requirement of an "imminent and substantial endangerment" has been construed broadly. Following the interpretation of the term "endangerment" in the landmark *Reserve Mining*[184] and *Ethyl Corp.*[185] cases, courts have interpreted section 7003 to mean "something less than actual harm. When one is endangered, harm is threatened."[186] The court measures the harm threatened by the risk of danger involved and uses an equitable balancing test to determine the appropriate relief.[187] Likewise, courts have loosened the traditional irreparable harm requirement for issuing injunctions, because in RCRA "Congress sought to invoke the broad and flexible equity powers of the federal courts ... where hazardous waste threatened human health."[188]

184. Reserve Mining Co. v. EPA, 514 F.2d 492 (8th Cir. 1975) (en banc).

185. Ethyl Corp. v. EPA, 541 F.2d 1 (D.C. Cir. 1976) (en banc), *cert. denied*, 426 U.S. 941 (1976).

186. *Id.* at 13.

187. United States v. Vertac Chemical Corp., 489 F.Supp. 870 (E.D. Ark. 1980); *see also* U.S. v. Valentine, 856 F.Supp. 627 (D. Wyo. 1994); Barry J. Trilling, *"Potential for Harm" As the Enforcement Standard for Section 7003 of the Resource Conservation and Recovery Act*, 2 UCLA J. ENVTL. L. & POLICY 43, 52–59 (1981).

188. U.S. v. Price, 688 F.2d 204, 211 (3d Cir. 1982); *see also* U.S. v. Aceto Agric. Chem. Corp., 872 F.2d 1373 (8th Cir. 1989).

2. *Actions Available to Private Citizens*

Despite an extensive armamentarium of tools, EPA's (and the states') enforcement resources are limited and the number of potential enforcement actions is large. To ensure broad—and motivated—enforcement, RCRA also provides for "citizen suits," actions which allow private citizens (or environmental groups representing affected citizens) either to enforce the law directly against a violator or to require EPA to take non-discretionary action to implement RCRA. Citizen suits are in many ways an additional set of teeth in RCRA, as they provide for enforcement when the government agency is either overwhelmed or reluctant.[189]

Citizen enforcement action, like government enforcement action, is predicated on information about facilities, and RCRA expressly provides for public access to key information from permits and inspections.[190] Based on that or any other information, section 7002(a)(1)(A) permits an action against any person, including the federal government, for a violation of "any permit, standard, regulation, condition, requirement, prohibition, or order."[191] Section 7002(a)(1)(B) permits citizens to bring in effect a section 7003 abatement action against past and present handlers of hazardous waste whose activities "may present an imminent and substantial

189. *See* Adam Babich, *Citizen Suits: The Teeth in Public Participation*, 25 ENVTL. L. REP. 10141 (1995).

190. RCRA § 3007(b), 42 U.S.C. § 6927(b) (with exceptions for confidential business information).

191. 42 U.S.C. § 6972(a)(1)(A).

endangerment, to human health and the environment."[192]

Citizen actions are, however, significantly limited in several ways. Constitutionally, the doctrine of standing restricts potential plaintiffs to ongoing violations (*i.e.*, not wholly past ones), who can demonstrate actual harm, and whose harm will be actually remedied by the suit.[193] Section 7002(b) sets up other important obstacles. In paragraph (A) suits, the citizen must give sixty days notice to EPA, to the relevant state, and to the violator before filing suit, and the Supreme Court has held that this limitation is absolute and jurisdictional.[194] Moreover, a suit is barred if the federal or a state government is "diligently prosecuting a civil or criminal action . . . to require compliance."[195] Somewhat greater obstacles are placed before the imminent and substantial danger suits,[196] in order to avoid complicating the corrective action process by having additional parties involved. Disputes have arisen over what kinds of compliance actions and what degree of vigor is required to constitute dili-

192. 42 U.S.C. § 6972(a)(1)(B).

193. Standing is a book in itself. The Supreme Court's latest major case on environmental standing is *Friends of the Earth, Inc. v. Laidlaw Envtl. Serv. (TOC), Inc.*, 528 U.S. 167 (2000), in which it retreated somewhat from a pattern of increasing hostility to citizen litigation.

194. RCRA § 7002(b)(1)(A), 42 U.S.C. § 6972(b)(1)(A); Hallstrom v. Tillamook County, 493 U.S. 20 (1989).

195. RCRA § 7002(b)(1)(B), 42 U.S.C. § 6972(b)(1)(B).

196. RCRA § 7002(b)(2)(A)–(D), 42 U.S.C. § 6972(b)(2)(A)–(D).

gent prosecution. A prevailing plaintiff can be awarded attorney's fees and costs.[197]

Finally, citizens can sue EPA to require it "to perform any act or duty ... which is not discretionary with the Administrator."[198] Suits against EPA for its failure to take statutorily mandated action under RCRA do not constitute enforcement *per se*. Moreover, given the doctrine of prosecutorial discretion, citizen plaintiffs are unlikely to be successful in forcing the agency to take enforcement action. Nevertheless, such actions can play a vital role in the development of the statute. Professor Robert Glicksman has gathered numerous examples of this kind of citizen suit which resulted in new regulatory programs or expanding or accelerating implementation of existing programs.[199]

3. State Hazardous Waste Programs

Most federal enforcement activity is handled by an EPA regional office, of which there are ten across the country, rather than EPA headquarters in Washington, D.C. However, Congress anticipated that RCRA would be applied primarily by the several states, especially in the areas of Subtitle C permitting and enforcement. RCRA provides for EPA approval of state hazardous waste programs (the

197. RCRA § 7002(e), 42 U.S.C. § 6972(e).

198. RCRA § 7002(a)(2), 42 U.S.C. § 6972(a)(2). The plaintiff must give EPA advance notice of these suits, as well. RCRA § 7002(c), 42 U.S.C. § 6972(c).

199. Robert L. Glicksman, *The Value of Agency–Forcing Citizen Suits to Enforce Nondiscretionary Duties*, 10 WIDENER L. REV. 353 (2004).

Subtitle D programs are already given almost entirely to the states), and the statute expresses its preference for state management with an oddly negative formulation: upon submission of a facially valid application for approval, a state "is authorized to carry out such program in lieu of the Federal program ... and to issue and enforce permits for the storage, treatment, or disposal of hazardous wastes ... *unless*" certain approval criteria are *not* met.[200] The state program must be "equivalent to" and "consistent with" the federal program.[201] In particular, each state program must have full enforcement authority,[202] and as a result, the foregoing governmental enforcement tools are applicable to state programs. Virtually all of the states have fully or partially authorized hazardous waste programs, and so the face of RCRA enforcement is most often a state regulator.

There are several incentives for states to adopt a hazardous waste program. Politically, states are generally inclined to handle intrusive regulatory programs themselves, because it allows them some degree of control over the effects that it will have on their industries and citizens. State programs may also be more stringent than the federal program,[203] which gives the states the ability, for example, to limit small-generator exemptions or to add to the group of listed wastes. In addition, hazardous waste

200. RCRA § 3006(b), 42 U.S.C. § 6926(b) (emphasis added).

201. RCRA § 3006(b)(1)–(2), 42 U.S.C. § 6926(b)(1)–(2).

202. RCRA § 3006(b)(3), 42 U.S.C. § 6926(b)(3).

203. RCRA § 3009, 42 U.S.C. § 6929.

is a particularly place-based problem—it does not move like air and water pollution—and state governments tend to be more familiar with the circumstances of particular locations. The disposition of hazardous wastes often implicates land use issues, and this is an area of intense state interest and traditional state autonomy.[204] RCRA provides assistance and significant funding for approved programs to encourage the states to adopt them.[205]

As in the other major delegated programs (air and water), EPA has concurrent enforcement authority with the states. EPA's continued ability to take direct enforcement action operates as both an additional enforcement resource and as a way to ensure vigorous enforcement by the states. Not surprisingly, this can give rise to tensions between federal and state regulators, and this tension has been most recently expressed in the "overfiling" controversy. Overfiling is a second enforcement action initiated by EPA after a state has resolved its issues with the violator under state law. Unlike the Clean Air Act and Clean Water Act, RCRA does not expressly provide authority for such federal actions. Section 3008 gives EPA broad authority to issue compliance orders or file suit "for *any* past or current violation,"[206] and it clearly anticipates federal activity in a state with an authorized program, because it

204. *See generally* Adam Babich, *Our Federalism, Our Hazardous Waste, and Our Good Fortune*, 54 MD. L. REV. 1516 (1995).

205. RCRA § 3011, 42 U.S.C. § 6931.

206. RCRA § 3008(a)(1), 42 U.S.C. § 6928(a)(1) (emphasis added).

provides for notice to the state under such circumstances and for federal enforcement of state-issued permits.[207] On the other hand, section 3006 speaks of the states carrying out their hazardous waste programs "in lieu of the Federal program." Defendants in overfiling cases have argued that the two provisions can only be reconciled by implying a prohibition on federal actions based on the same violations covered by a prior state action, unless the state program has been terminated or is otherwise inactive. This theory has enjoyed some influence, especially after it was embraced by the Eighth Circuit,[208] but subsequent courts, including the Ninth and Tenth Circuits, have rejected it,[209] as have most commentators.[210] The fact is that EPA needs tools less drastic than withdrawal of approval of an entire program[211] (which is a political nightmare, for obvious reasons) to be able to encourage and ensure vigorous state enforcement. Like citizen suits, concurrent authority and overfiling are valuable tools.

207. RCRA § 3008(a)(2)–(3), 42 U.S.C. § 6928(a)(2)–(3).

208. Harmon Indus., Inc. v. Browner, 191 F.3d 894 (8th Cir. 1999).

209. U.S. v. Power Engineering Co., 303 F.3d 1232 (10th Cir. 2002); U.S. v. Elias, 269 F.3d 1003 (9th Cir. 2001).

210. *See, e.g.*, Jeffrey G. Miller, *Theme and Variations in Statutory Preclusions Against Successive Environmental Enforcement Actions by EPA and Citizens, Part Two: Statutory Preclusion in EPA Enforcement*, 29 Harv. Envtl. L. Rev. 1, 83–93 (2005); Ellen R. Zahren, Comment, *Overfiling Under Federalism: Federal Nipping at State Heels to Protect the Environment*, 49 Emory L.J. 373 (2000).

211. RCRA § 3006(e), 42 U.S.C. § 6926(e).

Federal-state tension can flow in the opposite direction, too, when states attempt to enforce their hazardous waste programs against federal facilities in their states. Sadly, federal facilities, especially those of the Departments of Defense and Energy, are some of the worst polluters in the United States.[212] Just as the federal government has a legitimate interest in a minimum level of environmental protection across the country, the states have a genuine interest in establishing their own levels of environmental protection within their own territories.

The states are concerned, often with justification, that federal regulators are too lax in their treatment of sister agencies. For example, in *United States v. Colorado*, the state of Colorado sought to enforce its RCRA-authorized hazardous waste program against an Army chemical weapons facility that was being cleaned up under EPA's CERCLA supervision. The Department of Defense clearly preferred to have EPA as its sole regulator (among other things, under the unitary executive doctrine, EPA cannot take truly involuntary action against DoD[213]), but the Tenth Circuit upheld Colorado's power to enforce its own program.[214]

The primary limitation on the states' ability to regulate federal facilities is the doctrine of sovereign immunity, which insulates the federal govern-

212. *See* CASEBOOK, *supra*, at 1027–31.

213. CASEBOOK, *supra*, at 1041–43.

214. U.S. v. Colorado, 990 F.2d 1565 (10th Cir. 1993), *cert. denied*, 510 U.S. 1092 (1994).

ment from unconsented suits by citizens or, by implication from the Supremacy Clause of the Constitution, the states. RCRA, like all of the major federal environmental statutes, contains a general waiver of sovereign immunity for enforcement against federal facilities.[215] Uncertainty arose, however, over whether the waiver extended to all enforcement options.[216] In *Ohio v. U.S. Department of Energy*,[217] the Supreme Court interpreted RCRA to permit "coercive" penalties to induce compliance with orders and injunctions, but not to waive federal immunity from "punitive" penalties designed to punish *past* violations of environmental laws. The Court also held that a state generally could not use a citizen suit provision in a federal environmental statute to obtain civil penalties against the United States. In response, Congress passed the Federal Facility Compliance Act of 1992 (FFCA) to provide an unequivocal waiver of sovereign immunity.[218] The FFCA subjects federal agencies to civil penalties, both punitive and coercive, and waives federal employees' immunity from criminal prosecution. States can thus choose from a number of enforcement mechanisms, including administrative orders, civil penalties, and civil actions. Finally, if a state wishes to pursue its RCRA claims in a citizen suit, it may do so because the FFCA now defines a

215. RCRA § 6001(a), 42 U.S.C. § 6961(a). *See also* CASE-BOOK, *supra*, at 1044–55.

216. *See* U.S. v. New Mexico, 32 F.3d 494 (10th Cir. 1994) (reading "requirements" broadly).

217. 503 U.S. 607 (1992).

218. RCRA § 6001, 42 U.S.C. § 6961.

"person" subject to liability to include the United States.[219] By clarifying the concurrent role of the states where federal facilities are concerned, RCRA has permitted the development of a cooperative approach (or a division of labor) between federal and state regulators at these important hazardous waste sites.

* * *

To conclude, RCRA creates an extraordinarily complex regulatory regime for the management of hazardous wastes, reflecting the extent and variability of the hazardous waste problem in the United States. By and large, RCRA has been quite successful in defining the nature and scope of the problem and in bringing hazardous wastes under some degree of control. It has, however, been notably unsuccessful in coping with non-hazardous, and especially industrial, wastes. Its goals of waste minimization and pollution prevention—never a major focus of the statute, despite its title—have been largely ignored and at best indirectly pursued. A continuing issue for RCRA is the all-or-nothing character of the regulatory scheme, which places enormous pressure on the proper categorization of a substance as waste or not, as a precursor to the "hazardous" designation. In recent years, Congress and EPA have begun to address this feature of the statute with "C-/D+" programs; coordination of exit levels for the characteristic, disposal restriction, and delisting determinations; and risk-based management of hazardous waste identification, dis-

219.   42 U.S.C. § 6903(15).

position, and clean-up. These reforms have many attractions as "fine-tuning" of the regulatory requirements, but they also carry the dangers of imposing increasing administrative burdens on under-resourced federal and state agencies, of a general decline in the protectiveness of standards established by RCRA (especially after HSWA), and of jeopardizing existing incentives for waste minimization and the long-term protection of the environment.

CHAPTER III

CLEAN-UP: THE COMPREHENSIVE ENVIRONMENTAL RESPONSE, COMPENSATION, AND LIABILITY ACT

A. Introduction and Overview

The main federal statute governing the clean-up of sites already contaminated with hazardous wastes is the Comprehensive Environmental Response, Compensation and Liability Act (CERCLA). It authorizes and funds the remediation of inactive, leaking hazardous waste sites, and it defines the nature and scope of liability for past environmental harms. In essence, Congress enacted CERCLA to protect the public and the environment by requiring the clean-up of decades worth of hazardous waste dumping, and to ensure that the cost of such clean-up efforts were borne by the parties responsible for the contamination, instead of by taxpayers in general.

1. What is CERCLA?

CERCLA's current regulatory scheme is the result of two major enactments. The original Comprehensive Environmental Response, Compensation and Recovery Act, Pub. L. No. 96–510, 94 Stat.

2767, was enacted in 1980. In 1986, Congress reauthorized and revised CERCLA in the Superfund Amendments and Reauthorization Act (SARA), Pub. L. 99–499, 160 Stat. 1615. Known, collectively as CERCLA, 42 U.S.C. §§ 9601–9674, the statutes address two main issues: (1) the identification, investigation, and remediation of contaminated sites, and (2) the allocation of financial responsibility for clean-up activities.

CERCLA is not a traditional regulatory statute like the Resource Conservation and Recovery Act, the Clean Water Act, and the Clean Air Act. It is a *remediation* statute designed to impose *liability* for past conduct with present effects. There are numerous interactions between the remediation and liability aspects of CERCLA, but they are conceptually and statutorily quite different.

The *remediation* aspect of CERCLA identifies the kinds of sites ("facilities") that require attention, sets priorities among them, provides for their analysis, and specifies in some detail the nature and degree of clean-up activities.

The *liability* aspect of CERCLA is a retrospective statute that relies on tort-like liability to reach a range of private parties to pay the costs of cleaning up hazardous wastes sites.

As a *remedial* statute, CERCLA is designed to repair past waste disposal practices. If parties responsible for hazardous waste sites can be identified and located, they will be liable for both past and future clean-up costs of these sites, as well as the cost of preventing spills and releases of toxic and hazardous waste into the environment. If such parties cannot be found (*e.g.*, when hazardous waste sites have been abandoned by their original owners), or if the owners of the site have become bankrupt, the Superfund created by CERCLA serves as the monetary source from which the government may finance clean-up of these so-called "orphan" sites.

Although the text of CERCLA is ambiguous about the liability it imposes, subsequent court interpretations have established that the nature of the liability is *strict*; the scope of the liability is *joint and several*; and the effect of the liability is *retroactive*. Consequently, fault and causation are largely irrelevant; a person or entity responsible for a small percentage of the site's waste could be liable for 100% of the clean-up costs; and a party may be liable for extensive clean-up costs for disposal practices occurring before the enactment of CERCLA that were legal at the time the disposal took place. Not only is the liability scheme in CERCLA strict, broad, and backwards looking, it is also subject to only a few statutory defenses: acts of God; acts of war; acts or omissions of a third party not in contractual privity with the person asserting the defense; innocent landowners (or innocent purchasers) who can demonstrate both causation by a third party and adequate precautions by the buyer; and lenders who did not participate in the management of the waste site.

If a party's actions with respect to a waste site satisfy CERCLA's liability triggers (*i.e.*, there is a threatened release of a hazardous substance from a "facility"—a site or area where a hazardous substance has been deposited), and if the party becomes a "PRP"—a Potentially Responsible Party (*i.e.*, an owner, operator, etc.), then CERCLA provides that this unfortunate party is liable for "all costs of removal or remedial action incurred by the United States Government or a State or an Indian tribe not inconsistent with the [National Contingency Plan]."[1]

Courts have interpreted the phrase "all costs" quite literally, so that where the government takes action to investigate or monitor a release, or pays a contractor to perform work under agency direction, all of these costs can be reimbursed. Most courts allow the government to recover enforcement-related costs, indirect costs, such as rent and clerical supplies, and overhead, such as travel and legal expenses. Attorneys' fees are expressly authorized for government response actions, but not for private cost recovery actions.[2]

Another provision of CERCLA, § 107(a)(4)(c), imposes on PRPs the duty to pay for "injury to, destruction of, or loss of natural resources...." The federal government, state and local govern-

1. CERCLA § 107(a)(4)(A).

2. *See* Key Tronic Corp. v. United States, 511 U.S. 809 (1994) (holding that attorney's fees incurred in prosecuting a CERCLA liability action are not a "necessary cost of response," while allowing recovery of fees incurred by an attorney in tracking down other PRPs).

ments, and Indian tribal governments are designated as trustees empowered to sue for natural resource damages. Although cost recovery claims have dominated actions involving CERCLA, liabilities associated with natural resource claims may eventually exceed the billions of dollars spent on cleaning up waste sites. This is because (1) the term "natural resources" is given an extremely broad definition in the statute's definitions section, (2) unlike recovery of response costs, the government need not expend any money to recover natural resource damages, and (3) the appropriate measure of damages is not just the diminution of use values, but rather the cost of restoration and replacement of the damaged land and ecosystem.

Congress created a two-pronged approach to achieve its twin objectives—cleaning up hazardous waste sites and recovering costs. First, the *federal government* (through the EPA) was given authority to respond to hazardous releases at abandoned and inactive waste disposal sites. The federal government may (1) rely on the Superfund to clean up a site and then seek reimbursement from any responsible parties, (2) proceed directly against responsible parties, or (3) encourage "voluntary" clean-up by threatening responsible parties with court action and sanctions if they do not agree to the EPA's chosen action. Second, *private parties* may spend their own money to clean-up, and then sue those responsible to recover the clean-up costs. Even if private parties are partially responsible themselves, they may sue other responsible parties for their share of clean-up liability.

If either the government or a private party can identify and locate a party responsible for the hazardous waste site, that responsible party is subject to a particularly stringent form of liability. Under CERCLA, liability is not determined by traditional tort principles, which require some degree of causal link between the defendant's conduct and the actual harm to another person. Instead, CERCLA imposes automatic liability when there is a causal link between certain classes of defendants, the release of a hazardous substance, and the incurrence of clean-up costs. Neither harm nor carelessness nor the illegality of the defendant's conduct needs to be proven.

2. *What is the Superfund?*

The "Superfund" is a trust fund that exists to finance government-directed clean-up efforts, to pay claims arising from clean-up activities of private parties who are not liable as PRPs under CERCLA, and to compensate federal and state governments for damages to natural resources caused by a hazardous waste site. The Superfund receives its money from excise taxes on companies such as the petroleum and chemical industries.

To determine which sites are worthy of Superfund dollars, CERCLA authorized the EPA to create a list of the worst hazardous waste sites in the country, called the National Priorities List (NPL). To determine which sites should be placed on the

NPL, the EPA employs a Hazardous Ranking System (HRS) which assigns a score to each site, based on a few salient risk assessment criteria (*e.g.*, potential for contaminating drinking water, for producing a public health hazard, or for destroying sensitive ecosystems). Once a site is placed on the NPL, the National Contingency Plan (NCP) establishes the procedures and standards for responding to releases of hazardous substances from the site. CERCLA authorizes two kinds of responses: (1) short-term "removal" actions designed to alleviate immediate dangers, and (2) long-term "remedial" actions meant to provide a more permanent remedy.

Together, the NPL and NCP determine the *kinds of actions* that may be taken at hazardous waste sites, and the ability of the government and private parties to *recover costs* for cleaning up such sites. Placement of a site on the NPL is a prerequisite only to use of Superfund monies for clean-up; a non-federal party can always use its own money to clean up a facility and then, if possible, to recover from other responsible parties.

Although the Superfund is essential to the success of CERCLA, it is not free from criticism. Most of the problems surrounding CERCLA involve (1) inadequate funding, (2) the length of time required for completion of the clean-up process, and (3) the statute's high administrative costs.

First, to address inadequate funding, Congress passed SARA in 1986. After SARA, the size of the Superfund was expanded to $8.5 billion. Most of this money was to be raised by a so-called "Super-fund tax" collected from industries (*e.g.*, petroleum and chemical) whose products were judged to create most of the clean-up problem. At the end of 1995, Congress failed to reach an agreement on CERCLA reauthorization and the tax expired. Even though Congress has continually attempted to achieve consensus on a reauthorization bill, it has never been successful. As a result of the expiration of the Superfund tax, the EPA's CERCLA operations have been funded at only 75 percent of prior levels, curtailing clean-up activities at hundreds of NPL sites and forcing a dramatic reduction in remediation activities.[3]

Second, the Superfund clean-up process is criticized because of the long period of time that can elapse between the time a site comes to the EPA's attention, and the time when the remedial work is completed. Nearly four years can pass from the time a citizen or a state notifies the EPA of a possible CERCLA site, before that site is assessed and then receives a sufficiently high score on the HRS to be placed on the NPL for Superfund clean-up. After listing, there must be a remedial investigation and feasibility study completed before the EPA issues a Record of Decision (ROD) detailing the clean-up action that will be taken. This process can take five more years. The actual clean-up of the site can then begin, but it is not complete until a remedial "de-

3. *See* Lolly Merrell, Life in a Wasteland, High Country News, Dec. 9, 2002, at 1 (discussing plight of mining town in Utah that was named a priority site in Sept. 2002, while the EPA was running out of funds for clean-up projects).

sign" is finished, and subsequent remedial "action" has physically removed (or halted) contamination from the site. This clean-up work can last for four or more years. On average, the elapsed time is between 13 to 15 years. Additionally, further delays may arise if administrative and judicial challenges are brought by PRPs while the EPA is engaged in the clean-up process.

Third, CERCLA's high administrative costs have been a focus of concern. The Rand Corporation concluded that of the $2.6 billion paid out of the Superfund by the EPA through 1988, only $1.6 billion were devoted to remedial investigations and response actions at waste sites.[4] One billion had been spent on transaction costs—administration, management, laboratory, and litigation expenses. Of this $2.6 billion paid out of the Superfund, the EPA had recovered only $230 million of its costs through settlements at 328 sites.

B.   CERCLA in Context

CERCLA was the last of the major environmental statutes enacted during the "environmental decade," 1969–1980. By the mid–1970s, scientific and medical knowledge had grown considerably. The medical community was beginning to establish links between numerous chemical substances and negative health effects, especially cancer. Soon policymakers began to suspect that very low levels of

4. J. Action, Understanding Superfund: A Progress Report (1989).

many toxic chemicals in the environment could pose a threat to the public health.

1. *Love Canal and the Statute's History*

The disaster at Love Canal is credited with pushing the threat of hazardous waste sites on human health into the national spotlight, and inspiring the passage of CERCLA. The site at Love Canal was a classic abandoned waste dump. In the past, the standard disposal practice for factories, refineries, and mines was to place hazardous waste in barrels, drums, or open pits and then to bury and abandon them. Consistent with this practice, for ten years beginning in the 1940s, Hooker Chemical Company dumped tens of thousands of tons of chemical waste into an old canal near Niagara Falls, NY, covered it, and had given the site to the local board of education. The school board built a school on part of the land, and sold the remainder to a developer who built single-family homes. Residents began suffering abnormally high rates of miscarriages, birth defects, epilepsy, liver damage, and other illnesses. In response, in 1978, the state health department investigated the site and discovered that toxic chemicals migrating from the canal had contaminated the subsoil and groundwater throughout the entire area, and seeped into residential basements. The area's residents were quickly evacuated, and the problem of non-active waste sites was placed at the doorstep of Congress.

To remedy this newly discovered problem, Congress and the EPA had to address three main issues. First, they had to assess the gravity of the problem. Before enacting CERCLA, the EPA and congressional subcommittees estimated that there could be between 1,500–2,000 dump sites in the United States that contained waste so hazardous that they posed a risk to human health. The EPA concluded that virtually all hazardous wastes were being disposed of improperly, and that there were over 3,000 new spills of toxic chemicals each year. Second, Congress and the EPA had to determine who should pay for the clean-up of hazardous waste sites—the federal government or private parties. Third, if the site was not an "orphan" site (one for which the responsible parties are insolvent or unable to be located), they had to devise a system for reaching a range of liable parties that could pay for clean-up costs, often reaching into the tens of millions of dollars per site.

With respect to the first question, the fact that CERCLA was passed at all reflected congressional concern over the national scope and gravity of the hazardous waste problem. The second question was answered by establishing a program that combined the concepts of (1) federal responses to locations containing hazardous waste with (2) private party liability for past and ongoing releases of such substances. Congress responded to the third question by imposing strict, joint and several, and retroactive liability on parties deemed "responsible" for the contaminated sites.

CERCLA's structure was modeled after section 311 of the Clean Water Act (CWA), which establishes a revolving fund for use by the Coast Guard and EPA to respond to oil spills in navigable waters. Section 311 applies the principles of strict and joint and several liability to persons responsible for releases of "harmful quantities" of oil. Within this section lies the foundation for CERCLA. Section 311(b)(5) requires any person "in charge" of a vessel or facility discharging harmful quantities of oil to report the discharge to the EPA or Coast Guard. Section 103 of CERCLA requires reporting of releases of hazardous substances to the National Response Center. Under CWA § 311(c), the federal government may respond to the discharge or threatened discharge of oil or other hazardous substances into navigable waters, so long as the action is consistent with the National Contingency Plan (NCP). The initial costs of clean-up are paid out of the Oil Spill Liability Trust Fund. Similarly, section 104 of CERCLA authorizes response action consistent with the NCP, while CERCLA § 111 creates a Superfund which can be used to finance governmental response actions, and to reimburse private parties for costs incurred in carrying out the NCP. Section 311(f) of the CWA imposes liability for clean-up costs and natural resources damages on owners or operators of vessels or facilities from which spills have occurred or are threatened. Section 107 of CERCLA imposes liability on current and past owners and operators of facilities where hazardous substances are released, or threatened to be released.

Although CERCLA was an enormous expansion of the CWA's oil spill provisions, its passage was extremely hurried. The actual language was the statutory product of a last minute compromise by a small bipartisan group of influential senators. With virtually no debate, the statute passed in a lame-duck session by the Senate, and the House then agreed to accept the Senate version without even holding a conference committee. This rushed course of action produced unclear draftsmanship and very little legislative history.

Congress eventually helped to clarify the clean-up process and liability issues by adding two amendments to CERCLA. The Superfund Amendments and Reauthorization Act of 1986 (SARA) imposed a partial cleanup timetable (§ 116), mandated more extensive cleanups (§ 121), and increased the Superfund to $8.5 billion. SARA also added procedural changes designed to encourage settlement (§ 122), facilitate contribution among responsible parties (§ 113(f)), and enhance public participation (§§ 117, 310). In 1996, Congress passed the Asset Conservation, Lender Liability, and Deposit Insurance Protection Act, Pub. L. No. 104–208, clarifying the scope of lender liability and providing additional protections for fiduciaries.

KEY PROVISIONS OF CERCLA

§ 101 *Definitions*-"facility", "release"; "disposal"; "hazardous substance."

§ 104 *Removals* and *remedial action* authorized if consistent with the National Contingency Plan (NCP).

§ 105   National contingency Plan requires establishment of hazard ranking system and a National Priorities List (NPL).

§ 106   *Abatement* orders may be issued if actual or potential releases create imminent and substantial endangerment.

§ 107   *Liability* is imposed on potentially responsible parties (PRPs), defined as owners, operators, arrangers, and transporters of hazardous waste, for all costs of removal or remedial action incurred by the federal government not inconsistent with the NCP, for other response costs incurred by any person consistent with the NCP, or for damages to natural resources.

§ 111   Creates a *Superfund* to finance governmental response actions, and to reimburse private parties for costs incurred in carrying out the NCP.

§ 113   Prevents pre-enforcement *judicial review* of response actions; permits private *contribution* actions against PRPs.

§ 116   Sets out *schedules* for listing sites on the NPL, for undertaking remedial investigation and feasibility studies, and for taking remedial clean-up action at sites.

§ 121   Fixes standards for CERCLA clean-ups. There is a preference for permanent solutions where the site must be cleaned up to a level meeting a "legally applicable or relevant and appropriate standard, requirement, criteria or limitation" (*ARARs*) found in federal environmental

> law, or state law if it is more restrictive
> than federal law.

> § 122   Articulates standards for government-ini-
> tiated *settlements* with PRPs.

2.   *CERCLA and RCRA: A Comparison*

The Resource Conservation and Recovery Act
(RCRA) was passed to provide a comprehensive
structure for managing the generation, transport,
and treatment of hazardous and non-hazardous solid wastes, primarily at active waste disposal sites.
CERCLA, on the other hand, was intended to address ongoing problems associated with past improper waste disposal activities. The United States
Supreme Court in *Meghrig v. KFC Western, Inc.*[5]
explained:

Unlike [CERCLA], RCRA is not principally designed to effectuate the clean-up of toxic waste
sites or to compensate those who have attended
to the remediation of environmental hazards. *Cf.
General Electric Co. v. Litton Industrial Automa-
tion Systems, Inc.,* 920 F.2d 1415, 1422 (C.A.8
1990) (the "two * * * main purposes of CERC-
LA" are "prompt clean-up of hazardous waste
sites and imposition of all clean-up costs on the
responsible party"). RCRA's primary purpose,
rather, is to reduce the generation of hazardous
waste and to ensure the proper treatment, storage, and disposal of that waste which is nonetheless generated, "so as to minimize present and

5.   516 U.S. 479, 783 (1996).

future threat to human health and the environment." 42 U.S.C. § 6902(b).

Despite this difference in focus, there are some similarities and overlap between the two statutes. Jurisdictionally, there is an enormous overlap since CERCLA incorporates RCRA's list of hazardous wastes, and CERCLA includes corrective action provisions for cleaning up RCRA-permitted facilities. This provides the EPA with remedial choices when the contaminated site is also a "treatment, storage, and disposal facility" (TSDF) regulated under RCRA. The EPA may rely on either CERCLA or RCRA to bring about a clean-up at a TSDF. If the EPA proceeds under CERCLA, the owner/operator may object because CERCLA actions are often more public and less flexible, and because the owner/operator then becomes a PRP from whom response costs may be recovered. Despite these concerns, the rule is that RCRA does not limit CERCLA, and CERCLA may have applicability to a RCRA TSDF.[6]

There also is similarity between RCRA § 7003, which empowers the EPA to clean up hazardous waste sites that pose an "imminent and substantial endangerment to health or the environment," and CERCLA § 106(a), which empowers the EPA to issue a responsible party an abatement order when an actual or threatened release of hazardous sub-

6. Apache Powder Co. v. United States, 968 F.2d 66 (D.C. Cir. 1992) (EPA may include a TSDF subject to RCRA on the CERCLA National Priorities List); *see also* Chemical Waste Management, Inc. v. Armstrong World Indus., Inc., 669 F.Supp. 1285 (E.D. Pa. 1987) (a TSDF allegedly in violation of RCRA may nonetheless seek cost recovery under CERCLA).

stances presents an "imminent and substantial endangerment" to health or the environment. Initially, RCRA § 7003 was understood to apply only to
active hazardous waste sites. In 1984, Congress
amended RCRA so that § 7003 was applicable to
both "past and present handling, storage, treatment, or disposal" of hazardous wastes. As a result,
the EPA sometimes uses RCRA § 7003 and CECLA
§ 106(a) in tandem when it confronts a particularly
dangerous waste disposal site. If the EPA can identify a PRP at such as site, it might also proceed
under the cost-recovery provisions of CERCLA
§ 107 (setting out liability standards when cost
recovery actions are initiated for clean-up expenses).

CERCLA § 106 is available only to the federal
government; states and private parties seeking
abatement must use RCRA's citizen suit provision,
§ 7002(a)(1)(B), in conjunction with § 7003. Private
parties may not obtain compensatory relief for personal injury or property under § 7003 or § 7002,
since these RCRA provisions are equitable. CERC-
LA § 107 is the preferred statutory provision for
recovery of clean-up costs. RCRA § 7003 may also
be broader than CECRLA, since (1) RCRA includes
within its reach those who "contribute" to the
practices that create the endangerment; (2) RCRA's
provisions also extend to non-hazardous "solid
waste"; and (3) RCRA is not subject to CERCLA's
petroleum exclusion (CERCLA §§ 101(14) and
101(33)). Moreover, CERCLA has been interpreted
to require that the "hazardous substances" exist in

sufficient concentrations to subject a party to response costs.[7] On the other hand, the "hazardous substances" subject to CERCLA cover a broader range of materials than RCRA's "hazardous wastes." The CERCLA term includes RCRA hazardous wastes, as well as substances regulated under the Clean Air Act, Clean Water Act, and the Toxic Substances Control Act.[8]

3. CERCLA and State Law

CERCLA provides for the use of state law, while simultaneously preempting it in certain instances. The liability mechanism found in CERCLA—strict liability for abnormally dangerous activities—is a logical statutory extension of state common law tort doctrine. Moreover, CERCLA contains a broad savings clause, which provides that nothing in the statute "shall effect ... the obligations or liabilities of any person under ... State law, including common law, with respect to releases of hazardous substances or other pollutants or contaminants."[9] This savings clause acts to prevent the inference that CERCLA is intended to eliminate the common law of toxic torts, and be the exclusive remedy for harms that violate the statute. As such, it is common for actions against responsible parties for contaminating a waste site to be grounded both in CERCLA and state statutory and common law.

7. Amoco Oil Co. v. Borden, Inc., 889 F.2d 664 (5th Cir. 1989).

8. CERCLA § 101(14).

9. *Id.* § 302(d).

On the other hand, CERCLA preempts state laws and actions arising under state common law that would have the effect of preventing the accomplishment of federal statutory clean-up goals.[10]

Furthermore, while CERCLA has similarities to common law, it also has extended the realm of common law toxic tort liability, making recovery for hazardous waste disposal more efficient. There are at least three similarities between CERCLA and the common law. First, under CERCLA, an "owner" PRP is liable for clean-up costs irrespective of negligence or fault, and regardless of whether the government can prove actual harm stemming from the site. Likewise, many jurisdictions deem property owners subject to strict liability even though they had not disposed of any waste during their time on the contaminated property.[11] Second, CERCLA holds liable for clean-up costs companies that ar-

10. *See e.g.*, Fireman's Fund Ins. Co. v. City of Lodi, California, 302 F.3d 928 (9th Cir. 2002) (CERCLA preempted local liability scheme providing for joint and several liability with a right of contribution, where the state statute prohibited contribution actions against city, even if city was a PRP, while permitting city, as a PRP, to impose joint and several liability on other PRPs for the entire cost of clean-up); Arrest the Incinerator Remediation, Inv. v. OHM Remediation Services Corp., 5 F.Supp.2d 291 (M.D. Pa. 1998) (CERCLA preempts private state law nuisance action seeking to block ongoing clean-up of Superfund site); In re Pfohl Bros. Landfill Litigation, 68 F.Supp.2d 236, 249 (W.D.N.Y. 1999) (CERCLA preempts state statute of limitations that would otherwise have removed liability from those who Congress intended to be responsible for clean-up costs).

11. *See, e.g.*, State of New York v. Shore Realty Corp., 759 F.2d 1032, 1051 (2d Cir. 1985).

range for the disposal of hazardous wastes. Similarly, some courts have decided that a company's decision to generate and dispose of its wastes, either by itself or through an independent contractor, may be an "abnormally dangerous activity" subject to common law strict liability.[12] Third, just as CERCLA provides for recovery by the government for natural resources damages, which encompass environmental harms to "public" natural resources not owned by private parties, the common law also recognizes that a nuisance can be "public," when there is an unreasonable interference with a right common to the general public.

CERCLA has extended common law principles for toxic tort liability in at least four ways in order to remove some of the difficulties plaintiffs face in bringing common law tort actions. First, to eliminate the difficulty in proving causation when one brings a toxic tort action—proof is typically needed that the substance was in the defendant's control when it reached the plaintiff, and that the substance caused the harm—the drafters of CERCLA implemented a dramatically reduced standard of proof of causation. To establish CERCLA § 107 liability, only two conditions must be met: (1) a release of a hazardous substance must cause the incurrence of response costs; and (2) the defendant must fall within one of four categories of responsible parties based on its relationship to the waste or

12. *See, e.g.*, United States v. Hooker Chemicals and Plastics Corp., 722 F.Supp. 960 (W.D.N.Y. 1989) (generate and dispose of waste on company's own property).

to the site, rather than on the nature of the defendant's conduct. The first condition does not require proof that the defendant's hazardous waste actually migrated to the plaintiff's property; it is sufficient that legitimate response costs were incurred by the defendant.[13] The second condition assumes that CERCLA's strict liability standard is satisfied regardless of ignorance, action, or inaction of the defendant; all that is relevant is the defendant's status with respect to the waste.

Second, CERCLA eliminates the statute of limitations problem found in common law tort actions. In toxic tort actions, there is often a long latency period between the time of initial exposure to the harmful substance and the manifestation of the physical harm or illness that gives rise to the suit. By the time the resulting disease is discovered, the relevant statute of limitations period has already run, leaving the plaintiff with no cause of action. To address this problem, CERCLA § 309 provides that for injuries caused by exposure to hazardous substances, the statute of limitations for *state law* causes of action do not begin to run until the plaintiff has reason to know that the injury was caused by exposure to a hazardous substance.[14]

13. Dedham Water Co., Inc. v. Cumberland Farms Dairy, Inc., 972 F.2d 453 (1st Cir. 1992).

14. *See also* Freier v. Westinghouse Electric Corp., 303 F.3d 176 (2d Cir. 2002) (CERCLA section provides that discovery of cause of injury is uniform accrual date for state law claims based on exposure to hazardous substances, including state survival claims and wrongful death claims).

Third, under the common law, it is quite difficult for a property owner to pursue a strict liability claim against a former owner who has contaminated the property with hazardous waste. Tort actions are controlled by the doctrine of *caveat emptor*, which requires vendees to inspect the property prior to purchase, so that the vendor is not responsible to the vendee for the property's "defective" condition existing at the time of transfer. CERCLA avoids this problem by (1) allowing parties to allocate environmental risks between themselves pursuant to a contract,[15] and (2) permitting one PRP to sue other PRPs for reimbursement of costs of clean-up in a contribution action.[16]

Fourth, CERCLA alters the way in which damages are measured, to ensure that the actual cost of environmental remediation is covered, as opposed to basing damages on the plaintiff's loss. Unlike common law actions, CERCLA provides for a corrective action that benefits society, or nature, rather than the parties to the lawsuit. CERCLA § 107(c) permits damages for injury to natural resources, and § 107(d) includes as damages the total costs of health assessments to members of the public who may have been adversely affected by the waste site.

C. The Clean–Up Cornerstones

CERCLA is built on four cornerstones of remedial action. One side of the CERCLA structure rests on

15. CERCLA § 107(e)(1); Olin Corp. v. Yeargin, Inc., 146 F.3d 398, 407–08 (6th Cir. 1998).

16. *Id.* § 113(f)(1).

the two basic components of the statute's blueprint for action—the National Contingency Plan (NCP) and the National Priorities List (NPL). The NCP establishes the procedures and standards for responding to releases of hazardous substances. The NPL determines priorities among releases and threatened releases. On the other side of the CERCLA structure are the two kinds of clean-up or response actions that may be taken once a release or threatened release has been confirmed—"removal" actions and "remedial" actions. *"Removal"* actions are short-term responses aimed at preventing or minimizing immediate threats posed by a release. *"Remedial"* actions facilitate the final, long-term management of the site.

1. National Contingency Plan

CERCLA § 105 states that clean-ups of hazardous waste sites are to be governed by a master plan, called a National Contingency Plan. Section 105(a) explains that the purpose of the NCP is to "establish procedures and standards for responding to releases of hazardous substances, pollutants, and contaminants." As such, the NCP provides the following:

- methodologies for identifying sites most in need of remediation;

- analyses for determining the risks to human health and the environment posed by waste sites;

- requirements for state and community involvement in decision-making;
- systems for selecting cost-effective remedies;
- guidance for remedial actions that use Superfund money;
- standards for judging the extent and scope of clean-up; and
- the allocation of authority among federal, state, and local governments for implementing the plan's clean-up provisions.

To ensure that the NCP has teeth, CERCLA provides that response costs cannot be recovered if the response actions violate the NCP. Governmental parties (the EPA, states, or Indian tribes) can only recover "costs of removal or remedial action" which are "not inconsistent with the [NCP]."[17] Private plaintiffs can recover only response costs which are "consistent with the [NCP]."[18] This distinction is discussed in more detail below, in the section dealing with liability and cost recovery.

a. Evolution of the NCP. Originally, in developing the National Contingency Plan, the 1980 version of CERCLA called for a plan detailing a step-by-step process for dealing with a contaminated waste site. The 1980 NCP also established standards for determining the appropriate remediation measures. The SARA amendments in 1986 called for an additional revision of the NCP, particularly in the area of remedy selection. Pursuant to these

17. *Id.* § 107(a)(4)(A).
18. *Id.* § 107(a)(4)(B).

amendments, the NCP was to (1) give preference to the remedial actions that "permanently and significantly" reduce the volume, mobility, and toxicity of the contaminants at the site, and (2) incorporate a Hazard Ranking System (HRS) to be used to determine which sites should be added to the list. The HRS uses a risk assessment methodology that requires the EPA to assess the relative "degree of risk to human health and the environment posed by sites and facilities subject to review."[19]

The current product of these statutory commands is the 1990 National Contingency Plan.[20] This plan contains the following components:

- *National Response System*—The discharge of oil, or the release (but not a threat of a release) of a hazardous substance in reportable quantities, triggers a regulatory and statutory duty to notify the National Response Center. CERCLA § 103(a) sets forth the reporting requirements, which demand that any person who knows of a release of a "reportable quantity" of a hazardous substance to notify the National Response Center. The reportable quantity varies, depending on the on the nature of the contaminant involved. After being reported, a lead agency is assigned (usually the Environmental Protection Agency). This agency then designates an On–Scene Coordinator (OSC) and a Regional Project Manager (RPM) who coordinate clean-up activities at the site, manage costs paid out of the Superfund, and ensure compliance with the

19. *Id.* § 105(c)(1).

20. *See* 40 C.F.R. part 300.

NCP. State and local participation in response planning is provided by commissions and committees established under the Emergency Planning and Community Right-to-Know Act of 1986.[21]

- *Removals and Remedial Action*—The NCP lays out three steps that must be taken to clean up a site. First, the EPA, or other lead agency, uses the Preliminary Assessment and Site Inspection (PA/SI) process to identify the site, and to inspect it to ensure that it is worthy of placement on the National Priorities List. This step entails listing the site on the Comprehensive Environmental Response Compensation and Liability Information System—the CERCLIS list of over 30,000 sites. Second, a decision must be made as to whether the CERCLA response should be an emergency, short-term "removal" action, or a long-term "remedial" action. If a "remedial" action is chosen, a "remedial investigation/feasibility study" (RI/FS) must be completed to determine how best to clean up the site. Third, if a "remedial" action is selected, the NCP requires that the remedy chosen be cost-effective, a permanent solution, protective of human health and environment, and compatible with "applicable or relevant and appropriate" legal standards.

- *Enforcement*—The NCP provides guidance to the parties who may enforce various CERCLA provisions. It lays out what the EPA must include in the administrative record for proceedings conducted under § 106 administrative

21.   42 U.S.C. § 11001, *et seq.*

abatement authority. The NCP informs private parties of what actions "are consistent with the NCP" for purposes of cost recovery lawsuits under § 107. When natural resources damages are claimed under § 107(f)(2), the NCP identifies the trustees and sets out their responsibilities.

Even though the NCP appears quite detailed, the difficult issues are resolved by referring to hundreds of CERCLA "guidance documents." Guidance, which need not be subjected to the rulemaking requirements of the Administrative Procedures Act, is issued at both the national and regional levels, and the result is an enormous body of CERCLA "law" and practice that must be consulted and considered in choosing response actions.

b. NCP Procedures. The NCP establishes step-by-step procedures which the EPA and other government agencies must follow when responding to a contaminated waste site through either a removal or remedial action. This lengthy step-by-step process lays out what must be done, and who should do it, from the time a site is initially discovered to when the clean-up commences. The key steps in the process are as follows:

- *Preliminary Assessment and Site Investigation (PA/SI)*—A site must be identified as a site that may contain a hazardous waste. A site can be identified by neighbors, employees, site owners, interested passers by, environmental organizations, and local, state, or federal officials. For example, after finding out that a tank containing hazardous substances is leaking, the OSC and the EPA (or other lead agency) then go through a series of steps to determine if the site poses an immediate threat to the public health, or if instead it warrants a long-term federal response, or if no action is needed at all. More specifically, these steps are:

(1) *Removal site evaluation*—performed to determine if emergency "removal" measures are necessary. During this brief review, the agency evaluates readily available information such as personal interviews, photographs, and literature searches. The agency will perform a site evaluation if more information is needed.

(2) *Preliminary assessment*—the reviewing of existing information about the release, such as information on the nature of the release and exposure targets. This assessment either eliminates the site from further investigation if it poses no threat, or if there is a threat, helps to determine whether permanent remedial action is needed.

(3) *Site investigation*—helps to decide whether the site should be placed on the National Priorities List for remedial action. This step includes a thorough on-site and off-site field investigation of the impact of the release, or threat of release, on soil and groundwater. If the EPA determines that no further response action is needed, the agency will assign the site "No Further Response Action Planned" (NFRAP) status on the CERCLIS, and no further federal

action will be taken absent new developments or the discovery of new information. Otherwise, the site will be considered for inclusion on the NPL, discussed in more detail below.

- *"Removal" Actions*—These are rapid responses to the release or threat of release of a hazardous substance. They are addressed more fully below.

- *"Remedial" Action*—A *remedial investigation and feasibility study* (RI/FS) is the pre-decision assessment that permits selection of an appropriate remedy when long-term remedial action appears to be necessary at a site. Although separate activities, the RI and FS are conducted concurrently. The RI is a compilation of data gathered by the EPA regarding the conditions at the site. It "characterizes" the site by considering the nature of the hazardous substances there and the substances' threat to human health and the environment based on an estimate of actual or potential exposure, and then establishes "acceptable exposure levels for use in developing remedial alternatives."[22] The FS analyzes the remedial alternatives for a response that will satisfy CERCLA's clean-up requirements. It proposes a few alternatives, including a no action alternative, and evaluates them according to the substantive requirements of the NCP. As such, the purpose of this study is not to choose a specific remedy; rather, it permits the adoption of any remedy selected from a variety of alternatives, as long as the chosen alternative will protect human health

22.   40 C.F.R. § 300.430(d)(4).

and the environment, and conform to federal and environmental standards.

- *Proposed Plan*[23]—The proposed plan (PP) announces the EPA's initial conclusion from the RI/FS process; it states the EPA's preferred remedy derived from the suggested alternatives. Pursuant to § 117(a), this remedy is then made available for public comment both in writing and at a public meeting before a final decision is released. The relevant state must also concur with the remedy by agreeing that it will play a role with respect to future maintenance of the remedial action.[24]

- *Record of Decision*—The EPA then reassess the decision made in its PP by factoring in the new information provided by the public and other governmental agencies during the comment period.[25] The agency then issues a Record of Decision (ROD) memorializing its final decision on the remedy. The ROD describes the site and its risks; alternative remedial actions available; why the final remedy was chosen; how the action complies with the NCP; the remediation goals for the site; the extent to which hazardous substances will remain after the clean-up is done; how community involvements affected the final plan; and commits to further analysis if needed.[26]

23. *Id.* § 300.430(f)(2).

24. CERCLA § 104(c)(3). The state should have had meaningful involvement in the selection of remedies. *Id.* § 121(f).

25. 40 C.F.R. § 300.430(f)(4).

26. *Id.* at 300.430(f)(5).

- *Remedial Design and Remedial Action*—Performance of the remedial design and remedial action (RD/RA) is the last step before a construction and clean-up contract is awarded to a private contractor. The RD/RA sets out the action design of the remedy and the construction that will occur to achieve the remedy's goal. After the RD/RA, construction begins and eventually is completed.

    c. *NCP Substantive Standards.* There are two substantive aspects to determining the appropriate remedial action at the Superfund site: (1) the method of clean-up (the actual remedy, such as excavation, incineration, capping, liners, etc.), and (2) the degree of clean-up (often referred to as the "how clean is clean" question). These two standards must comply with § 121, which sets out the standards the EPA is to apply when selecting a remedy. In drafting the NCP, the EPA created nine criteria, each of which was assigned a particular weight in remedy selection. The § 121 criteria are discussed in greater detail below. There are two kinds of response actions contemplated by the NCP: "removal" actions and "remedial" measures.[27]

2. *National Priorities List*

    CERCLA may be used to clean up any contaminated site, but Congress also wanted to identify and clean up the most dangerous sites in the United States. This goal is accomplished by § 105(a)(8)(B), which requires that a National Priorities List (NPL) be established. The NPL ensures that the most

  27. CERCLA § 104(a).

dangerous hazardous sites receive monies from the Superfund.

a. The Listing Procedure

• *Preliminary Assessment and Site Investigation*—The road to the NPL begins with the Preliminary Assessment and Site Investigation (PA/SI) phase of the NCP. One of the purposes of this phase is to determine whether a site warrants listing on the NPL.

• *Hazard Ranking System*[28]—The Hazardous Ranking System (HRS) is the most commonly used mechanism for placing a site on the list. It works by assigning a "score" to each site based on (1) various risk assessment criteria (*e.g.*, the likelihood of release, the nature of the hazardous substance, the probability of dilution, the distance from the site to the threatened target, and the nature of the endangerment to the human population or environment); and (2) the potential exposure "pathways" to threatened humans and the environment (*e.g.*, soil, surface water, groundwater, and air). The resulting score represents an estimate of "the probability and magnitude of harm ... from exposure of hazardous substances as a result of contamination of groundwater, surface water, [soil], or air."[29] A score of 28.50 or greater permits a site to be listed on the NPL.

• *State Designation*—Section 105(a)(8)(B) allows each state to designate a facility which presents

28. 40 C.F.R. Part 300, Appendix A.

29. Eagle–Picher Indus. v. United States EPA, 759 F.2d 905 (D.C. Cir. 1985).

the greatest danger in its state. These facilities are placed on the NPL regardless of HRS score.

- *Toxic Substances and Disease Registry*—If the Toxic Substances and Disease Registry issues a health advisory recommending "disassociation" of individuals from the site, the site may be listed on the NPL regardless of HRS score.[30]

b. Consequences of an NPL Listing. Listing on the NPL has little significance for the EPA, except that it works as a limit to the EPA's clean-up authority. Unless a site is listed on the NPL, the EPA cannot use Superfund monies to clean it up with *remedial* action.[31] However, there are many other clean-up avenues the government can pursue under CERCLA. Among the more important non-NPL actions are:

- the EPA may perform short term *removal* actions with Superfund money;

- the EPA may order parties to undertake short and long-term clean-up measures pursuant to its abatement authority under § 106;

- state governments, local governments, or private parties may clean up a site and then bring a § 107 action to recover their response costs; and

- settlement through consent decrees can take place under § 122.

30. 40 C.F.R. § 300.425(c)(3).

31. *See also* Honeywell Int'l, Inc. v. E.P.A., 372 F.3d 441 (D.C. Cir. 2004) (EPA's listing of site on the NPL did not obligate agency to discuss or give notice of potential remedial actions to be taken at the site).

Listing has much more significant consequences for a site owner. Listing means that the EPA has determined that out of 40,000 sites on the CERCLIS, this site poses significant enough of a danger to human health and the environment to warrant a full and federal investigation and possible response.[32]

   c. Delisting and Deletions. There is no administrative procedure in place for bringing about a "delisting" of an area that is not in fact contaminated and therefore improperly listed. The only way to get a site *delisted* is to overturn the EPA's listing decision in court. Since NPL—listing is done by rulemaking, affected parties can obtain pre-enforcement judicial review. Hence, NPL listing decisions have engendered a large amount of litigation. However, the standard of review for an EPA listing is "arbitrary and capricious"—a standard that causes courts to be very deferential to the agency. As such, plaintiffs have little success in these suits. An EPA decision to list a site usually will only be reversed if the agency makes a listing call based on (1) criteria other than those specified by CERCLA, or (2) assumptions about the nature and extent of contamination that are not supported by the record.

   Sites can be *deleted* for a number of reasons, such as completion of all necessary response actions. However, if the EPA discovers that the threat of a

   32. *See also i.d.* (listing site on the NPL for clean-up under CERCLA neither requires owner or operator to take any action nor assigns liability to any party).

dangerous release remains, due to a flawed clean-up, the agency can relist the site.

3.   *"Removal" Actions*

Section 101(23) defines "removal" to include clean-up action necessary to deal with a threatened release.[33] Removal actions are simple, short-term clean-ups at sites posing an immediate "threat to the public health or welfare."[34] Examples are installation of fences and warning signs; removal of tanks that leak and spill; excavation or removal of highly contaminated soils that could migrate; stabilizing dikes or impoundments; and evacuating individuals threatened by a release.[35] In theory, none of these responses are intended to be effective in the long term; rather, they are short-term actions that are expected to be replaced with long-term, permanent plans.

An important part of the EPA's initial investigation of a site is to ascertain whether the immediacy of the threat requires removal action, or whether there is a long-term risk sufficient for an NPL

33. *See also* Village of Milford v. K–H Holding Corp., 390 F.3d 926, 934 (6th Cir. 2004) (removal actions include "such actions as may be necessary to monitor, assess, and evaluate the release or threat of release of hazardous waste").

34. 40 C.F.R. § 300.415(b). *But see* Village of Milford v. K–H Holding Corp., 390 F.3d 926, 934 (6th Cir. 2004) (characteristic of hazardous waste as posing an "immediate threat" is not a requirement for finding the costs of an action recoverable as removal costs).

35. *See* State of Colorado v. Sunoco, Inc., 337 F.3d 1233 (10th Cir. 2003) (installing adit plug and adit monitoring wells constituted removal, rather than remedial action).

listing and remedial action. To help organize this process, in 1993, the EPA adopted the Superfund Accelerated Clean-up Model which places sites into three categories: (1) non-NPL-sites which need time-critical action; (2) NPL-caliber sites deserving of non-emergency early action; and (3) NPL sites where remedial responses are justified. This determination is important since the NCP prevents the EPA from undertaking remedial action unless the site qualifies for an NPL-listing.

Oftentimes removal and remedial actions overlap and the proper response could fall under either category. Two factors may influence the agency to categorize the action as "removal" instead of "remedial:" (1) the Superfund may be used to finance removal actions at sites not listed on the NPL; and (2) the procedures for removal actions allow the EPA to act more quickly than it may under its remedial action authority. To prevent agencies from labeling "remedial" actions as "removal" actions, § 104(c) provides that removal action at a site cannot continue after $2 million has been spent for response work, or one year has elapsed from the date of the initial agency response.

The decision to take "removal" action is based on factors including: (1) actual or potential exposure of humans, animals, or the food chain to the hazardous substance; (2) actual or potential contamination of the drinking water supply and sensitive ecosystems; (3) hazardous substances in bulk containers that threaten release; (4) high levels of hazardous substances in soil that may migrate; (5) weather conditions that may cause such migration; and (6) the threat of fire or explosion.[36] Once the agency determines that removal action is warranted,[37] a series of steps occur. First, the agency must "begin as soon as possible to abate, prevent, minimize, stabilize, mitigate, or eliminate the threat...."[38] Second, the public should be informed and be allowed to provide input to the decision-makers.[39] Third, when the removal action is being planned, the NCP provides that all Superfund-financed removal actions are, to the extent practicable, to meet the "applicable or relevant and appropriate requirements" (ARARs) that determine the clean-up standard. ARAR compliance is only necessary for those actions that are directly part of the removal action, but not for other clean-up steps that are not encompassed by the removal plan. Fourth, when the response action is removal in nature, the party seeking cost recovery must prove that its actions were in "substantial compliance" with those portions of the NCP that pertain to removal actions. Fifth, the potentially responsible party must provide the EPA

36. 40 C.F.R. § 400.415(b)(2).

37. *See also* APWU v. Potter, 343 F.3d 619 (2d Cir. 2003) (where President delegated his removal authority to heads of executive departments and agencies in non-emergency situations, anthrax contamination was not an "emergency" requiring the EPA to conduct the removal action because the situation did not call for action within hours, and the United States Postal Service was able to perform the removal itself).

38. 40 C.F.R. § 300.415(b)(3).

39. *Id.* § 300.415(m).

with information about the hazardous nature of the site and physical access to the site.[40]

If a removal action is completed by the EPA, it will file suit to recover the costs if a PRP is available. Section 107 provides that a PRP "shall be liable for all costs of removal ... incurred by the United States Government...." Cost recovery actions are addressed in greater detail below.

4. "Remedial" Actions

The other response action contemplated by CERCLA is remedial action, generally encompassing more extensive, long-term, permanent cleanups of contaminated sites. Section 101(24) defines "remedial action" as an action "consistent with a permanent remedy," taken "instead of or in addition to removal actions" so as to "prevent or minimize the release of hazardous substances...." Examples include removing contaminated groundwater, excavating contaminated soil, disposing of hazardous materials offsite, constructing barriers above, below, or around sites to prevent migration, and relocating residents.[41] The site must be listed on the NPL for the EPA to undertake these cleanup measures.

The EPA must take care to comply with all the procedural and substantive requirements of the NCP. For example, § 104(c) provides that the EPA may not implement remedial action unless the state

40. CERCLA § 104(e).

41. *See also* United States v. Tarkowski, 248 F.3d 596 (7th Cir. 2001) (holding that the EPA could not enter private property pursuant to an access order to undertake remedial action pursuant to CERCLA).

in which the site is located agrees to pay 10 percent of the clean-up costs; assures maintenance of the site upon completion of remedial action; and demonstrates a 20-year capacity for the treatment and destruction of all resulting wastes. As is the case with removal actions, the EPA is authorized under § 107 to sue any of the parties responsible for the contamination to recover the EPA's costs of performing remediation activities. For sites not listed on the NPL, the EPA often mandates that other parties take remediation measures.

Under § 121, CERCLA provides clean-up criteria for determining what remedial action the EPA should choose. This section was added by SARA and lists six factors the EPA must consider when deciding on a final remedy. This section applies to all remedial action carried out under § 104 (clean-up performed by the government) and § 106 (clean-up mandated to private parties by an administrative order). The remedial action should: (1) be cost-effective taking into consideration the short-term and long-term costs, including costs of operations and maintenance;[42] (2) comply with the NCP "to the extent practicable;"[43] (3) normally involve permanent treatment to reduce volume, toxicity or mobility of the hazardous substance, rather then offsite transport of the material without treatment;[44] (4) protect human health and the

42.   CERCLA § 121(a), (b)(1).

43.   Id. § 121(a).

44.   Id. § 121(b)(1).

environment;[45] (5) utilize alternative treatment technologies or resource recovery technologies "to the maximum extent practicable;"[46] and (6) normally meet ARARs—attain the clean-up level required by any "legally applicable or relevant and appropriate" standard under federal environmental law, and under any state law that is more stringent than federal law.[47]

However, the EPA adopted regulations amending the NCP to address inconsistencies in these § 121 criteria. The NCP now contains nine criteria the EPA uses to select an appropriate remedy, including:

(1) overall protection of human health and the environment;

(2) compliance with ARARs;

(3) long-term effectiveness and permanence;

(4) reduction of toxicity, mobility, or volume;

(5) short-term effectiveness;

(6) the ease of implementing the alternative;

(7) cost;

(8) state acceptance of the remedy; and

(9) community acceptance of the remedy.

The NCP establishes a three-step process for applying these criteria to determine the best remedy. First, all of the proposed remedies must meet the

45. *Id.* § 121(b)(1), (d)(1).

46. *Id.* § 121(b)(1).

47. *Id.* § 121(d)(2).

first two criteria ("threshold" criteria)—overall protection of human health and the environment, and compliance with ARARs. Second, the EPA evaluates the remaining potential remedies using criteria (3) through (7) ("primary balancing criteria"), with permanence and cost being the two most important of these five criteria. Third, after receiving state and community input, the EPA considers the final two criteria ("modifying criteria")—state and community acceptance. These are regarded as "modifying criteria," because they only come into play after a remedy has been tentatively selected. Adverse comments may result in the choice of another remedy.[48] The most significant of the criteria are discussed below.

  a. Protectiveness. The protection of human health and the environment, the first of the NCP threshold criteria, must be met before a remedial alternative is acceptable. Protectiveness means the acceptable exposure level representing concentrations to which humans (including sensitive ones) may be exposed without adverse effect.[49] To make this determination, the EPA performs a two-part risk assessment analysis. For known or suspected carcinogens, the appropriate level for CERCLA sites is defined in the NCP as a range between 10 to 10 individual lifetime cancer risk.[50] The toxicity por-

  48. Ohio v. EPA, 997 F.2d 1520 (D.C. Cir. 1993).

  49. 40 C.F.R. § 300.430(e)(2)(i)(A)(1).

  50. *See* United States v. Burlington Northern Railroad Co., 200 F.3d 679 (10th Cir. 1999) (a risk level of 1 in 100,000 does not mean that 100,000 people need to be exposed for one person

tion of the equation is based on the contaminants of concern. The exposure portion is based on a "reasonable maximum exposure" (RME) scenario which calculates the amount of exposure to the harm-producing substances that may still remain after remediation is completed, and the likelihood that it still poses a risk to human health. This calculation of exposure is based on the cumulative effect of multiple contaminants, the potential for human exposure to toxic pathways from the site in light of exposure frequency and duration, the sensitivities of the population that may be in contact with the site, as well as some uncertainty factors. The "protectiveness" goal is met when there would be less than a 1 in 500 chance that an individual exposed to a cleaned up Superfund site would receive exposure greater than the RME.

b. ARARs. Section 121(d)(2) provides guidance as to how clean a site should be once the remedial actions is completed. This section states that any "legally applicable" or "relevant and appropriate" rule under federal or state law (ARAR) must be achieved for on-site clean-ups, or explicitly waived for specific reasons. This means that sites are judged under other federal environmental standards, such as the Resource Conservation and Recovery Act, the Safe Drinking Water Act, the Clean Water Act, and the Toxic Substance Control Act, or their state counterparts (if more stringent than the federal standards).

to contract cancer; it means that for every person exposed there is a .00001% chance the person will get cancer).

The NCP makes a distinction between "applicable" and "relevant and appropriate" requirements. An "applicable" requirement includes "those clean-up standards, standards of control, and other substantive requirements ... under federal environmental or state ... laws that specifically address a hazardous substance...." This language means that if a law would be legally enforceable at the site, regardless of CERCLA remediation, it must be attained unless grounds for waiver exist. Section 121(d)(4) permits waiver of an ARAR if one of a number of conditions are present, such as: compliance with the ARAR will result in greater risk than alternative options; compliance with an ARAR is technically impractical; and the ARAR derives from state law, but the state has failed to consistently apply it.

"Relevant and appropriate" requirements are "clean-up standards ... that, while not 'applicable' to a hazardous substance, pollutant, contaminant, remedial action, location, or other circumstance at a CERCLA site, address problems sufficiently similar to those encountered at the CERCLA site that their use is well suited to the particular site."[51] Unlike "applicable" requirements, which are largely objective, "relevant and appropriate" requirements are discretionary, and assume that "best professional judgment" will be used to decide if a proposed remedy addresses the problem at the site (*i.e.*, is relevant), and is suited to the particular characteristics of the site (*i.e.*, is appropriate). The EPA also

51.   40 C.F.R. § 300.5.

uses a third category, "to be considered," for standards that are neither applicable nor suitable for direct adoption, but which may provide useful guidance.

An ARAR, particularly one based on the "applicable" requirement, can come from any number of federal or state laws. Most commonly, an ARAR is pegged to a health or risk-based numerical value, such as the maximum contaminant levels set under the Safe Water Drinking Act (SWDA) that establish limits on contamination in the water of a public water system.[52] An ARAR can be a technology or activity-based requirement, such as RCRA's land disposal restrictions for RCRA "hazardous wastes" (which may have been disposed of at a CERCLA site). If a RCRA waste has been dumped at a CERCLA site, the RCRA requirement is the applicable requirement, even if the wastes were disposed of at the site prior to the statutory date that they were deemed hazardous.[53] Location-specific ARARs are also possible, if a legal restriction is triggered solely because the hazardous substance is in a specified location, such as a wetland, a protected wildlife habitat, or a water body subject to an anti-degradation law under state law.[54]

   c.   *Permanence*. While protectiveness and compliance with ARARs are "threshold" criteria, long-

52.   42 U.S.C. § 300(f) *et seq.*

53.   Chemical Waste Management, Inc. v. United States EPA, 869 F.2d 1526, 1535–37 (D.C. Cir. 1989).

54.   United States v. Akzo Coatings of America, Inc., 949 F.2d 1409, 1439–50 (6th Cir. 1991).

term effectiveness and "permanence" constitute one of the "primary balancing criteria" which may be used to decide among different clean-up strategies. A closely related balancing criteria is "reduction of toxicity, mobility, or volume through treatment." Both are designed to assure that remedial action will in fact be final, and that the problem will not reappear in the future. Thus, the statute states a distinct preference that "treatment" or other "permanent" solutions be a "principal part" of any remedy.

The NCP assumes that some residual hazardous waste will still exist after clean-up is completed. As such, the permanence standard is satisfied if the threat posed by the hazardous substances remaining can be adequately managed by "engineering or institutional controls." On the other hand, while it is expected that some wastes will still be present, the EPA also endorses a guideline that achieves between 90 to 99 percent reduction in toxicity or mobility. A strict standard is necessary because over 26% of the sites on the NPL are expected to become residential, while 80% will likely have residents surrounding the site.[55] These are seemingly contradictory impulses: treatment because people are likely to come into contact with the contamination in the future, and yet acceptance of significant amounts of residual contamination.

d. Cost. CERCLA § 121(a), (b)(1) requires that a remedy by "cost effective." The EPA and NCP have derived two alternative interpretations for this slip-

55.   60 Fed. Reg. 29595, 29596 (June 5, 1995).

pery term that are mirror images of each other. On the one hand, a cost-effective remedy is simply a means of achieving a predetermined clean-up goal. The EPA decides what level of environmental protection is appropriate (*i.e.*, what level is protective and permanent), and then selects the remedy that will be the cheapest way of obtaining that desired level. In making this decision, "[t]he decisionmaker should both compare the cost and effectiveness of each alternative individually and compare the cost and effectiveness of alternatives in relation to one another."[56] Alternative comparable technologies that are more costly will be rejected. On the other hand, the NCP takes the view that "cost effective" is achieved by performing a cost-benefit analysis. The theory is that cost can help decide the appropriate level of environmental clean-up (the goal) by being weighed against the benefits conferred by a certain level of clean-up. If the costs are disproportionate to the benefits, the clean-up standard itself can be loosened.

5. *Judicial Review*

There are several reasons why a private party might wish to bring a lawsuit challenging a decision under CERCLA. The general public, including environmental organizations, may believe that an EPA regulation is too lax, or may be concerned that a specific clean-up operation will be inadequate. By contrast, a PRP may wish to attack a rule or a particular clean-up decision for being too harsh. In

56.   55 Fed. Reg. 8728 (Mar. 8, 1990).

such cases, two CERCLA provisions allowing for a *citizens' suit* are key.

Section 310(a)(1), (2) "giveth"—it permits suits against (1) any person alleged to be in violation of any CERCLA rule,[57] or (2) any federal official who has failed to perform a non-discretionary act under CERCLA.[58] Section 113(h) "taketh away"—it restricts federal court jurisdiction to entertain challenges to EPA decisions with respect to the clean-ups of a hazardous waste site. It bars most pre-implementation review, and possibly even pre-enforcement review. Congress has limited the federal courts' jurisdiction to hear such actions because these suits can greatly delay the clean-up of a site.[59]

There are additional statutory restrictions and rules that plaintiffs must follow to initiate a suit. First, plaintiffs may not sue in cases in which the government is "diligently prosecuting" a similar action.[60] Second, the plaintiffs must give appropri-

57. CERCLA § 310(a)(1).

58. *Id.* § 310(a)(2).

59. *But see* United States v. Colorado, 990 F.2d 1565 (10th Cir. 1993) *cert. denied* 510 U.S. 1092 (1994) (holding that an action by Colorado to enforce a compliance order issued by the EPA pursuant to RCRA for property placed on the National Priorities List and where clean-up action was on the way was not a challenge to the Army's CERCLA response action and therefore was permitted despite the bar on pre-implentation review); United States v. Princeton Gamma–Tech, Inc., 31 F.3d 138 (3d Cir. 1994) (where irreparable harm to public health or the environment is threatened, an injunction may be issued even though the clean-up may not yet be completed).

60. *Id.* § 310(d)(2). *See* Frey v. EPA, 270 F.3d 1129 (7th Cir. 2001) (citizens precluded from bringing air pollution enforce-

ate notice. At least 60 days before filing suit under § 310(a)(1), the plaintiff must have given notice of the alleged violation to the EPA, to the state in which the alleged violation occurs, and to the perpetrator of the violation.[61] Similarly, at least 60 days prior to commencing an action under § 310(a)(2), the plaintiff must notify the EPA or other federal department, agency, or instrumentality alleged to be in violation of CERCLA.[62] Third, in an action under either §§ 301(a)(1) or (a)(2), the plaintiff may not sue for purely past violations; the defendant must either still be "in violation,"[63] or in some jurisdictions, the violation must be "continuous" or likely to recur in the future.[64] The notice provision, therefore, gives governmental defendants an opportunity to take the demanded action, and private defendants the opportunity to sin no more without facing litigation.

There are limitations restricting the federal court's jurisdiction to hear suits regarding the clean-up of specific sites. CERCLA § 113(h) provides that "[n]o Federal court shall have jurisdiction under federal law ... to review any challenges to removal or remedial action selected" by the EPA under § 104 or § 106(a), except in cost-recovery or

ment action where citizens failed to exhaust their administrative remedies and the state was diligently pursuing clean-up of sites).

61. CERCLA § 310(d)(1).

62. *Id.* § 310(e).

63. *See, e.g.,* Coalition for Health Concern v. LWD, Inc., 60 F.3d 1188 (6th Cir. 1995).

64. Lutz v. Chromatex, Inc., 718 F.Supp. 413 (M.D. Pa. 1989).

enforcement lawsuits in which money or response actions are actually demanded.[65] Federal courts have interpreted section 113(h) to mean that they have no jurisdiction to review challenges to removal or remedial actions *until those actions have been completed.*[66] In other words, pre-implementation review is forbidden.[67] Although this rule seems to be a barrier to lawsuits that may prevent excessive or *ultra vires* expenditures, in enacting § 113(h) "Congress intended to prevent time-consuming litigation which might interfere with CERCLA's overall goal of effecting the prompt clean-up of hazardous waste sites."[68] The rule apparently is to clean up first and ask questions later.

Some courts have taken this philosophy to its logical extreme. In *Voluntary Purchasing Groups,*

65. Gopher Oil Co. v. Bunker, 84 F.3d 1047, 1051 (8th Cir. 1996); Arkansas Peace Ctr. v. Arkansas Dept. of Pollution Control & Ecology, 999 F.2d 1212, 1216 (8th Cir. 1993).

66. *See* Schalk v. Reilly, 900 F.2d 1091, 1095 (7th Cir. 1990) ("The obvious meaning of this statute is that when a remedy has been selected, no challenge to the clean-up may occur prior to the completion of that remedy."); *see also* Frey v. EPA, 270 F.3d 1129 (7th Cir. 2001) (holding that the district court was required to determine if remedial action was "complete" in order to determine if citizens had stated a claim upon which relief could be granted under CERCLA); Frey v. EPA, 403 F.3d 828, 834 (7th Cir. 2005) (concluding that § 113(h) is not an open ended prohibition to citizen's suits, and therefore, following initial clean-up, to halt a lawsuit under this provision, the EPA must "point to an objective referent that commits it and other responsible parties to an action or plan for further clean-up.")

67. Alabama v. EPA, 871 F.2d 1548 (11th Cir. 1989).

68. United States v. City and County of Denver, 100 F.3d 1509, 1514 (10th Cir. 1996).

Inc. v. Reilly,[69] the court barred pre-enforcement review. According to the court, the PRPs at the site could not challenge a fully implemented clean-up decision until the EPA had filed a cost-recovery action against them. Despite the fact that a post-implementation, pre-enforcement lawsuit could not halt the already completed remedy, that court concluded there was "no indication [that section 113(h)] only applies when a delay in clean-up would ensue."[70]

D. Liability

CERCLA's primary task aims at protecting the public and the environment by responding to hazardous spills and releases of contaminated waste, and by bringing about a prompt clean up of hazardous waste sites through the four clean-up cornerstones—the NCP, NPL, and remedial and removal actions. CERCLA's second purpose is to ensure that the cost of clean-up is borne by the parties responsible for causing the release or threatened release of the hazardous substances. To accomplish this goal, CERCLA creates a new cause of action; the statute establishes the nature of the new liability, the identity of who may be liable, and the triggers for liability, remedies, and defenses to liability.

If the conditions to liability are met, and the defenses are unavailable, the consequence, accord-

69. 889 F.2d 1380 (5th Cir. 1989).

70. *Id.* at 1388–89.

ing to § 107(a)(4), is that the responsible party is liable for three types of costs incurred as a result of the release or threatened release of the hazardous waste: (1) governmental response costs (incurred by the federal government, Indian tribes or states); (2) private party response costs (incurred by private parties if consistent with the NCP); and (3) damages to natural resources.

1. *The Standard of Liability*

Section 107(a) states that certain "person[s]" meeting CERCLA's test for responsible parties "shall be liable." Courts interpret this phrase to impose (1) strict, (2) joint and several, and (3) retroactive liability. All of these elements were established in judicial decisions shortly after CERCLA was enacted. Since Congress had the opportunity to modify these results in the 1986 SARA amendments, its failure to do so must be considered an affirmance of these judicial interpretations.

a. Strict Liability. The standard of liability under § 107(a) is strict liability, even though the statute nowhere expressly demands this result. Section 101(32) defines "liable" as "the standard of liability which obtains under [§ 311 of the Clean Water Act]." Since most courts have interpreted § 311 as imposing strict liability, the same standard has been applied to CERCLA. Strict liability means that a plaintiff, governmental or private, need not prove that the release of hazardous substances was due to the defendant's negligent conduct, nor that the defendant's conduct was intentional or unreasonable. To establish the defendant's liability and responsibility for response costs, the plaintiff only has to prove four elements: (1) the site is a "facility"; (2) the defendant is a responsible "person"; (3) a release or threatened release of a "hazardous substance" has occurred; and (4) the release has caused the plaintiff to "incur response costs."

Another important consequence of strict liability is that causation, normally a central component to a common law toxic tort action, is relevant in a completely new way. To meet the causation element for CERCLA claims, plaintiffs do not have show that the responsible parties actually caused the presence or release of a hazardous waste. Current and prior owners and operators of hazardous waste sites, as well as generators of hazardous wastes, may be liable irrespective of whether they in fact caused the hazardous waste to occur. Rather, the required linkage is whether the *release* (or threat of release) caused response costs to be incurred.[71] This very weak causal link has several benefits: (1) companies are given a powerful incentive to internalize their waste clean-up costs; (2) clean-up costs will usually be borne by the businesses that generate and dispose of the wastes, not by affected neighbors or taxpayers; and (3) the Superfund (*i.e.*, taxpayer money) is conserved. A generator of wastes or owner of a facility can be liable even if it was not at fault or if, since due care is not a defense to strict

71. New York v. Shore Realty Corp., 759 F.2d 1032 (2d Cir. 1985).

liability, it took every precaution when disposing of its wastes.

b. *Joint and Several Liability.* Although CERC-LA is silent on the issue, § 107(a) has been universally interpreted as allowing joint and several liability among potentially responsible parties.[72] Joint and several liability means that the entire burden can be shifted to any contributor to the harm, even one that has only a tiny role, leaving to that party the task of seeking contribution from other defendants, if possible.

In joint and several liability cases, the defendant has the burden of proving that the harm is *divisible*, and therefore can be apportioned among two or more parties (as opposed to the defendant being responsible for the entire cost of clean-up). To meet this burden, the defendant must show that its waste has produced a separate, identifiable harm which is distinct from all other harms. The defendant may seek to show its separate contribution to the single harm, for example, where many generators of the same kind of toxic waste in a non-leaking site can calculate the exact percentage of the total quantity of waste for which they were responsible. If the defendant meets this considerable burden, then each party will only be responsible for the percentage of harm it caused. When the defendant fails to meet this burden (and the harm is *indivisible*), a

72. United States v. Chem–Dyne Corp., 572 F.Supp. 802 (S.D.Ohio 1983). *See* United States v. Hercules, Inc., 247 F.3d 706 (8th Cir. 2001) (chemical manufacturer was an "arranger" for purpose of CERCLA liability and was therefore correctly held jointly and severally liable).

court may find any given defendant jointly and severally liable for any hazardous substance found at the site, whatever its source, and regardless of that defendant's percentage of contribution of the overall waste problem at the site.[73]

Joint and several liability can be unfairly harsh in cases where 100% of the cost of clean-up falls on a small generator of waste, a naïve purchaser of the contaminated property, or a former lessee with only fleeting contact with the waste site, each of whom had little to do with dumping significant waste quantities there. In the SARA amendments in 1986, Congress added two important provisions to mitigate these sometimes unfair consequences of joint and several liability. First, pursuant to § 122(g), the EPA is directed to offer early settlements to defendants who are responsible for only a small portion of the harm, so called *de minimis* settlements. Second, § 113(f)(1) now permits a statutory cause of action in *contribution*, which allows courts to "allocate response costs among liable parties using such equitable factors as the court determines are appropriate." Both of these provisions are addressed more fully below.

73. United States v. Alcan Aluminum Corp., 315 F.3d 179 (2d Cir. 2003) (failure to prove that harm was divisible where defendant merely argued that the waste it caused was minimal and benign); Chem–Nuclear Systems v. Bush, 292 F.3d 254 (D.C. Cir. 2002) (party responsible for 80 drums of hazardous waste not entitled to reimbursement absent proof beyond preponderance of the evidence that additional waste at the site was not also attributable to this source); United States v. Township of Brighton, 153 F.3d 307 (6th Cir. 1998); Town of New Windsor v. Tesa Truck, Inc., 919 F.Supp. 662 (S.D.N.Y. 1996).

In addition, some courts have tried to moderate the impact of joint and several liability in appropriate cases. Both the Second and Third Circuits inject causation into the liability question (although the burden of proof remains on the defendant) by permitting an otherwise responsible party to avoid § 107(a) liability if it can prove that the wastes, when mixed with other hazardous wastes, "did not [or could not] contribute to the release and the resultant response costs [or contributed at most to only a divisible portion of the harm]."[74] Other courts have stretched the joint and several liability doctrine to find the harm to be divisible and the resulting liability capable of apportionment. The leading case is *In the Matter of Bell Petroleum Service, Inc.*[75] In *Bell Petroleum*, three parties had successfully operated a business that discharged one contaminant (chromium) into groundwater. The Fifth Circuit decided it could apportion damages based on circumstantial evidence of the volumes of chromium-contaminated water discharged by each party.

    c.   *Retroactive Liability.* CERCLA has additionally been interpreted to impose retroactive liability, that is, the statute's liability standards apply to hazardous waste deposited years (or decades) before the statute's enactment in 1980. Responsible parties find themselves liable even though at the time they

74. United States v. Alcan Aluminum Corp., 990 F.2d 711, 722 (2d Cir. 1993); United States v. Alcan Aluminum Corp., 964 F.2d 252, 270–71 (3d Cir. 1992).

75. 3 F.3d 889 (5th Cir. 1993).

dumped the hazardous wastes it may have been perfectly legal to discard wastes at a site now listed on the NPL.

Although defendants have frequently attacked CERCLA on constitutional grounds for being retroactive, all of these claims have been unsuccessful. These cases conclude that CERCLA did not create retroactive liability at all, because it simply imposed post-enactment prospective obligations for past, pre-enactment private actions. Alternatively, since one of the triggers for liability is a present or threatened release, CERCLA can be understood to apply prospectively to remedy current problems, not punish past conduct.[76]

2. *Potentially Responsible Parties*

Potentially responsible parties (PRPs) are the possible defendants in a CERCLA action. Pursuant to § 107(a), CERCLA liability applies to four classes of PRPs:

(1) the "owner and operator" of a hazardous waste site or "facility";

(2) "any person who at the time of disposal of any hazardous substance owned or operated" a site or facility where "hazardous substances were disposed of";

(3) "any person who by contract, agreement, or otherwise arranged for disposal or treatment, or who arranged with a transporter for trans-

76. Usery v. Turner Elkhorn Mining Co., 428 U.S. 1 (1976); Concrete Pipe and Products of California, Inc. v. Construction Laborers Pension Trust for Southern California, 508 U.S. 602 (1993).

port for disposal or treatment" of hazardous substances; or

(4) "any person who accepts or accepted any hazardous substances for transport" to "facilities ... or sites" for disposal or treatment.

The parties within these categories may be liable for all of the costs specified by the statute, under strict, joint and several, and retroactive standards of liability. Since each of the PRPs at one time had *control* of the hazardous substance as issue, the theory is that each had the ability to prevent or minimize the harm. Note especially that these categories are not exclusive. There is no reason that a PRP cannot be liable cumulatively or alternatively under any category that fits.

a. Current Owners and Operators. Section 107(a) imposes liability on the "owner and operator" of a facility. Although the word "and" makes this test appear conjunctive, suggesting that the owner must also operate the facility or site, courts have read it to be disjunctive—*either* the present owner *or* operator may be liable.[77] Additionally, the time for determining owner or operator status is when the cost-recovery action is filed.

If one wishes to receive guidance on the question of who is an "owner," and who is an "operator," the statute's basic definition is vague at best. Section 101(20)(A) defines "owner or operator" as "any person owning or operating." One is left with the commonsense notion that Congress must have

77. Redwing Carriers, Inc. v. Saraland Apartments, 94 F.3d 1489 (11th Cir. 1996).

intended to hold strictly liable those parties whose status puts them in a position to do something about the waste at the site—the present owner has the most immediate control over how the land is used, and the operator in some way manages the activity that resulted in the release of hazardous substances. Since this liability is based only on status, and not the quality of the defendant's actions, the plaintiff need not prove that the current owner or operator (1) caused the release, (2) knew about the release, or (3) owned or operated the facility at the time of the release. As such, the mere status of being a current owner or operator makes these parties liable even though they neither owned nor operated the site or facility at the time of the disposal or release of the hazardous substance.[78]

i. Owners. A current owner is liable under § 107(a)(1) so long as that owner holds title in fee simple absolute. When dealing with a fee simple property interest, it is irrelevant that the waste disposal was done by someone other than the owner, such as a lessee.[79] Harder cases arise, however, with respect to ownership involving lesser property interests, such as an easement holder.

In the case of a person holding less than fee simple interest, liability hinges on the extent to which the defendant has the legal right to control

78. State of New York v. Shore Realty Corp., 759 F.2d 1032 (2d Cir. 1985); City of Phoenix v. Garbage Services Co., 816 F.Supp. 564 (D. Ariz. 1993).

79. United States v. Monsanto Co., 858 F.2d 160 (4th Cir. 1988).

the premises. Courts generally hold that easement holders, such as utility companies, are generally not owners because they exercise little control over the waste site. The Ninth Circuit in *Long Beach Unified School District v. Dorothy B. Godwin California Living Trust*,[80] concluded that imposing CERCLA liability on an easement holder would unfairly penalize "legitimate, non-polluting actors such as telephone and electric companies which, in running pipelines and cables, have no greater responsibility for the nation's toxic waste problem than the public at large." Lessees, on the other hand, are more likely to be liable if they maintain substantial "site control,"[81] or have power over decisions regarding waste disposal at the site.[82]

Aside from lessor/lessee liability, two other common relationships that give rise to CERCLA litigation include secured creditors and innocent purchaser liability. Confusion arises for secured creditors because there is an explicit statutory exclusion from the "owner or operator" category of a person "who, without participating in ... management ... holds indicia of ownership primarily to protect his security interest in the ... facility."[83] A secured creditor seemingly fits into this excluded category. In *United States v. Fleet Fac-*

80. 32 F.3d 1364 (9th Cir. 1994).

81. United States v. A & N Cleaners and Launderers, Inc., 788 F.Supp. 1317 (S.D.N.Y. 1992).

82. United States v. McLamb, 5 F.3d 69 (4th Cir. 1993); Lansford–Coaldale Joint Water Auth. v. Tonolli Corp., 4 F.3d 1209 (3d Cir. 1993).

83. CERCLA § 101(20)(A)(iii).

tors Corp.,[84] however, the Eleventh Circuit found liable a secured creditor whose "involvement with the management of the facility is sufficiently broad to support the inference that it could affect hazardous waste disposal decisions if it so chose." As such, if a secured creditor maintains a certain amount of management (or control) over a facility, even with the exclusion language, that creditor nonetheless may be liable; the theory is that the party could have used its management power to prevent or minimize the harm. The holding in *Fleet Factors* has been limited by courts and the EPA to immunize secured creditors who do not actually participate in the management of the contaminated site; because they have no control over the waste, they cannot be held responsible for its contamination.

In the case of *innocent purchaser liability*, if a buyer of a contaminated site becomes the "owner" of the site, that purchaser may become liable under § 107(a). To prevent this result in the case of truly innocent purchasers, the SARA amendments clarify that such buyers can be relieved of liability if they had no knowledge of the hazardous substance when the land was acquired, and if at acquisition the buyer conducted "all appropriate inquiry into the previous ownership and uses of the property."[85] Since these purchasers never had the opportunity to prevent or minimize the harm, they cannot be held liable for its clean-up. Inadequate preacquisition

84. 901 F.2d 1550, 1558 (11th Cir. 1990).

85. CERCLA § 101(35)(B).

inquiry, however, will void the innocent purchaser defense.

ii. Operators. Non-owners can be liable if they are termed "operators." Generally, an "operator" is one who has legal authority to control the activities at the site, and who actually exercises that control. Most courts follow the "actual control" test, attaching "operator" liability only upon a finding that (1) the defendant had the authority to determine whether and how there would be a disposal of hazardous wastes, and (2) that defendant actually exercised the authority, either personally performing the tasks necessary to dispose of the hazardous waste, or by directing others to perform those tasks.[86] The Eighth Circuit explained in *United States v. Gurley*,[87] that this approach is consistent with the ordinary meaning of "operator," which connotes "some type of action or affirmative conduct"; omissions do not suffice. Additionally, the Supreme Court in *United States v. Bestfoods*,[88] had occasion to take up the meaning of "operator" specifically within the context of CERCLA. The Court concluded that to be a CERCLA operator, one "must manage, direct, or conduct operations specifically related to pollution, that is, operations having to do with the leakage or disposal of hazardous

86. United States v. Gurley, 43 F.3d 1188 (8th Cir. 1994); Lansford–Coaldale Joint Water Authority v. Tonolli Corp., 4 F.3d 1209, 1221 (3d Cir. 1993).

87. 43 F.3d 1188 (8th Cir. 1994).

88. 524 U.S. 51 (1998).

waste, or decisions about compliance with environmental regulations."[89]

Courts are divided on the issue of where a defendant holds the legal right to control a site, but does not actually exercise that control. Some early decisions adopted the "authority to control" test, finding operator liability if the defendant had authority to control the facility, even if he did not exercise such control. The best-known decision following this approach is *Nurad, Inc. v. William E. Hooper & Sons Co.*,[90] where the Fourth Circuit reasoned that the "authority to control" test "is one which properly declines to absolve from CERCLA liability a party who possessed the authority to abate the damage caused by the disposal of hazardous substances, but who declined to actually exercise that authority by undertaking efforts at a clean-up."

Governmental entities can also be liable as operators. One leading case, *FMC Corp. v. United States Dept. of Commerce*,[91] found that the United States qualified as an operator of the plaintiff's facility where it required a company to manufacture a product that yielded a hazardous waste product and maintained a significant degree of control over the

89. *See also* American Cyanamid Co. v. Capuano, 381 F.3d 6, 23 (1st Cir. 2004) (finding operator liability to be not clearly erroneous where party developed the idea for using the site, prepared the site for dumping, arranged for waste to be dumped at the site, showed transporters where to dump on the site, and collected payment and transmitted a share to the owner of the site for allowing the dumping).

90. 966 F.2d 837, 843 (4th Cir. 1992).

91. 29 F.3d 833 (3d Cir. 1994).

production process through regulations and on-site inspectors. The court also concluded that the federal government could be liable when it "engaged in regulatory activities extensive enough to make it an operator ... even though no private party could engage in the regulatory activities at issue."[92] Conversely, other cases have tended to reject the argument that the government could be liable under CERCLA merely for its regulatory activities.[93]

b. Past Owners/Operators "at the Time of Disposal". Section 107(a)(2) states that a PRP may be "any person who at the time of disposal of any hazardous substance owned or operated any facility at which such hazardous substances were disposed of." Under this provision, *past* owners and operators may be liable.[94] This provision can be divided into two further classes. The first class contains persons who owned the land at the time a "disposal of any hazardous substance" took place. Section 101(29) defines "disposal" by borrowing RCRA's broad definition, which includes "the discharge, de-

92. *Id.* at 840.

93. *See* United States v. Brighton, 153 F.3d 307, 315–16 (6th Cir. 1998) (mere regulation does not suffice to make a government entity liable, but actual operation and "macromanagement" does); United States v. American Color and Chemical Corp., 858 F.Supp. 445 (M.D. Pa. 1994) (United States not an "operator" when it is acting in a regulatory capacity to bring about a clean-up).

94. *See* Crofton Ventures Ltd. Partnership v. G & H Partnership & Cyphers, 258 F.3d 292 (4th Cir. 2001) (landowner not required to show that former owners and operators actually dumped waste or had knowledge of dumping or leaking in order to recover response costs).

posit, injection, dumping, spilling, leaking, or placing of ... any hazardous waste into or on any land
or water so that such solid waste or hazardous
waste or any constituent thereof may enter the
environment or be emitted into the air or discharged into any waters, including ground waters."[95] Following this definition, if a party owned
land on which wastes were "deposited" or
"dumped" or "discharged," that party would be a
past owner PRP under § 107(a)(2).[96]

The second class of past owners is the class of
persons who owned or operated the waste site *after*
the time the initial disposal took place, but *before*
the time the CERCLA liability suit was filed. The
main question facing courts for this class is whether
the past owners/operators may also be liable under
§ 107(a)(2) if the wastes may have, without human
intervention, migrated further into the soil or
groundwater during the alleged PRP's ownership or
operation of the site. The definition of "disposal" is
ambiguous when applied to the issue of passive
disposal. As such, courts are split on whether to
interpret "disposal" broadly (and include passive
owners), or narrowly (immunizing passive owners
from CERCLA liability).

The leading case opting for the broad definition of
"disposal" is *Nurad, Inc. v. William E. Hooper &*

95. RCRA § 1004(3).

96. *See* Bob's Beverage, Inc. v. Acme, Inc., 264 F.3d 692 (6th
Cir. 2001) (predecessor warehouse owner was not liable for
response costs and his action of replacing the septic system did
not cause a "disposal" of hazardous waste).

Sons.[97] The court there believed that the definition contemplates action that has a passive component, encompassing leakage or spillage without any active human participation. The rationale is that without liability for passive disposal there would be no disincentive for past owners who did nothing while hazardous wastes slowly contaminated the surrounding environment.

Alternatively, many courts follow a narrow definition of "disposal," requiring that a person introduce ("place") formerly controlled or contained hazardous substances into the environment to be responsible. Only prior owners or operators who had a relationship with the site at the time the hazardous substances were actively added may be liable. In *Carson Harbor Village v. Unocal Corp.*,[98] a mobile park owner and operator purchased property that decades before was leased by a corporation that dealt in petroleum products. In addition to the contamination caused by the petroleum by-products, lead-contaminated storm water and runoff from adjacent cities would drain into wetlands located on the property. As a result of the wetlands, and the slope of the land, the hazardous substances eventually spread across the property. After undertaking clean-up efforts, the current-owner/operator plaintiffs filed a suit under CERCLA to recover its clean-up costs against the petroleum producer, the past owner/operator who owned the property during the time of petroleum production, and the govern-

97.   966 F.2d 837 (4th Cir. 1992).

98.   270 F.3d 863 (9th Cir. 2001).

ment responsible for the lead runoff. The Ninth Circuit, sitting *en banc*, held that "disposal" did not encompass passive migration of contaminants. As such, the past owners/operators who did not actively dispose of any wastes on the site were not liable.

In making this decision, the court examined the plain meaning of the terms in the statutory definition of "disposal" and applied each term to the facts of the case. The court determined that the actions taken by the hazardous substances in this case, which included "spreading," "migration," "seeping," and "oozing" were not synonymous with "discharge . . . injection, dumping, . . . placing" or other terms in the definition of "disposal" used to hold parties liable under CERCLA; the terms did "not describe the passive migration that occurred here." The court then concluded that its interpretation of the "disposal" was in accordance with the purpose of CERCLA as a whole because it (1) "made sense" with the statute's liability provisions, (2) preserved the scope and the role of CERCLA's statutory defenses, and (3) was consistent with the provisions that allocate liability among PRPs.

The rationale supporting "active disposal" is this: Since CERCLA's primary policy is to enforce a "polluter pays" principle, prior owners and operators should not be liable for mere passive migration because these parties are not true polluters. Additionally, some courts take the view that the terms in the definition of "disposal" that are interpreted to include passive migration—"leak" and "spill"—

both seem to assume something other than slow, passive, migration of wastes.[99]

   c. *Persons Who "Arranged for Disposal or Treatment".* Section 107(a)(3) includes in the categories of PRPs persons who "by contract, agreement, or otherwise arranged for disposal or treatment, of hazardous substances" which they "owned or possessed." The most common pattern of arranger liability involves a *generator* defendant—the factor, refinery, smelter, or other industrial complex—that generates hazardous wastes. A second group that is liable under this provision is an *arranger*. A generator becomes an arranger when it hires a transporter to haul its wastes. As such, a generator of wastes cannot ignore how its wastes will eventually be treated or discarded; if a hazardous substance generated by a private party is sent to a site where a release occurs (or is threatened), that party is subject to CERCLA liability. The general rule of strict liability applies. So even if a generator was not at fault and exercised due care with regard to disposal of its wastes, that generator is liable if the transporter leaves behind a contaminated waste site.

   A generator of wastes may be liable for a release even absent proof that its own wastes were released. In the leading of *United States v. Monsanto Co.*,[100] generator defendants argued that the United States had failed to establish that the defendants'

---

99. *See* Idylwoods Assocs. v. Mader Capital, Inc., 915 F.Supp. 1290 (W.D.N.Y. 1996); In re Tutu Wells Contamination Litigation, 994 F.Supp. 638, 668 (D. Virgin Islands 1998).

100. 858 F.2d 160 (4th Cir. 1988).

wastes were still present at the facility when the release occurred. Recognizing the "technological infeasibility of tracing an improperly disposed of waste to its source," the Fourth Circuit rejected the "proof of ownership" standard for cases involving multiple generators. The court held that the plaintiff need only to prove that (1) the generator's waste was shipped to the site, and (2) hazardous substances similar to those belonging to the defendant generator's waste remained present at the site at the time of release.

Following the Fourth Circuit's reasoning, most courts have adopted a four-element test for determining generator liability: (1) the generator in some fashion disposed of its hazardous substances at the site in question; (2) the site now contains hazardous substances like those disposed by the generator; (3) there has been a release (or threat of release) of some hazardous substance (not necessarily the generator's or wastes like the generator's); and (4) which has caused the incurrence of response costs.[101]

One recurring question is whether the *sale of a product* that might later be dumped or discarded is tantamount to *arranging* the disposal of a hazard-

101. United States v. Monsanto, 858 F.2d 160 (4th Cir. 1988); United States v. Mottolo, 695 F.Supp. 615, 625 (D.N.H. 1988); United States v. Wade, 577 F.Supp. 1326 (E.D. Pa. 1983). *See also* Morton Int'l, Inc. v. A.E. Staley Mfg. Co., 343 F.3d 669 (3d Cir. 2003) (the most important factors in determining arranger liability are ownership or possession of a material, knowledge that processing will release a hazardous substance, or control over the production process).

ous substance. There are three general tests courts use to determine when a party is truly engaged in the sale of a product, or if the transaction is a disguised arrangement for a disposal. First, most courts have adopted the "useful product" test. If a product has little or no remaining value for its original purpose, and it contains a hazardous substance, its sale is likely to be seen as an "arrangement for disposal" which creates CERCLA liability. Second is the "intent-causation" test. Some jurisdictions ask whether the ultimate disposal of the product was intended or caused by its sale, or whether its disposal was a transaction, or event, that was independent of the sale. This test seems most appropriate with respect to products, such as asbestos materials or PCB-contaminated transformers, that were sold not because the seller wanted or intended to rid itself of a hazardous substance, but because the seller intended for the products to satisfy some market demand.[102] Third, a test employed by the Ninth Circuit asks whether the material being arranged for disposal would qualify as a "solid waste" under RCRA. In *Catellus Development Corp. v. United States*,[103] for example, the court found that the seller of spent automotive batteries to a lead reclamation plant could be liable for arranging a disposal, primarily because spent

102.   Prudential Ins. Co. v. United States Gypsum Co., 711 F.Supp. 1244, 1254 (D.N.J. 1989) (asbestos); Florida Power & Light Co. v. Allis Chalmers Corp., 893 F.2d 1313 (11th Cir. 1990) (PCBs).

103.   34 F.3d 748 (9th Cir. 1994).

batteries would be considered a solid waste under RCRA.

Another issue is determining what it means to be an arranger by "contract, agreement, or otherwise," and how far arranger liability extends under this phrase. The Eighth Circuit in *United States v. Aceto Agricultural Chemicals Corp.*,[104] gave the most expansive view of arranger liability when it found that producers who contracted with another company to formulate commercial grade pesticides had "arranged for" the releases that occurred at the formulator's factory site.[105] This conclusion was based on the assumption that the escape of contaminated waste products was "inherent" in what the formulator did. The formulators had caused the wastes to be released as a result of the contract with the producers, while the producers had retained title to the pesticide at all times. Moreover, the final product had been shipped back to the producer or to the producer's customers. The prevailing view, however, is that the holding in *Aceto* is too extreme. Most courts demand that the alleged arranger have some direct participation in the waste disposal action.[106]

104. 872 F.2d 1373, 1379 (8th Cir. 1989).

105. *See also* GenCorp, Inc. v. Olin Corp., 390 F.3d 433 (6th Cir. 2004) (finding arranger liability where even though the company did not realize that its business would create hazardous waste when it entered into its business agreement, it "necessarily appreciated this reality" when it approved the plant's construction plans which provided that the waste would be placed in drums and buried at an offsite location).

106. *See* Berg v. Popham, 412 F.3d 1122 (9th Cir. 2005) (holding that actual involvement encompasses actions such as

d. *Transporters Who "Selected" a Disposal or Treatment Site*. Section 107(a)(4) defines a PRP as a person who accepts hazardous substances for transport "to disposal or treatment facilities, incineration vessels or sites selected by such person." The "selected by" language excludes transporters or shippers involved with releases during transportation resulting from circumstances beyond their control.[107] Congress intended to aim this definition at transporters who helped cause the pollution problem by picking up a hazardous substance and then dumping it at a location of their choice.[108] This category includes both legitimate "full service" waste disposal companies who transport and dispose of their customers' hazardous waste, and so-called midnight dumpers who dispose of waste illegally. Transporter liability is not so far-reaching, however, that anyone who has ever transported waste material to a site becomes a PRP. To impose liability, a CERCLA plaintiff must prove that the defendant transported material containing a hazardous substance to the site.[109] Having to meet this burden excuses from transporter liability those who transport wholly innocuous waste materials to a site. Additionally, the transporter has to have a

recommending the use of PCE and then designing and installing the system that disposes of the waste).

107. United States v. M/V Santa Clara I, 887 F.Supp. 825 (D.S.C. 1995).

108. *See, e.g.*, United States v. Bliss, 667 F.Supp. 1298, 1303 (E.D. Mo. 1987).

109. Prisco v. A & D Carting Corp., 168 F.3d 593 (2d Cir. 1999).

substantial role in the actual selection of the site to incur transporter liability. In *Tippins Inc. v. USX Corp.*,[110] for example, the transporter surveyed potential disposal sites for hazardous dust, identified two landfills which would accept the dust, gathered financial information concerning both sites, and provided this information to its client. Even though the client ultimately selected the site, the Third Circuit found that the transporter had such substantial input into the site selection decision that he also was liable.

The Ninth Circuit set the outer limits of transporter liability in *Kaiser Aluminum & Chemical Corp. v. Catellus Development Corp.*[111] There, while excavating a development site, a building contractor spread soil containing lead and asbestos that already existed on his land. Noting that § 101(26) defines "transport" to include "the movement of hazardous substances by any mode," the court found the grading of the soil to be "transportation" of hazardous substances to a site selected by the transporter.

e. Corporations. Corporations present unique problems when it comes to determining the PRP status of such entities.

i. Officers, Directors, and Employees. Courts have ruled that individuals owning or working for a corporation may be personally liable as "operators" or "arrang[ers] for disposal" under § 107(a) if cer-

110. 37 F.3d 87, 94 (3d Cir. 1994). B.F. Goodrich v. Betkoski, 99 F.3d 505, 520 (2d Cir. 1996).

111. 976 F.2d 1338 (9th Cir. 1992).

tain conditions are met. The theory is that the term "person" in CERCLA includes both corporations and individuals, and not does not exclude corporate officers and employees. Individuals within a corporation may be liable under § 107 if they personally participate in the conduct that violates CERCLA.

Courts are split, however, on the appropriate standard for "operator" liability when it comes to corporate officers or employees. There are basically three tests various courts use to determine such liability. First, some courts agree that an officer or employee is liable if he had the authority to exercise control over the hazardous substance that was released into the environment, even if he never actually exercised such control. In *United States v. Carolina Transformer Co.*,[112] the Fourth Circuit declared the corporation's president was an "operator" where he was in charge of the company and responsible for its operations. The court reasoned that he was liable because he had the power to prevent the release of hazardous waste.

Second, courts on the other side of the spectrum conclude that an individual qualifies as an operator only if the operator had the authority to exercise control over the substance released into the environment, and in fact exercised this control. These courts reason that the ordinary meaning of "operator" requires affirmative conduct. In *Riverside Market Development Corp. v. International Bldg. Products, Inc.*,[113] the Fifth Circuit concluded that a

112.   978 F.2d 832 (4th Cir. 1992).
113.   931 F.2d 327 (5th Cir. 1991).

majority shareholder whose only corporate activities were visiting the facility on occasion, reviewing financial statements, and attending periodic officers' meetings, was not an "operator." The shareholder was not actually involved with the handling of the hazardous substance.[114]

A third test which satisfies a middle ground was suggested in *Kelley v. Thomas Solvent Co.*[115] Here, the court considered several criteria: (1) the individual's degree of authority with respect to hazardous waste disposal; (2) the individual's position in the corporate hierarchy; (3) actual responsibility undertaken for waste disposal practices; and (4) evidence of responsibility undertaken and neglected, as well as affirmative attempts to prevent unlawful hazardous waste disposal.

Corporate officers, directors, or employees may also become PRPs if they are deemed to be "arrangers." Courts may impose arranger liability if the individual either "owned or possessed" the wastes as issue. Ownership may stem from the individual's ownership rights to the corporation that conducted the disposal operation. The best-known case defining what possession means under CERCLA is *United ed States v. Northeastern Pharmaceutical & Chem.*

114. *See also* Raytheon Constructors, Inc. v. Asarco Inc., 368 F.3d 1214 (10th Cir. 2003) (even though president of mining company was an "operator" for purposes of the mining company, this role did not suffice to make him an "operator" with regard to a predecessor minority shareholder company for which he was also president, where there was no evidence that he acted on behalf of the predecessor rather than the corporation).

115. 727 F.Supp. 1532 (W.D. Mich. 1989).

Co.,[116] where a corporate vice-president authorized the transport of hazardous substances to an unlicensed farm for disposal. The Eighth Circuit ruled that the officer "possessed" the wastes because he (1) had actual control over the waste, (2) approved an arrangement for their transportation, and (3) was directly responsible for deciding how and where they would be discharged.

ii. Parent-Subsidiary. The leading case determining under what circumstances a parent corporation can be held responsible for it subsidiary's CERCLA liability is *United States v. Bestfoods.*[117] In *Bestfoods*, the United States Supreme Court concluded that CERCLA does not displace traditional common law rules under corporate law. As such, the Supreme Court stated that only "when the corporate veil may be pierced, may a parent corporation be charged with derivative CERCLA liability for its subsidiary's actions." The Court looked at the plain language of the statute to conclude that an entity must "operate" a facility to be liable for the cost of cleaning up the pollution; there must be direct liability on the part of the parent for it to incur liability, something not created by the mere existence of a parent-subsidiary relationship. The court continued by explaining that "The question is not whether the parent operates the subsidiary, but rather whether it operates the facility, and that operation is evidenced by participation in the activities of the facility, not the subsidiary."

116.   810 F.2d 726 (8th Cir. 1986).

117.   524 U.S. 51 (1998).

CERCLA imposes a different liability test regarding parent corporations in the context of being an "arranger for disposal." In *United States v. TIC Investment Corp.*[118] the Eighth Circuit stated:

> while a parent corporation need only have the authority to control, and exercise actual or substantial control, over the subsidiary in order to incur direct [operator] liability, we believe that, in order for a parent corporation to incur direct arranger liability for a subsidiary's off-site disposal practices, there must be some causal connection or nexus between the parent corporation's conduct and the subsidiary's arrangement for disposal, of the off-site disposal itself.

iii. Successor Corporations. When a corporate entity "takes over" another corporate entity, two CERCLA liability questions arise. First, can the corporation that has been acquired by another avoid liability as a result of the transaction? The answer is no. CERCLA § 107(e) has a prohibition on transferring liability (in the absence of an indemnification agreement) in order to prevent companies from shifting responsibility for their waste problem to another corporation. Second, is a successor corporation responsible for the waste disposal practices of the corporate entity it has acquired? While the issue in not expressly resolved by the plain language of CERCLA, courts universally agree that Congress intended successor liability to apply. The successor corporation becomes responsible for the waste disposal practices of the corporation it acquired.

118. 68 F.3d 1082, 1091–92 (8th Cir. 1995).

On the other hand, where a successor only buys the assets of its predecessor, the general common law rule is that an asset purchaser *does not* acquire the liabilities of the seller. However, there are four exceptions to this general rule:

(1) *The purchaser expressly or impliedly agrees to assume liabilities*—To fall within this exception courts are interested in whether the purchase agreement expressly contains language transferring "all liabilities" to the purchaser. Implied liability can result if the purchaser knew of the pollution problems at the site it acquired.[119]

(2) *The transaction is a de facto merger or consolidation*—Courts consider the following factors to determine if a purported sale of assets is actually a *de facto* merger or consolidation: continuity of management, personnel, physical location, assets, and general business operations; continuity of shareholders resulting from the successor corporation paying for the acquired assets with shares of its own stock; and whether the successor assumed obligations of the predecessor necessary for uninterrupted continuation of business operations.[120]

(3) *The purchaser is a "mere continuation" of the seller*—This standard applies when a corporation transfers its assets to another corporation, so that post-transfer there is only one corporation with stock, stockholders, and directors identical to the

119. United States v. Iron Mountain Mines, 987 F.Supp. 1233 (E.D. Cal. 1997).

120. North Shore Gas Co. v. Solomon Inc., 152 F.3d 642 (7th Cir. 1998).

acquired corporation. Alternatively, some courts have adopted the "substantial continuation" (or "continuity of enterprise") standard, in which the plaintiff must establish that the predecessor and successor share continuity of employees, supervisory personnel, location, product, company name, and assets, and the successor holds itself out as a continuation of the seller.[121] In the absence of these findings, successor liability fails to attach.[122] Some courts also require that the successor must have actual notice of the predecessor's liabilities.[123]

(4) *The transaction is an effort to fraudulently escape liability*—Courts who reject the "substantial continuation" exception do so with the rationale that when this exception has been applied to hold a successor liable, there has almost always been some fraudulent intent or collusion, in which case the successor would have been liable under the fraudulently-entered transaction exception. For example, in the leading "substantial continuation" case, *United States v. Carolina Co.*,[124] the children of the seller's owner were the sole shareholders of the successor, giving the "unmistakable impressions that the transfer was part of an effort to continue

121. United States v. Carolina Transformer Co., 978 F.2d 832 (4th Cir. 1992).

122. *But see* New York v. National Services Indus., 352 F.3d 682 (2d Cir. 2003) (rejecting substantial continuity test in light of the holding in United States v. Bestfoods (discussed *supra*) because it is not part of general common law).

123. Louisiana–Pacific Corp. v. Asarco, Inc., 909 F.2d 1260 (9th Cir. 1990).

124. 978 F.2d 832 (4th Cir. 1992).

the business in all material respects yet avoid environmental liability."

iv. Dissolved Corporations. CERCLA makes "persons" liable as PRPs, but does not explicitly include dissolved corporations within the statute's definition of "persons." The question that emerges is whether dissolution under state law, coupled with the typical state law prohibition against corporations being sued within two years of their dissolution, defeats a CERCLA § 107(a) claim against a former owner. Or, does CERCLA preempt state laws that prevent dissolved corporations from being sued? On the one hand, Federal Rule of Civil Procedure 17(b) states that a corporation's capacity to be sued must be determined by the state law where the corporation is organized. As such, if the dissolved corporation is no longer a legal entity pursuant to state law and 17(b), then it follows that a § 107(a) lawsuit must fail. On the other hand, if such state law stands as an obstacle to the accomplishment of CERCLA, then the state law is preempted.

The courts are divided on the preemption issue. Some say that since 17(b) is a "procedural" rule, it is not superseded by CERCLA's substantive imposition of liability.[125] Other courts hold that CERCLA preempts state laws. In *United States v. Sharon Steel Corp.*,[126] after noting Congress's intent "to

125. *See, e.g.,* Levin Metals Corp. v. Parr–Richmond Terminal Co., 817 F.2d 1448, 1451 (9th Cir. 1987); Citizens Electric Corp. v. Bituminous Fire & Marine Ins. Co., 68 F.3d 1016 (7th Cir. 1995).

126. 681 F.Supp. 1492, 1498 (D. Utah 1987).

hold responsible parties liable for clean-up costs '[n]otwithstanding any other provision or rule of the law,'" the court held that CERCLA preempted F.R.C.P. 17(b) "to the extent the rule might otherwise shield a dissolved corporation from liability."

For jurisdictions that conclude that state law is preempted, they must determine the extent to which a dissolved corporation is subject to CERCLA liability. Some courts differentiate between corporations that are "dead" (dissolved entities) and those that are "dead and buried" (dissolved and all assets distributed). Most courts have held that only "dead" corporations are amenable to suit.[127] The rationale is that "dead and buried" corporations are no longer entities that can be sued or defend themselves against suit, and therefore should be excluded from CERCLA liability.[128] Other courts have refused to make this distinction, emphasizing that CERCLA's language places no limitation on the term "corporation" as used in the statute.[129]

f. Lenders. Lender liability under CERCLA has changed many times. Originally, lenders escaped liability due to an exclusion in CERCLA's definition of "owner or operator." Section 101(20) stated that an entity that held an "indicia of ownership" in a facility primarily to protect its "security interest,"

127. Idylwoods Assocs. v. Mader Capital, Inc., 915 F.Supp. 1290 (W.D.N.Y. 1996).

128. Burlington Northern and Santa Fe Ry. Co. v. Consolidated Fibers, Inc., 7 F.Supp.2d 822, 828 (N.D. Tex. 1998).

129. United States v. SCA Services of Indiana, Inc., 837 F.Supp. 946, 953 (N.D. Ind. 1993).

without "participating in the management" of the facility, was not considered an owner or operator. Under this definition, a passive lender could avoid § 107 liability. However, this standard caused two issues to remain unclear. First, what level of lender activity amounted to enough "participation in management" to create liability? In *United States v. Fleet Factors Corp.*,[130] the Eleventh Circuit suggested that the lender's mere "capacity to influence" the borrower's operational decisions could trigger liability. Second, did liability attach if the lender acquired the property through foreclosure? Some cases suggested that it could.[131]

In 1992, the EPA issued an interpretive rule rejecting the Eleventh Circuit's "capacity to influence" standard, by requiring lenders to have an active role in waste disposal decisions in order to be liable under CERCLA.[132] This rule also allowed lenders to escape liability in the event of foreclosures and repurchase at a foreclosure sale. In 1994, however, this rule was struck down by the D.C. Circuit on the basis that the EPA lacked authority to define through regulation the scope of § 107 liability.[133] Once again, lenders' rights to control borrowers waste sites could, in some jurisdictions, create owner/operator liability under CERCLA.

130.   901 F.2d 1550 (11th Cir. 1990).

131.   *See e.g.,* Guidice v. BFG Electroplating and Manufacturing Co., 732 F.Supp. 556 (W.D. Pa. 1989).

132.   40 C.F.R. § 300.1100(c)–(d).

133.   Kelley v. EPA, 15 F.3d 1100 (D.C. Cir. 1994).

Two years later, lender liability was again minimized when Congress amended § 101(20) to address the original concerns regarding lender liability. The Asset Conservation, Lender Liability, and Deposit Insurance Protection Act of 1996 rejects the capacity-to-influence test. Section 101(2)(F)(i)(I)–(II) now states that "participation in management" means "actually participating in the management or operational affairs" of the borrower. A lender will be considered to participate in management only if it: (1) exercises control over the facility's environmental compliance; or (2) exercises general control of the facility at a level "comparable to that of a manager."[134] Additionally, a lender will not become an owner or operator simply by acquiring contaminated property by foreclosure or by undertaking related post-foreclosure activities (*e.g.*, carrying on business activities, taking response action, and winding up operations).[135] To receive these protections, however, a lender must try to resell or transfer the contaminated facility or waste site "at the earliest practicable, commercially reasonable time...."[136]

g. Fiduciaries, Estates, and Beneficiaries. Section 107(n)(5)(A) defines "fiduciary" to include trustees, executors, administrators, custodians, guardians, conservators, or personal representatives. The term also encompasses a trustee under a financing arrangement, such as a trustee on a deed

134. CERCLA § 101(20)(F)(ii).

135. *Id.* § 101(20)(E)(ii).

136. *Id.* § 101(20)(E)(ii).

of trust. Although a fiduciary may be liable as a PRP, liability cannot exceed the "assets held in the fiduciary capacity."[137] CERCLA also lists activities in which fiduciaries can participate without incurring liability such as: (1) conducting response action at the facility; (2) inspecting the facility; and (3) administering an already-contaminated facility. These protections do not apply if the fiduciary's negligence causes or contributes to the release or threatened release.[138] There is no private right of action against a fiduciary.[139]

CERCLA does not expressly impose liability on the estates of those found to be PRPs. Section 101(21) fails to include as a "person" a beneficiary of an inheritance. Instead, Congress created an exception to § 107 liability within the "innocent landowner defense."[140] Under this defense, which is discussed in detail below, a person who inherits contaminated property, thereby becoming an "owner" and a PRP, is entitled to assert this defense and escape liability. Thus, beneficiaries do not become PRPs under CERCLA simply because they inherited a hazardous waste site from someone who was a PRP.

h. Federal, State and Local Governments. Section 101(21) defines "person" to include the "United States Government, [a] State, municipality,

137. Briggs & Stratton Corp. v. Concrete Sales & Services, 20 F.Supp.2d 1356 (M.D. Ga. 1998).

138. CERCLA § 107(n)(1)–(4).

139. *Id.* § 107(n)(5)(A)(i), (n)(5)(B).

140. *Id.* § 107(b)(3).

commission, political subdivision of a state, or any interstate body." In the case of the federal government, CERCLA partially waives sovereign immunity for facilities owned and operated by the federal government, such as military facilities. This immunity is not waived, however, in instances when the United States is acting only in its regulatory capacity (*e.g.,* by performing remedial work pursuant to CERCLA § 104). Section 120(a)(1) also provides that the United States is subject to CERCLA to the same extent as any private, non-governmental entity.

Although states are included in the definition of "person" subject to CERCLA liability, several doctrines reduce their risk. When a private PRP sues a state for "contribution" under § 113(f), such a suit runs up against the case of *Seminole Tribe of Florida v. Florida.*[141] *Seminole Tribe* holds that Congress cannot abrogate, by statutes passed under the commerce power, the states' Eleventh Amendment immunity from private suits. This case seems to prevent private parties from suing states from contribution under § 113(f). States can also avoid liability by proving that the site was only regulated, but not owned, by the state.[142]

Municipalities may be liable under § 107(a)(3) for having arranged to dispose of municipal solid waste

141. 517 U.S. 44 (1996). *See also* Board of Trustees of Univ. of Alabama v. Garrett, 531 U.S. 356 (2001).

142. United States v. Dart Indus., 847 F.2d 144 (4th Cir. 1988).

at sites where CERCLA response actions took place.[143]

3. Triggers of Liability

To make a prima facie case for liability under § 107, the plaintiff must prove that there (1) has been a "release" or there is a "threat" of release, (2) of a "hazardous substance," (3) from a "facility," and that the release (4) caused the plaintiff (the government or some "other person") to incur "response costs" which are "not inconsistent with" (or are "consistent with") the NCP.

a. "Release" or Threatened Release. Section 101(22) broadly defines a "release" to include "any spilling, leaking, pumping, pouring, emitting, emptying, discharging, injecting, escaping, leaching, dumping, or disposing into the environment. . . ." Courts have interpreted the language to cover virtually all avenues by which pollutants can escape and do damage to human health and the environment. Almost any *movement* of hazardous substances into the general environment will constitute a release. Plaintiffs generally do not have to provide evidence demonstrating how the hazardous substance moved into the environment; mere presence is enough.[144]

143. Goodrich Corp. v. Town of Middlebury, 311 F.3d 154 (2d Cir. 2002) (municipalities which contributed to waste mixture at landfill sites were "liable parties," and thus subject to contribution claims from non-municipal parties).

144. *But see* Niagara Mohawk Power Corp. v. Jones Chem., Inc., 315 F.3d 171 (2d Cir. 2003) (passive movement of hazardous substance over defendant's property from another's property was not a "disposal" or "release" where the chemicals spread onto defendant's property without defendant's fault).

Additionally, a number of actions are specifically exempted by CERCLA. The following are exempted by § 101(22) because they are covered by other federal statutes: releases in the workplace, emission from motor vehicles, nuclear material from a processing site, and "the normal application of a fertilizer." Section 104(a)(3) instructs federal authorities not to initiate removal or remedial actions in response to a release of a "naturally occurring substance in its unaltered form," from "products which are part of the structure of, and result in exposure within, residential ... business or community structures," or into "public or private drinking water supplies due to deterioration of the system through ordinary use."

Potential future releases into the environment are also included by the words "threat of release." Most courts require that two conditions be met before potential future releases trigger liability: (1) there must be evidence of the presence of a hazardous substance at the facility, and (2) there should be evidence of unwillingness of a party to assert control over the substances.[145] In the leading case on point, *New York v. Shore Realty Corp.*,[146] the Second Circuit noted that a "threat of release" included the storage of toxic substances in corroding and deteriorating tanks, the owner's lack of expertise in

145. G.J. Leasing Co. v. Union Elec. Co., 854 F.Supp. 539 (S.D. Ill. 1994), *aff'd* 54 F.3d 379 (7th Cir. 1995); Amland Properties Corp. v. ALCOA, 711 F.Supp. 784 (D. N.J. 1989).

146. 759 F.2d 1032 (2d Cir. 1985).

handling hazardous wastes, and the failure to license a facility.

Lastly, the "release" or "threat" of release must occur "into the environment."[147] Section 101(8) defines "environment" to include all surface water, groundwater, drinking water supply, land surface or subsurface strata, or ambient air within the United States or under its jurisdiction.

b. "Hazardous Substance". A CERCLA "hazardous waste" includes a broad range of pollutants, contaminants, and wastes. Since the statute uses the language "substance," liability can even be triggered when there is no "waste," applying to virgin materials, consumer products, and manufacturing by-products. To the extent municipal wastes contain hazardous substances, and there is a release or threatened release into the environment, such wastes fall within the CERCLA liability framework. CERCLA may additionally impose liability on municipalities disposing of household wastes that contain hazardous substances.

Chemicals are designated hazardous wastes in three ways. First, § 101(14) defines "hazardous substances" by incorporating lists of substances regulated under other federal environmental statutes, such as the Resource Conservation and Recovery Act, Clean Water Act, Clean Air Act, and Toxic Substances Control Act. Second, § 102(a) permits the EPA to designate as hazardous any substance that "may present substantial danger" when re-

147. CERCLA § 101(22).

leased into the environment. The EPA has listed 2,000 such "hazardous substances."[148] Third, CERCLA extends to mixtures of hazardous and non-hazardous substances if a CERCLA hazardous substance is somewhere within the mixture.[149]

There is no minimum level of concentration or quantity required for CERCLA to be triggered.[150] As such, PRPs are still liable when faced with clean-up costs for waste that contains hazardous substances in such minute amounts that they cannot be considered dangerous. The primary rational for this conclusion is that the CERCLA definition refers simply to "any substance,"[151] and the accompanying EPA regulations provide no minimum levels. CERCLA is only concerned with *presence*. Appearing as a defendant in *City of New York v. Exxon Corp.*[152] and *United States v. Alcan Aluminum Corp.*,[153] Alcan Aluminum Corporation pointed out that the concentration of hazardous substances in its wastes was lower than those found in milk, breakfast cereal, or even the paper and ink which comprised the government's own brief. Although Alcan's wastes were not actually dangerous to humans to the environ-

148. 40 C.F.R. § 302.4, Table 302.4.

149. B.F. Goodrich v. Betkoski, 99 F.3d 505 (2d Cir. 1996).

150. United States v. Alcan Aluminum Corp., 990 F.2d 711 (2d Cir. 1993); United States v. Alcan Aluminum Corp., 964 F.2d 252 (3d Cir. 1992); B.F. Goodrich Co. v. Murtha, 958 F.2d 1192 (2d Cir. 1992).

151. CERCLA § 101(14).

152. 744 F.Supp. 474 (S.D.N.Y. 1990).

153. 755 F.Supp. 531 (N.D.N.Y. 1991).

ment, they were still deemed "hazardous substances" under CERCLA.[154]

There is one statutory exclusion—the petroleum exclusion—from the definition of "hazardous substance." Section 101(14) states that the term "hazardous substance" does not include either (1) "petroleum, including crude oil or any fraction thereof which is not otherwise specifically listed or designated" as a hazardous substance, or (2) various natural and synthetic gas products. Although petroleum-based wastes may contain other toxic constituents, they were exempted because petroleum product spills into navigable waters were already covered by § 311 of the Clean Water Act, and because at the time Congress was considering CERCLA, it was also debating a parallel land-based oil spill bill (which never passed). However, even though petroleum waste is statutorily excluded, courts interpret this exception very narrowly.

The defendant bears the burden of proving that it is not liable based on the exclusion.[155] The easiest way to meet this burden is to show that an otherwise hazardous substance occurs *naturally* in the petroleum. For example, in *Wilshire Westwood Assoc. v. Atlantic Richfield Corp.*,[156] the Ninth Circuit held that refined gasoline was within the petroleum

154. *But see* Amoco Oil Co. v. Borden, Inc., 889 F.2d 664 (5th Cir. 1989) (suggesting that a "release" does not occur unless the quantity of the hazardous substance involved actually threatens public health and safety).

155. Organic Chemicals Site PRP Group v. Total Petroleum, Inc., 6 F.Supp.2d 660 (W.D. Mich. 1998).

156. 881 F.2d 801 (9th Cir. 1989).

exclusion, even though it contained lead, benzene, and other additives which would normally be considered hazardous substances. The exclusion also applies if the hazardous substance is *added* during the refining or production process,[157] if there is no indication that the petroleum products used waste oil or that they were contaminated with hazardous substances,[158] or if petroleum products are mixed with soil that itself is non-hazardous.[159] The exclusion does not apply, however, if the hazardous substance is added *after* the refining process.[160]

Courts have also considered an exclusion for municipal solid waste (MSW). About 200 million tons of MSW is generated each year, and most is dumped into municipal landfills. A small fraction consists of hazardous substances (*e.g.*, cleaning supplies, paint, pesticides). The argument in favor of the exclusion is that if MSW is considered a hazardous substance, then virtually all local governmental entities which collect and dispose of MSW would be liable under CERCLA for billions of dollars. In *B.F. Goodrich v. Murtha*,[161] the Second Circuit considered this issue. In rejecting the plea to recognize an exemption for

157. United States v. Gurley, 43 F.3d 1188, 1199 (8th Cir. 1994).

158. Foster v. United States, 926 F.Supp. 199, 205–06 (D.D.C.).

159. Southern Pacific Trans. Co. v. Caltrans, 790 F.Supp. 983, 985–86 (C.D. Cal. 1991).

160. United States v. Alcan Aluminum Corp., 964 F.2d 252 (3d Cir. 1992) (oil which became contaminated with hazardous substances when used to lubricate machinery was not exempt).

161. 958 F.2d 1192 (2d Cir. 1992).

MSW, the court looked to the plain language of the definition and held that MSW is a hazardous substance if "that waste contains a hazardous substance, found in any amount." It is widely anticipated, however, that future CERCLA amendments will include some form of MSW exception.

   c.   "Facility" or "Vessel". Section 101(9) defines "facility" to include "any site or area where a hazardous substance has been deposited, stored, disposed of, or placed, or otherwise come to be located." The end of this definition ("or otherwise come to be located") has come to be known as a catch-all phrase that basically includes any place where a hazardous substance can be found. Courts have found facilities to include sewer pipes, manufacturing equipment, a 220–mile strip of highway, a dragstrip, mine tailings at the base of a dam, and mines.

   More difficult than defining "facility" is determining the scope of the site to be cleaned up. A large geographic area could be defined as a facility based on the presence of a hazardous substance in one portion of it.[162] Or, the facility could be defined with such precision to include only those specific cubic meters of a PRP's property where hazardous substances were deposited or eventually found. The words of the statute (§ 101(9)) suggest, however,

   162. *See* Sierra Club v. Seaboard Farms Inc., 387 F.3d 1167 (10th Cir. 2004) (holding that a farm complex as a whole, as opposed to every barn, lagoon, and land application area on the complex, constituted a single "facility").

that the bounds of a facility should be defined at least in part by the bounds of the contamination.

Section 101(28) defines "vessel" as "every description of watercraft or other artificial contrivance used, or capable of being used, as a means of transportation on water." Very few CERCLA cases involve vessels.

d. "Cause" the "Incurrence of Response Costs". If there is a "release or threatened released" of a "hazardous substance" at a "facility," liability cannot attach unless the above conditions "cause" the "incurrence of response costs." The final liability trigger is comprised of three elements: (1) the action of the PRP must have brought about (however indirectly) the release or threatened release; (2) the release or threatened release must have caused response costs to be incurred[163]; and (3) the costs incurred must be within the scope of recoverable response costs.

Courts typically need only one connection between the PRP and the release or threatened release: the PRP delivered hazardous substances to the site where there is now, or may be, a release. There does not need to be a specific connection between the delivery and the threat of release, or between the release and the environmental damage.[164] Plaintiffs do not need to trace ownership of a specific waste to a specific PRP-defendant.[165]

163. Dedham Water Co., Inc. v. Cumberland Farms Dairy, Inc., 972 F.2d 453 (1st Cir. 1992).

164. United States v. Wade, 577 F.Supp. 1326 (E.D. Pa. 1983).

165. Outlet City v. West Chemical Products, 60 Fed. Appx. 922 (3d Cir. 2003).

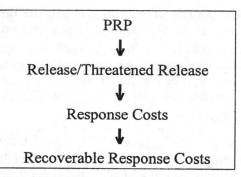

The plaintiff must also prove that it incurred costs in responding to the release or threatened release. Especially when the release is merely threatened, the question arises whether there is a sufficient causal link between the defendant's conduct that gives rise to the threat and the incurrence of response costs. Since most courts do not require the plaintiff to show that the defendant's wastes caused the threat, the plaintiff instead must demonstrate that it incurred response costs *because* of the threat of release. To meet this standard the plaintiff must prove: (1) it had a "good faith belief" that action was desirable to address a "particular environmental threat," and (2) its response was "objectively reasonable."[166]

Some courts believe that the plaintiff's requirement of proving the incurrence of response costs applies *only* to the "threat of release." For example, in *Westfarm Associates L.P. v. International Fabri-*

166. Dedham Water Co., Inc. v. Cumberland Farms Dairy, Inc., 972 F.2d 453 (1st Cir. 1992).

care Institute,[167] the court analyzed § 107(a) to mean that CERCLA "imposes liability for releases, and *also* for threatened releases which cause the incurrence of response costs. Therefore, only in the case of threatened releases does it appear that a plaintiff must demonstrate any degree of causation." (Emphasis in original).

It must also be shown that the response costs incurred are "justified." The Fifth Circuit in one leading decision stated that the liability requirement is met if it is shown that "any release violates ... any applicable [ARAR], including the most stringent."[168]

Jurisdictions are split on which party has the burden of proving or disproving the causal nexus between the release and the incurrence of response costs. Some jurisdictions assume that after the plaintiff makes a prima facie case showing that defendant's conduct caused a release, then "the burden of proof falls on the defendant to disprove causation."[169] Other jurisdictions not only hold that the plaintiff must establish causation between a release and incurrence of response costs, but they also conclude that such causation is not shown if

167. 846 F.Supp. 422 (D. Md. 1993).

168. Amoco Oil Co. v. Borden, Inc., 889 F.2d 664, 670 (5th Cir. 1989). *But see* United States v. Western Processing Co., 734 F.Supp. 930, 942 (W.D. Wash. 1990) (government need not show particular defendant's waste caused ARAR to be violated).

169. Westfarm Assocs. Ltd. Partnership v. Washington Suburban Sanitary Com'n, 66 F.3d 669, 681 (4th Cir. 1995); Town of New Windsor v. Tesa Tuck, Inc., 919 F.Supp. 662, 669 (S.D.N.Y. 1996).

response costs are incurred merely because of a finding of hazardous substances above background levels.[170]

4. Recoverable Costs

Section 107(a)(4)(A) states that once a PRP is found liable, it is responsible for "all costs of removal or remedial action incurred by the United States Government or a State or an Indian Tribe not inconsistent with the National Contingency Plan." Moreover, where applicable, a PRP may also be liable for "damages . . . to . . . natural resources."[171] In challenging the amount of costs recoverable under § 107(a)(4)(A), two questions arise: (1) what does "all costs" mean?, and (2) when is cost "inconsistent" with the NCP? When assessing damages to natural resources, the main issue is what are, and how does one measure, "damages to natural resources"?

a. *"All Costs"*. The federal government or another listed plaintiff can recover *all* payments made to effect removal or remediation action, including costs for investigating, monitoring, and assessing a release, as well as the government's payments reimbursing contractors who actually perform the § 104 remediation work. Indirect costs may be covered as well. These costs include planning, overhead (salaries of personnel involved, travel expenses, legal expenses, rent, utilities, supplies), and oversight

170. United States v. Dico, Inc., 136 F.3d 572 (8th Cir. 1998); Liccardi v. Murphy Oil U.S.A. Inc., 111 F.3d 396 (5th Cir. 1997).

171. CERCLA § 107(a)(4)(C).

costs. While some courts have left open the question of whether unreasonable, unnecessary, or excessive costs can be recovered, others have simply assumed that the modifier "all" permits recovery of even apparently unreasonable costs. For example, the Fifth Circuit in *Matter of Bell Petroleum Services, Inc.*[172] took the position that Congress did not intend to give the EPA such unrestrained spending discretion as to be able to recover even "unreasonable and unnecessary costs." On the other hand, the Tenth Circuit in *United States v. Hardage*[173] explained that this subsection "does not limit the government's recovery to 'all reasonable costs;' rather, it permits the government to recover '*all* costs....'" (Emphasis in original). Section 107(a)(4) additionally allows the government to obtain prejudgment interest.[174]

Future costs are another important issue. While CERCLA does not contemplate awards of future monetary damages, § 113(g)(2) permits courts to enter a declaratory judgment on liability for "further response costs or damages." When there is such a judgment, PRPs may be liable to CERCLA plaintiffs for future costs not inconsistent with the NCP. *Kelley v. E.I. DuPont de Numours & Co.*[175] is the leading case interpreting this provision. In this decision, the defendants contended that because the

172. 3 F.3d 889 (5th Cir. 1993).

173. 982 F.2d 1436 (10th Cir. 1992).

174. Goodrich Corp. v. Town of Middlebury, 311 F.3d 154 (2d Cir. 2002).

175. 17 F.3d 836 (6th Cir. 1994).

required clean-up had been completed, any future costs were speculative and that there was no existing "case or controversy" as required by Article III of the Constitution to justify judicial action. In rejecting this argument and concluding that a declaratory judgment was mandatory, the Sixth Circuit explained that in CERCLA cases: (1) the "probability of subsequent activity . . . is more likely than remote;" and (2) it would waste state, corporate, and judicial resources to require relitigation of liability whenever subsequent response is taken.

Even under the "all costs" standard, however, the total amount of recoverable costs cannot exceed the limitations listed in § 107(c)(1). The maximum liability of a responsible person for a release from a non-incineration vessel which carries a cargo of hazardous substances (including response costs, natural resources damages, etc.), for example, cannot exceed $300 per gross ton or $5 million, whichever is greater. Most facilities, however, fall under § 107(c)(1)(D), which allows recovery of "the total of all costs of response" plus $50 million for natural resource damage and other items.

b. *"Not Inconsistent with the National Contingency Plan"*. Section 107(a)(4)(A) also requires that the governmental party's actions giving rise to the costs to be recovered be "not inconsistent with" the NCP.[176] This double-negative construction has been read to mean that the *challenger* of the costs of a

---

176. Private parties' costs must be "consistent with" the NCP. CERCLA § 107(a)(4)(B). The meaning of this distinction is discussed below in connection with private cost recovery actions.

removal has the burden of proving that response costs were inconsistent with the NCP, and thus not recoverable. PRPs may succeed only if they can establish that the NCP's substantive or procedural requirements were not followed, making the government's clean-up order arbitrary and capricious.

The government's failure to follow substantive requirements of the NCP may constitute inconsistency. In the leading case of *Matter of Bell Petroleum Services, Inc.*,[177] the defendant challenged the EPA's decision to provide an alternate public drinking water supply during remedial work to clean up groundwater contaminated with chromium. Although the NCP allows such an alternate water supply when there is a "substantial danger to public health or the environment," the defendant argued that the administrative record failed to demonstrate any danger. Applying the arbitrary and capricious standard, and after searching through over 5,000 pages of the administrative record, the Fifth Circuit held that the EPA decision was unsupported and thus inconsistent with the NCP.

Inconsistency may also be present if there is a government violation of the NCP's procedural standards. In *Washington State Dept. of Transp. v. Washington Natural Gas Co.*,[178] the plaintiff sought recovery of over $4 million incurred for remedial work in connection with tar waste discovered during freeway construction. The plaintiff failed, however, to refer to the NCP for guidance on how to

177.   3 F.3d 889 (5th Cir. 1993).
178.   59 F.3d 793 (9th Cir. 1995).

manage the contaminants at the site. As such, the Ninth Circuit found that the plaintiff failed to meet the NCP requirements. In particular, it did not conduct an adequate remedial investigation, evaluate alternative remedies, or provide opportunity for public comment. Finding this inconsistency with the NCP to be arbitrary and capricious, the court denied the plaintiff from recovering any of its response costs.[179]

c. Natural Resources Damage. Section 107(a)(4)(C) provides that a PRP may also be liable for "damages for injury to, destruction of, or loss of natural resources." Such natural resources damage (NRD) claims can be staggering—sometimes costing two to three times the amounts involved in cost-recovery claims.[180] There are four major differences between cost-recovery and NRD actions. First, the government need not spend any money first in order to seek natural resource damages. Second, any monetary recovery received for such damages may only be used to "restore, replace, or acquire the equivalent of such natural resources."[181] Third, there is an exception to the normal rule of unlimit-

179. *See also* Outlet City, Inc. v. West Chemical Products, 60 Fed. Appx. 922 (3d Cir. 2003) (if procedural deviations are "immaterial" of "insubstantial" they should not deemed inconsistent with the NCP).

180. *See* E. Lynn Grayon et al., The Business Dilemma: 21st Century Natural Resource Damage Liabilities for 20th Century Industrial Progress, 31 Envtl. L. Rep. 11356 (2001) (discussing the uncertainty and chaos businesses face from having to pay future natural resource damage liabilities as a result of past industrial progress).

181. CERCLA § 107(f)(1).

ed retroactive CERCLA liability, in that § 107(f)(1) precludes recovery where the release, and damages from the release, occurred prior to CERCLA's enactment.[182] Fourth, § 113(g) sets out special statutes of limitations for NRD claims.[183] The following section describes the requisite terminology involved in an NRD action.

i. *"Natural Resources"*. Section 101(16) broadly defines "natural resources" to include "land, fish, wildlife, biota, air, water, ground water, drinking water supplies, and other such resources" which are owned, controlled, managed, or held in trust by the United States, other governmental entities, or Indian Tribes. This language encompasses virtually all effects a hazardous substance can have on nature, so long as that which is affected is somehow owned or controlled or held in trust by a government entity.

ii. *"Injuries Caused by a Release"*. Section 107(a)(C) requires that natural resources damages "result from [a] release." In order to establish this standard of causation, the Department of Interior—

182. State of Montana v. Atlantic Richfield Co., 266 F.Supp.2d 1238 (D. Mont. 2003) (holding that the State of Montana could not recover natural resource damages because the injury to the environment occurred before enactment of CERCLA).

183. For federal facilities on the NPL, and those subject to remedial action, the statute of limitations does not begin to run until three years after completion of remedial work. For all other sites, the statute runs three years after the discovery of the loss, or the date on which regulations are promulgated for assessing natural resources damages, whichever is later. *See* 43 C.F.R. § 11.91(e).

which was given authority to issue NRD regulations—has established criteria that must be proven
by the party bringing the natural resource damage
claim. The party must show that the injury alleged
to have occurred is a "commonly documented" response to releases of such hazardous substances;
that the hazardous substances are known to cause
such injury in field studies or controlled experi-
ments; and that the injury can be measured by
practical techniques and has been "adequately documented in scientific literature."[184] Natural resources damages are limited by the boundaries of
the NPL site described in the original NPL listing,
and may not be expanded to a surrounding area,
despite the presence of hazardous substances in a
larger area.[185]

Although these criteria have been sustained,
questions persist about the standard of proof required to demonstrate that natural resources injuries "result from" a particular release. Specifically,
it is unclear whether the causation-of-injury standard should be less demanding than the common
law standard. And courts must decide whether speculative assessments of causation are permitted by
§ 301(c)(2)'s requirement that "best available procedures" be used to determine natural resources
damages.

In *Natural Ass'n of Manufacturers v. Dept. of the*

184. 43 C.F.R. § 11.62(f)(2).

185. United States v. ASARCO Inc., 28 F.Supp.2d 1170 (D.
Idaho 1998).

Interior,[186] the D.C. Circuit considered both issues. Regarding the causation-of-injury standard, the court reiterated its previous findings that CERCLA is ambiguous on the question of whether the standard under § 107(a)(4)(C) should be less demanding than that of common law. It further explained that while the statutory language requires some causal connection between the element of damages and the injury, Congress has failed to specify what this relationship should be. In addressing the issue regarding "best available procedures," the court stated:

> While we have noted that the "best available procedures" language of subsection 301(c)(2) indicates that it would be inconsistent with CERCLA to permit "unduly speculative assessments," ... we have never held that simply because assessment procedures are in some measure "speculative" or "predictive" they are contrary to CERCLA's "best available procedures" admonition. Rather, predictive submodels that represent rational scientific judgments about the probability that a particular release will cause a specific type and amount of injury are consistent with the Congress's intent to develop a "standardized system for assessing such damage which is efficient as to both time and cost."

iii. Who May Bring Suit. Unlike the rest of § 107 which permits any responder to sue, pursuant to § 107(f)(1) only certain public "trustees" may sue for natural resources damages—the United States, the states, and Indian tribes, and local gov-

186. 134 F.3d 1095, 1105 (D.C. Cir. 1998).

ernments with the proper authorization from a state.

iv. Damages. Section 107(a)(4)(C) provides that public trustees may recover "damages for injury to, destruction of, or loss of natural resources," while § 107(f)(1) cautions that these damages "shall not be limited by the sums which can be used to restore or replace such resources." On the other hand, § 107(f)(1) also limits recovery by barring it if the resources involved were specifically identified as an "irreversible and irretrievable commitment" of natural resources in an environmental impact statement and the permit or license ultimately issued authorizes this commitment.

Most of the controversy in the area of natural resource damages concerns the appropriate measure of damages. To assist with disputes, § 301(c) directs the Department of Interior to promulgate two kinds of assessment methodologies for measuring natural resources damages: Type A rules "for simplified assessment requiring minimal field observation," and Type B rules "for conducting [more complex] assessments in individual cases to determine the type and extent of short-and long-term injury, destruction or loss." Pursuant to § 107(f)(2)(c), a damage assessment made in accordance with these regulations is entitled to a rebuttable presumption of validity.

The Interior Department's initial "Type B" regulations issued under this authority sparked controversy. They provided that the dollar amounts recoverable would be either restoration/replacement costs, or diminution of use values, whichever was less. These regulations chose to measure "use" values in large part according to *market values*. Only when it or a similar resource was not traded in the market would contingent valuation be acceptable. A *contingent valuation* method uses surveys to measure how much potential users of an area might pay to enhance its environmental quality sufficiently to justify a visit there. Since no limit exists on these values, it is possible that a contingent valuation assessment could calculate natural resources damages at very high levels.

The regulations also largely excluded non-use values in the damages calculation. Such *existence value* seeks to calculate either the value that people place on an environmental improvement for its own sake, or the value that some people place on the fact that other people at another time may enjoy the improvement.

Finding this standard inconsistent with the intent of Congress, the D.C. Circuit in *Ohio v. Dept. of the Interior*,[187] invalidated significant parts of the Type B regulations. Using an example based on the effect of a hazardous substance spill which killed a rookery of fur seals, the *Ohio* court explained the practical problems associated with the "lesser of" rule:

The loss value of the seals . . . would be measured by the market value of the fur seals' pelts (which

187.   880 F.2d 432 (D.C. Cir. 1989).

would be approximately $15 each).... Even if, as likely, that use value turns out to be far less than the cost of restoring the rookery ... , it would nonetheless be the only measure of damages....

The court concluded that Congress "was skeptical of the ability of human beings to measure the true 'value' of a natural resource," and thus intended restoration cost as the basic measure of damages. The revised Type B regulations replaced the "lesser of" rule with a standard based on "restoration, rehabilitation, replacement, and/or acquisition or equivalent." However, because regulations suggest that "natural recovery with minimal management actions" may be sufficient "restoration" under certain conditions, this standard may also be inconsistent with the holding in *Ohio*.

In *Colorado v. U.S. Department of the Interior*,[188] the Type A regulations were also invalidated in part for the same reasons that the *Ohio* case invalidated much of the Type B regulations. The revised Type A regulations were later upheld in *Nat'l Assoc. of Manufacturers v. U.S. Dept. of Interior*.[189]

d. CERCLA Liens. Section 107(*l*)(1) provides that "[a]ll costs and damages for which a person is liable to the United States ... shall constitute a lien in favor of the United States" upon all real property owned by the PRP which is subject to removal or remedial action. The First Circuit, however, declared this provision unconstitutional in

188.   880 F.2d 481 (D.C. Cir. 1989).

189.   134 F.3d 1095 (D.C. Cir. 1998).

Reardon v. United States,[190] based on the fact that the lien could be imposed without prior notice to the property owner and a hearing, thus violating one's rights to procedural due process. Although other courts have not addressed the topic of CERCLA liens, it appears that *Reardon* has voided this section of CERCLA.

E. Defenses and Exclusions

Instead of using defenses applicable to common law tort actions, parties facing CERCLA liability must (1) negate the elements of the plaintiff's case described above (consistency with the NCP, PRP status of defendant, causation, etc.); (2) assert one of the four statutory defenses to CERCLA liability set out in § 107(b); or (3) rely on one of the few non-§ 107(b) defenses that are available. This section focuses on the statutory and non-statutory defenses.

1. *Section 107(b) Defenses*

Section 107(b) sets forth the four key defenses to CERCLA liability, often called the "statutory defenses." In order for a defendant successfully to employ a § 107(b) defense, there must be proof by a preponderance of the evidence that the "damages resulting [from a release]" were "caused solely" by some other source—an "act of God," or an "act of war," or "an act or omission of a third party" with whom the defendant does not have a "contractual

190. 947 F.2d 1509 (1st Cir. 1991).

relationship." The SARA Amendments of 1986 added a definition of "contractual relationship" (§ 101(35)(A)) which was intended to exclude from liability innocent landowners or buyers. Thus, if the defendant contributed in any way to the release or amount of damages incurred, the defense is unavailable. Courts generally construe these defenses narrowly to further the statute's remedial purpose.

a. Act of God. The first statutory defense in an "act of God." Section 107(b)(1) defines an "act of God" as "an unanticipated natural disaster or other natural phenomenon of an exceptional, inevitable, and irresistible character, the effects of which could not have been prevented or avoided by the exercise of due care or foresight." The operative words here are "unanticipated" and "could not have been ... avoided by ... due care." Based on these terms, courts have defeated act of God claims by finding that the defendant should have exercised due care in preparing for the catastrophic but foreseeable event. Even conditions such as unpredictable winds, heavy rains or flood condition, high ocean waves, and hurricanes have not been able to support an act of God defense. CERCLA only permits the defense if the release of the hazardous substance has been caused solely by the act of God. If other factors contribute to the release, such as lack of due care, then the defense must fail.

b. Act of War. The second statutory defense in an "act of war." Although CERCLA does not define this defense, which is found at § 107(b)(2), its scope is quite small. The leading case on point is *United States v. Shell Oil Co.*[191] In this case, the defendants, who manufactured aviation fuel during World War II, had dumped resulting acid sludge wastes into unlined pits. The company asserted the "act of war" defense, arguing that they contaminated the site only because their wartime contract with the government required the production of such large quantities of aviation fuel. Their claim was that spillage and leaks were the inevitable consequences, pursuant to the government contracts, of producing such an enormous amount of the hazardous substance. The court reasoned, however, that an "act of war" required: (1) the use of force by one government against another; or (2) the seizure or capture of property belonging to an enemy nation; or (3) the wartime destruction of property to injure an enemy. None of these scenarios could be found when there was simply a contractual relationship between the United States and the defendant.

c. *Third Party Defenses.* Section 107(b)(3) states that if the release or threatened release was solely caused not by the defendant, but by some other party whose "act or omission" did not occur "in connection with a contractual relationship," then the defendant may escape liability if two other conditions are met: the defendant (1) exercised due care with respect to the hazardous materials concerned, and (2) "took precautions against foreseeable acts or omissions of any such third party."

191. 841 F.Supp. 962 (C.D. Cal. 1993), *aff'd* 294 F.3d 1045 (9th Cir. 2002).

This defense really only applies where a total outsider or unrelated third party disposed of the hazardous wastes on the defendant's property.

In effect, then, the defendant must prove four elements in order to prevail: (1) that the release was cause *solely* by a third party; (2) that third party's act or omission did not occur "in connection with a contractual relationship" with the defendant; (3) that the defendant exercised "due care" with respect to the hazardous substance; and (4) that the defendant "took precautions against foreseeable acts or omissions" of third parties. Establishing all four of these elements is difficult. As such, there are only a handful of cases in which this a third party defense has proved successful.

i. Release Caused Solely by Third Party. In order to satisfy the element requiring that the release be caused solely by a third party, the release must be wholly attributable to a total outsider or unrelated third party. This, however, is the rare case. Typically, the third party has some legal link with the defendant.

ii. Contractual Relationship. Much of the litigation surrounding the "third party defense" has focused on the kinds of legal relationships between defendant and dumper that arguably fall within the "in connection with a contractual relationship" language. Courts have extended this definition to include not only instances in which a contractor does the dumping according to the defendant's instructions, but to virtually any legal relationship between defendant and dumper, no matter how causal or disconnected to waste disposal activities. A leading decision demonstrating the broad definition courts give the term "contractual relationship" is *United States v. Monsanto Co.*[192] Here, the Fourth Circuit established that a lease between a property owner and tenant constituted a "contractual relationship" for purposes of CERCLA liability. The property owner could not use the third party defense to escape liability for the tenant's acts. Courts following this view agree that *any* contractual relationship between the defendant and the dumper is enough to preclude the defendant from raising the third party defense.

Other courts view the "contractual relationship" language more narrowly, requiring some linkage between the release and the contract. The Second Circuit in *Westwood Pharmaceuticals, Inc. v. Nat'l Fuel Gas Dist. Corp.*,[193] looked at the text of § 107(b)(3) more closely, noting that the phrase "in connection with" modifies "contractual relationship." As such, the court concluded that the defendant is only precluded from asserting the defense "if the contract . . . somehow is connected with the handling of hazardous substances" or "if the contract allows the landowner to exert some control over the third party's actions so that the landowner fairly can be held liable for the release." Courts following this holding take the approach that only *certain* contractual relationships between the dum-

192. 858 F.2d 160 (4th Cir. 1988).

193. 964 F.2d 85 (2d Cir. 1992).

per and the defendant will preclude the third party defense.

iii. Exercise of Due Care. The "due care" inquiry tends to focus on whether the defendant had knowledge of the contamination and release, and if so, what steps it took to limit the harm. This element therefore deals with the defendant's conduct *after* discovery of the release. If, upon discovery, the defendant takes no action to correct the problem, to prevent it from worsening, or even fails to warn others of the contamination, the party will be precluded from raising the third party defense. In *Idylwoods Assoc. v. Mader Capital, Inc.,*[194] the court found that the defendant failed to exercise due care where after discovering a release the party did not post warning signs, employ security, or erect a fence around the site. On the other hand, if the defendant did not know of the release, it may be excused from its failure to exercise due care.

iv. Precautions against Foreseeable Acts or Omissions. As with the "due care" element of the third party defense, the "taking precautions" requirement asks if the defendant knew or should have known about the release. Unlike the "due care" element, however, the precautions requirement focuses on the defendant's conduct *before* discovery of the release. Courts tend to look at whether the defendant could and should have taken precautionary steps to prevent the release, as opposed to focusing on the defendant's conduct upon discovery. The critical element here is wheth-

194. 915 F.Supp. 1290 (W.D.N.Y. 1996).

er the waste disposal acts (or omissions preventing disposal) of the third party were foreseeable. If so, the defendant must take precautionary measures to prevent such occurrences. Failure to take such precautions precludes the assertion of this defense.

This element is well illustrated by a pair of cases with similar facts. In both *Westfarm Assoc. v. Washington Suburban Sanitary Comm'n*[195] and *Lincoln Properties, Ltd. v. Higgins,*[196] one or more dry cleaning companies dumped a hazardous substance into sewer pipes, which ultimately leaked the contaminant into the groundwater. The public sewer authority in both instances raised the third party defense. In *Lincoln*, the sewer authority was successful. The Court held that the defendant took reasonable precautions because (1) it was unaware of the dumping by the dry-cleaning companies; (2) a local ordinance prohibited such dumping; and (3) the sewer lines were built and maintained according to industry standards. Conversely, in *Westfarm*, the third party defense failed. The defendant knew that the dry cleaner was dumping a hazardous substance into the sewer pipes, and knew that the pipes contained cracks, but took no reasonable precautions, such as repairing the pipes or prohibiting the discharge of toxic substances into the pipes, against the foreseeable result that a hazardous waste would be released into the sewer.

  d. Innocent Landowner Defense. The "innocent landowner" is an offshoot of the third party de-

195. 66 F.3d 669 (4th Cir. 1995).

196. 823 F.Supp. 1528 (E.D. Cal. 1992).

fense. Prior to 1986, real estate deeds, land contracts, and other instruments transferring title were deemed "contractual relationships" that prevented the use of the third party defense by an unsuspecting buyer of previously contaminated property. SARA changed this result in 1986 by adding § 101(35)(A), which states that purchasers are not in a contractual relationship for the purposes of the third party defense when:

(1) the "facility" on which there is a hazardous substance was acquired *after* disposal of the hazardous substance; and

(2) at the time of the acquisition, the defendant "did not know and had no reason to know that any hazardous substance . . . was disposed of on, in, or at" the newly acquired property.[197]

After meeting the requirements of § 101(35)(A), the "innocent landowner" or "innocent buyer" can then avoid liability if the other third party defense elements, discussed above, are satisfied, including:

(3) release caused solely by someone other than the buyer,[198]

(4) due care, and

(5) adequate precautions taken by the buyer.

197. CERCLA § 101(35)(A)(i). Western Properties Service Corp. v. Shell Oil Co., 358 F.3d 678 (9th Cir. 2004) (where landowner knew about hazardous waste when it bought the property, it was precluded from asserting innocent landowner defense).

198. Dico, Inc. v. Amoco Oil Co., 340 F.3d 525 (8th Cir. 2003) (landowner did not qualify for innocent landowner defense where it released a hazardous substance onto the property).

The essence of this narrow defense is that the buyer had no reason to know that any hazardous substance had contaminated the property. Section 101(35)(B) provides that to establish the "no reason to know" standard requires that "all appropriate inquiry [be made] into the previous ownership and uses of the property consistent with good commercial and customary practice...." This section additionally requires that in determining whether the landowner took "all appropriate inquiry," the court must consider the following factors: (1) the defendant's specialized knowledge or expertise, if any; (2) the relationship of the purchase price to the value of the property if uncontaminated; (3) commonly known or reasonably ascertainable information about the property; (4) the obviousness of the contamination at the property; and (5) the ability to detect such contamination by appropriate inspection. These provisions in effect require the purchaser to undertake some pre-purchase action such as performing an environmental assessment of the property.

Failure to engage in the proper inquiries may preclude a landowner from using this defense. In the easy case of *Foster v. United States*,[199] Foster purchased an industrial property from the government that had been contaminated with several hazardous substances, including lead, mercury, and PCBs. Foster raised the innocent landowner defense, contending that the federal government had contaminated the site. The court denied the de-

199. 922 F.Supp. 642 (D.D.C. 1996).

fense, however, holding that Foster had failed to make "all appropriate inquiry" because: (1) he did not inspect the property prior to purchase; (2) he performed no environmental investigation of the site before purchase; (3) the soil was "visibly" stained with PCB contaminated oil at the time of purchase; (4) he failed to inspect federal records which would have put him on notice of the fact that PCBs where contained on the property; (5) he had expertise in commercial real estate transactions; and (6) comparable properties in the area were valued on the market at five times the purchase price of his site.

Although it is often difficult to determine how much pre-purchase inquiry in necessary, both courts and the EPA have provided some guidance. Judicial interpretation of the legislative history underlying § 101(35) suggests three levels of scrutiny: (1) commercial transactions are held to the strictest standard; (2) private transactions for personal or residential use are afforded more leniency; and (3) inheritances and bequests are given the most leniency.[200] EPA innocent purchaser guidance states that two other important variables are (1) known prior uses of the property (was it used as a residence or waste disposal site?), and (2) the date of purchase (was is bought in 1950 or 1980?).[201]

200. In re Hemingway Transport, Inc., 993 F.2d 915, 933 (1st Cir. 1993); United States v. Pacific Hide & Fur Depot, Inc., 716 F.Supp. 1341 (D. Idaho 1989).

201. EPA Guidance on Landowner Liability (June 6, 1989) at 11–12.

There are two exceptions to the § 101(35)(A)(i) requirement that the purchaser be actually unaware and have "no reason to know" of the presence of hazardous substances. Sections 101(35)(A)(ii)–(iii) except from the definition of "contractual relationship" situations where (1) the defendant is a government entity which acquired the facility through escheat, involuntary transfer, or eminent domain, or (2) the defendant acquired the facility by inheritance or bequest. Parties who fall into one of these two categories will still qualify for the defense.

Under certain circumstances, a defendant who would normally qualify for the innocent landowner defense will lose its protection. Section 101(35)(C) provides that if a non-liable defendant obtains actual knowledge of the release or threat of release during the defendant's ownership, and then sells the facility without disclosing this knowledge, the defendant "shall be treated as liable." This provision forces an obligation of disclosure on innocent buyers.

2. *Other Defenses*

In addition to CERCLA's § 107(b) statutory defenses, a PRP has a number of other statutory and non-statutory defenses it can raise to avoid or minimize liability. These include: statute of limitations, equitable defenses, indemnity or hold-harmless agreements, and constitutional defenses.

a. Statute of Limitations. Section 113(g) establishes the limitations period for bringing a cost recovery claim. The period of time depends on the nature of relief sought. To seek recovery for the cost of a *removal action*, the claim must be filed within three years after "completion of the removal action." To seek recovery for the cost of a *remedial action*, the claim must be filed within six years after "an initiation of physical on-site construction of [a] remedial action"[202]; if remedial action is initiated within 3 years after completion of the removal action, costs incurred in the removal action may also be recovered.[203] It is important to determine whether the clean-up is a removal or remedial action. The general rule is that the investigation and study of clean-ups is "removal" action, even when a party is developing and testing—but not implementing—the contamination source control remedy.[204] "Remedial" actions are response actions conducted in accordance with a Record of Decision (ROD) over an extended period of time.[205] For remedial actions,

202. *See also* California ex rel. Dept. of Toxic v. Neville Chem., 358 F.3d 661 (9th Cir. 2004) (limitations period cannot accrue until after final adoption of remedial action plan).

203. *See also* State of Colorado v. Sunoco, Inc., 337 F.3d 1233 (10th Cir. 2003) (if environmental clean-up response activity occurs after limitations period for cost recovery action has run, cost of that activity may be recovered if initial cost recovery action for site was timely filed and subsequent action is filed no later than three years after cessation of all response activity at site).

204. Kelley ex rel. State of Michigan v. E.I. duPont de Nemours, 786 F.Supp. 1268 (E.D. Mich. 1992), *aff'd*, 17 F.3d 836, 840 (6th Cir. 1994).

205. Advanced Micro Devices, Inc. v. National Semiconductor Corp., 38 F.Supp.2d 802 (N.D. Cal. 1999); United States v. Azko Nobel Coatings, Inc., 990 F.Supp. 897, 904 (E.D. Mich. 1998).

the pertinent statute of limitations question is when "physical on-site construction" occurs. An event often must meet several criteria to be considered the initiation of physical on site construction: (1) there is some "physical" action; (2) that physical action happens on the site; (3) the action is part of the remedial action; (4) the action constitutes "initiation" of the remedial action; and (5) the action plays a critical role in implementation of the permanent remedy.[206]

For response costs incurred after the government obtains a declaratory judgment of liability for future response costs, a second suit to collect such costs must be filed "no later than three years from the date of completion of all response action."[207]

To seek recovery for natural resource damages, § 113(g)(1) requires that a suit be filed within three years of the latter of the following: (a) the "date of discovery of the loss and its connection with the release in question;" or (b) the date upon which regulations are promulgated under § 301(c). The Ninth Circuit has held that the limitations period linked to § 301(c) regulations began on March 20, 1987, and thus ended on March 20, 1990.[208]

b. Equitable Defenses. Most courts read § 107(a) literally when it states that CERCLA liability is "subject only to the defenses" of § 107(b). This

206. *See* State of California v. Hyampom Lumber Co., 903 F.Supp. 1389, 1393–94 (E.D. Cal. 1995).

207. CERCLA § 113(g)(2).

208. California v. Montrose Chem. Corp., 104 F.3d 1507 (9th Cir. 1997).

means that while equitable considerations such as laches, estoppel, unclean hands, and caveat emptor may have a role in a contribution action, they will not be considered in actions to determine whether a party is liable as a PRP in the first place.[209]

c. *Indemnity and Holds Harmless Agreements.* If a person or company wishes to minimize the risk of financial liability in connection with a property sale, it is common to enter into an indemnification or hold harmless agreement with the other party to the transaction. Such risk allocation agreements do not constitute a defense in an EPA enforcement action as against a non-party to the agreement, but they do permit the parties to allocate environmental responsibility among themselves. Section 107(e) recognizes the enforceability of indemnification and hold harmless agreements among responsible parties.

The two issues that arise with respect to such agreements are whether the language of the agreement is broad enough to cover CERCLA liability, and whether a party may contract to indemnify or hold harmless another for environmental liability, even though CERCLA was not in existence at the time of the contracting. An "as is" or "all claims" clause, or a narrowly written clause may not be sufficient to include CERCLA liability.[210] But

209. California ex rel. Dept. of Toxic v. Neville Chem., 358 F.3d 661 (9th Cir. 2004) (the three defenses to CERCLA liability expressly listed in statute are the only defenses available, and thus traditional equitable defenses are unavailable).

210. Fina, Inc. v. ARCO, 200 F.3d 266 (5th Cir. 2000).

CERCLA liability is encompassed by language that evinces a strong intent to cover all liability arising in connection with occupancy or use of the property (*e.g.*, "Party A should indemnify and hold harmless Party B against all claims, actions, demands, losses, or liabilities arising from the use or operation of the land.").[211] A party may also contract with another with respect to allocation of environmental liability even if the contract arose pre-CERCLA, so long as the language is sufficiently broad to suggest an intent to cover all possible liability claims.[212]

d. Constitutional Defenses. In limited circumstances, the constitution may provide a defense to CERCLA actions, but most constitutional challenges have proven unsuccessful. The Eleventh Amendment, for example, has been effectively used as a defense to bar a state's participation where the state has not consented to suit in federal court under CERCLA.[213] Less successful was a challenge to CERCLA under the Commerce Clause. The Eleventh Circuit rejected a claim that the extension of CERCLA liability to clean up an aquifer was prohib-

211. *See* Velsicol Chem. Corp. v. Reilly Indus., 67 F.Supp.2d 893 (E.D. Tenn. 1999).

212. Kerr–McGee Chem. Corp. v. Lefton Iron & Metal Co., 14 F.3d 321, 327 (7th Cir. 1994); E.I. Du Pont de Nemours and Co., Inc. v. United States, 365 F.3d 1367 (Fed. Cir. 2004) (pursuant to a pre-CERCLA indemnification agreement where the government agreed to hold contractor harmless against any loss, expense, or damage "of any kind whatsoever" for construction and operation of World War II ordnance plant, the government was obligated to reimburse contractor for CERCLA costs incurred).

213. *See, e.g.*, Thomas v. FAG Bearings, 50 F.3d 502 (8th Cir. 1995).

ited under this clause.[214] Challenges to CERCLA liability under the Tenth Amendment have also been futile.[215] Another failed constitutional challenge to CERCLA occurred in *United States v. Alcan Aluminum Corp.*,[216] where the Second Circuit concluded that holding a manufacturer jointly and severally liable for clean-up costs did not result in an unconstitutional takings pursuant to the Fifth Amendment, or a deprivation of the company's Fourteenth Amendment rights to due process.

3. *Exclusions from CERCLA Coverage*

CERCLA's coverage is limited by various exclusions found within its text. Many of these exceptions arise in the Act's definitions of key terms. For example, § 101(22)—the definition of "release"—expressly excludes work place contamination, motor vehicle exhaust, and fertilizer application. Section 107 contains three exclusions, each based on the premise that they are covered by another federal environmental statute:

(1) *Application of registered pesticides*—Section 107(i) excludes applications of registered pesticides. This section provides that response costs or damages stemming from the application of a pesticide registered under the Federal Insecticide, Fungicide, and Rodenticide Act (FIFRA) cannot be recovered. The disposal of such a pesticide, however, can trigger CERCLA liability.

214.   United States v. Olin, 107 F.3d 1506 (11th Cir. 1997).

215.   *See, e.g.,* Bolin v. Cessna Aircraft Co., 759 F.Supp. 692 (D. Kan. 1991).

216.   315 F.3d 179 (2d Cir. 2003).

(2) *Federally permitted releases*—Section 107(j) bars the recovery of response costs or damages resulting from a "federally permitted release." Section 101(10) defines this term as a release authorized by a federal permit issued under another statute (*e.g.*, the Clean Air Act or Clean Water Act).

(3) *Releases at closed RCRA-permitted TSD facilities*—Section 107(k) states that owners and operators of RCRA-permitted TSD facilities which are closed pursuant to RCRA are protected from CERCLA liability; any such liability is assumed by a special post-closure liability fund.

F. Cost-Recovery Actions and Apportionment of Liability

CERCLA allows government entities (the Federal Government, the states and Indian Tribes) and private parties to initiate clean-up actions with or without prior EPA approval.

1. Government Cost-Recovery and Enforcement Actions

When a government (federal, state, or tribal) takes the lead in responding to a release or threatened release of a hazardous substance, it may choose among several courses of action. As discussed above, the EPA may investigate and then clean up the contaminated site. In such a case, § 104(a) permits the EPA to spend Superfund money as long as the response actions are consistent with the NCP. After the EPA has incurred response costs, it may recover those costs from PRPs found liable under § 107(a).

In addition to cost recovery under section 107, section 106 authorizes the United States (but not states, tribes, or private parties) to "secure such relief as may be necessary" from a court "as the public interest and equities of a case may require," or to "take other action ... including ... issuing such [administrative] orders as may be necessary to protect public health and welfare and the environment when (a) there may be an imminent and substantial endangerment, (b) because of an actual or threatened release of a hazardous substance." Thus, under § 106 the EPA can compel a responsible person to clean up the contaminated site, either by obtaining a court injunction or by issuing an administrative order.

Section 106 was partly derived from RCRA § 7003, which authorized the federal government to order responsible persons to clean up hazardous waste contamination if an "imminent and substantial endangerment to health or the environment" may occur. But there are important differences between the two sections. RCRA § 7003 has primary applicability to emergencies at active sites; § 106 includes emergency and non-emergency situations at both active and inactive sites. RCRA § 7003 is triggered when there is endangerment to public health or the environment; § 106 also protects "public welfare." RCRA § 7003 requires that the endangerment arise from the handling or storage of solid or hazardous waste; § 106 requires endangerment from a "release or threatened release of a hazardous substance." On the other hand, RCRA § 7003 encompasses the petroleum wastes excluded from CERCLA. Moreover, RCRA § 7003 is enforceable by private parties (and states) through RCRA's more generous citizen suit provision (§ 7002).

Section 106 offers several advantages over the §§ 104/107 approach. First, § 106 clean-ups are financed by the responsible parties, eliminating the need to use scarce Superfund monies. Second, § 106 clean-ups are faster and less expensive than government-led § 104 clean-ups, especially when implemented by an administrative order. Third, whereas remedial action under § 104 is limited to sites on the NPL, the EPA can enforce § 106 clean-ups for sites not listed on the NPL. However, the EPA is hesitant to use § 106 when: (1) the responsible parties lack the financial capacity to cleanup the site; (2) there are many responsible parties; or (3) the response action required cannot with clarity be completely defined in advance.

a. *Judicial Relief.* Although § 106 uses the same terms as § 107 to describe the conditions in which CERCLA liability is triggered—"an actual or threatened release" of a "hazardous substance" from a "facility"—the language of this section is silent on the issues of who is liable and what is the standard of liability. To remedy this problem, courts found congressional intent to incorporate § 107(a) liability standards into § 106(a). As such, the four

PRPs listed in § 107(a)—current owners/operators, past owners/operators at the time of disposal, arrangers, and transporters—are also liable under § 106(a). Furthermore, as with § 107(a), most courts interpret § 106(a) as imposing strict liability.

The elements of § 106 liability include:

- An "imminent and substantial endangerment" to the public health, welfare, or the environment of

- an "actual or threatened release"

- of a "hazardous substance"

- from a "facility" or "vessel"

- which justifies an injunction or order against a § 107(a) PRP.

The last four elements were discussed above; this section focuses solely on the first element.

The key element of proof in section 106 actions is the requirement of "may be an imminent and substantial endangerment to the public health or welfare of the environment." In the leading case of *United States v. Conservation Chemical Co.*,[217] virtually every one of the words in that phrase were broadly construed so as to encompass non-emergency situations when there is only the potential threat of harm. According to the court, the word "imminent" does not require proof that harm will occur "tomorrow," only that factors are present now giving rise to future endangerment. "Substantial" does

217. 619 F.Supp. 162 (W.D. Mo. 1985).

not require quantification of the endangerment, merely reasonable cause for concern that someone or something may be exposed to a risk of harm. "Endangerment" does not require quantitative proof of actual harm, just threatened or potential harm (the language of § 106 is triggered when there "may" be endangerment). The risk that humans might be exposed to hazardous substances which migrated from the site by way of groundwater, surface water, or air is sufficient to trigger § 106. Also, the court stressed that § 106 relief is available when *either* "the public health" *or* "welfare" *or* "the environment" is endangered. The majority of courts have adopted this liberal construction. Some courts, however, still limit the scope of § 106 to emergency situations.

Section 106 is silent on the subject of defenses. Most courts acknowledge that the statutory defenses set forth in § 107(b)—act of God, act of war, third party, and innocent landowner—are impliedly incorporated into § 106(a). Courts, however, disagree on whether equitable defense are also available under § 106 liability. Unlike § 107, § 106 expressly refers to equitable principles. It states that "the public interest and the equities of the case" should be considered when determining relief when the government sues for an injunction. Some courts construe this language to permit traditional equitable defenses (*e.g.*, laches, estoppel, and unclean hands).

ACTIONS UNDER § 106 AND § 107 COMPARED

DIFFERENCES

Authority to bring § 106 action	A § 106 action may be initiated only by the federal Government, not states, *New York v. Shore Realty Corp.*, 759 F.2d 1032, 1049–50 (2d Cir. 1985), not citites, *Mayor and Council v. Klokner & Klockner*, 811 F.Supp. 1039 (D.N.J 1993), and not private parties. *Cadillac Fairview/California, Inc. v. Dow Chemical Co.*, 840 F.2d 691, 697 (9th Cir. 1988). A § 107 action is available to federal and state governments, Indian tribes, and certain private parties.
Who pays?	Under § 106, "responsible" parties pay directly for the clean up.
Speed of clean-up	Section 106 can bring about a clean-up much more quickly, because it avoids the procedural hurdles of § 104.
National Priorities List	A site subject to § 106 need not be on the NPL; remedial action under § 104 is limited to sites on the NPL.
Triggers	Section 107 becomes relevant when there is a release /threatened release that causes the incurrence of response costs; § 106 is triggered when there is also an imminent and substantial endangerment because of a release/threatened release.
Defenses	While equitable defenses are generally unavailable in a § 107 context, they are available under § 106(a), which provides that courts should grant such relief "as the public interest and the equities of the case" require.

SIMILARITIES	
Liable parties	Both §§ 106 and 107 apply to persons qualifying as PRPs under § 107(a).
Standard of Liability	Most courts interpret § 106(a) as imposing the same standard of liability as is applicable for § 107(a), *i.e.*, strict liability. *United States v. Price*, 577 F.Supp. 1103, 1113 (D.N.J. 1983); *United States v. Outboard Marine*, 556 F.Supp. 54 (D. Ill. 1982).
Defenses	Although § 106 does not acknowledge any defenses, § 106(b)(2)(C) & (D) authorize parties who must remediate a site under § 106 to seek reimbursement from the Superfund, provided that they are not otherwise liable for response costs under § 107. One can construe this proviso as making available to § 106 defendants all the statutory defenses available under § 107(b).

b.　Administrative Orders. Section 106(a) permits the President (through the EPA) to "issue such orders as may be necessary to protect public health and welfare and the environment." This administrative mechanism has several advantages over the judicial route. A "unilateral" order is much quicker, and it permits the EPA to control the nature of the remedy imposed. Preenforcement judicial review of these orders is precluded by § 113(h), and according to § 113(j), if a challenge to the order mounted after the clean-up is complete, courts must defer to the order unless it is arbitrary and capricious or illegal.

Administrative orders usually result from one of two scenarios. The EPA may notify the responsible party of its decision to require the clean-up of a site where the site is under the control of the responsible party (*e.g.*, an owner). The responsible party then contacts the EPA, and the two begin to negotiate an order that will be acceptable to both. Based on these negotiations, the EPA issues a § 106 consent order that is binding on the responsible party. Alternatively, the responsible party may choose to resist the order, and not negotiate.[218] In this case, the EPA gathers evidence, compiles an administrative record, and then issues a unilateral order directing the responsible party to remediate the site. The recalcitrant party receives no hearing (only notice and an opportunity to respond in writing), and is denied the right to pre-enforcement judicial review by § 113(h).[219] Although this rule has been attacked several times on due process grounds, courts have consistently upheld its constitutionality. The Second Circuit in *Wagner Seed Co. v. Daggett*,[220] explained the rationale for the ban on preenforcement review: "To introduce the delay of court proceedings at the outset of a cleanup would conflict with the strong congressional policy that directs cleanups to occur prior to a final determina-

---

218. One reason why a responsible party may be inclined to resist an EPA § 106 order is that such order may require the party to clean up all hazardous substances at the site, including those that were not the result of that party's disposal practices. *See* Employers Insurance of Wausau v. Clinton, 848 F.Supp. 1359 (N.D. Ill. 1994).

219. Solid State Circuits, Inc. v. United States EPA, 812 F.2d 383 (8th Cir. 1987); Wagner Seed v. Daggett, 800 F.2d 310 (2d Cir. 1986).

220. 800 F.2d 310 (2d Cir. 1986).

tion of the parties' rights and liabilities under CERCLA."

The EPA encourages liable parties to accept § 106(a) orders by threatening severe monetary penalties for noncompliance. If the responsible party fails "without sufficient cause" to undertake the removal or remedial action mandated by the order, § 107(c)(3) mandates that the party may be liable to the United States for both the resulting response costs and for punitive damages up to three time the response costs. Furthermore, pursuant to § 106(b)(1), a party who ignores an order "without sufficient cause" may also be fined up to $25,000 for each day of noncompliance. However, courts disagree on whether "sufficient cause" is an objective standard requiring the responsible party to have an objectively reasonable basis for believing the order is invalid,[221] or a subjective standard, where the responsible party must show a subjective good faith belief that the order is invalid.[222]

The permissible scope of § 106(a) orders is quite broad; parties may be forced to clean-up waste for which they are not even potentially responsible. In *Employers Insurance of Wausau (EIW) v. Clinton*,[223] the EPA ordered EIW and others to clean up a site contaminated with PCBs and various volatile organic compounds (VOCs). Although EIW was arguably

221. Solid State Circuits v. United States EPA, 812 F.2d 383 (8th Cir. 1987).

222. Aminoil, Inc. v. United States, 646 F.Supp. 294 (C.D. Cal. 1986).

223. 848 F.Supp. 1359 (N.D. Ill. 1994).

a responsible party in connection with the disposal of PCBs, the company was in no way connected with the VOCs. The court, however, rejected this argument, explaining that is it not "inconsistent with the broad goals of the statute" to require a party responsible for a portion of the contamination to clean up the entire area and then seek reimbursement from the government.

2. Settlements and Consent Decrees

CERCLA enforcement is primarily accomplished through settlements negotiated between the EPA and PRPs, not through litigation. Settlements are often memorialized in a consent decree, an order of the court, agreed to by all parties, which sets out in greater or lesser detail the remedy selected and the allocation of liability. There are incentives and disincentives both for the government (EPA) and private parties to avoid litigation. The EPA has only a certain amount of congressionally appropriated enforcement funding, and the Superfund monies are likewise limited. The EPA does not have enough personnel to oversee the work of government-hired clean-up contractors at every NPL site. It is preferable for the EPA to shift the costs of CERCLA compliance to the PRPs, and to have responsible parties (and their contractors) do the clean-up work, after these parties have conceded their liability in a settlement. In accordance with this reasoning, § 122(a) encourages the EPA to enter into settlement agreements with PRPs that are "in the public interest and consistent with the National

Contingency Plan in order to expedite effective remedial actions and minimize litigation."

Likewise, PRPs would rather not face the prospect of extended § 107 litigation or preemptory § 106 orders. Private parties would prefer to reduce the costs they could incur from litigation and liability by entering into a settlement agreement. CERCLA adds a further critical incentive to settlement: pursuant to § 113(f)(2), PRPs who settle are protected against additional, future liability, and may even seek contribution against non-settling PRPs.[224]

The first step toward a final settlement often begins when the EPA determines that a site is contaminated with a hazardous substance. The EPA then collects data on possible levels and sources of contamination and tries to identify the individuals or companies who are PRPs. The next step is then to estimate the cost of remediating the site, and putting together an initial list of PRPs and an assessment of their financial wherewithal. CERCLA provides the EPA with two sources of authority for collecting pertinent information: § 104(e) permits the EPA to seek information about all environmental matters, as well as about "the ability of a person to pay for or perform a clean-up," and § 122(e)(3)(B) gives the EPA power to issue subpoenas in order to implement the settlement provisions of § 122.

It is most often the case that the EPA first notifies the PRPs of their impending liability with a

224. United States v. Colorado & Eastern Railroad Co., 50 F.3d 1530 (10th Cir. 1995).

"general notice" or "104(e) letter." The letter notifies recipients about the site, lists the other identified PRPs, and warns of the potential liability for response costs. The EPA can usually identify between 20 and 100 PRPs for a site, making settlement with each very difficult. As such, the letter states that the EPA prefers to negotiate with all the PRPs as a single entity, and requests that the PRPs create a steering committee whose representative can enter into settlement discussions on behalf of the entire group of PRPs. A number of actions could follow.

The PRPs create subgroups in order to facilitate negotiations with the EPA. There are generally two types of groups at a major site—one or a few "major parties" who contributed most of the hazardous waste, and many "de minimis parties" who contributed only a small volume.

The EPA may try to encourage settlement by preparing a "nonbinding preliminary allocation of responsibility" (NBAR) which provides an estimate of the liability of each PRP.[225]

If the EPA has already incurred response costs, it may use the threat of future § 107 liability to encourage settlement. The EPA can then have the PRPs repay the Superfund according to their financial ability to pay.[226]

225. CERCLA § 122(e)(3).

226. United States v. Bay Area Battery, 895 F.Supp. 1524 (N.D. Fla. 1995).

The EPA may employ the "special notice" procedures set forth in § 122(e). The EPA begins this process by sending the PRPs a "special notice" letter, which includes the names and addresses of all the PRPs, the volume and nature of the substances contributed by each PRP to the site, and a ranking by volume of the substances at the site. The PRPs have the opportunity to make a proposal within 60 days to perform or finance a government cleanup. If settlement is not reached within the 90–120 days, the EPA may perform the work and seek reimbursement in a cost recovery action. During this negotiation-settlement time period, the EPA is prohibited from imposing response actions under § 104(a) and unilateral administrative orders under § 106.

A PRP, or a subgroup of PRPs, may decide not to settle (typically because they believe that the proposed settlement imposes a disproportionate burden). When this happens, the non-settlers face lawsuits from both the EPA (§ 107 liability) and from other settling PRPs (§ 113 contribution). Lawsuits filed by non-settlors challenging the settlement inevitably fail.[227]

a. Major Party Settlements and Consent Decrees. Before the EPA can begin negotiations with the major contributors to a site, it first must cull those that had only a de minimis role. For those parties, CERCLA encourages specialized and flexible "de

227. *See* In re Tutu Water Wells CERCLA Litigation, 326 F.3d 201 (3d Cir. 2003) (upholding approval of consent decree over objections of non-settling parties).

minimis settlements" under § 122(g). The EPA then engages in settlement negotiations with the major parties, in which the ultimate goal is for them to sign a consent decree embodying the proposed settlement terms. The proposed consent judgment is sent to the federal district court and made available for public comment for at least 30 days. If ultimately approved by the court, it is then entered as a final judgment.[228] The trial court must review the proposed settlement to ensure that it is "reasonable, fair and consistent with the purposes of CERCLA."[229] In practice, courts generally uphold such settlements.

The settling parties pay for and/or perform the RI/FS and all remedial activity at the site. Most important, they agree to an allocation of responsibility among themselves. The EPA or a professional facilitator may act as a mediator in order to achieve some consensus, often using the NBAR as a starting point. Allocation is usually based on harm,[230] which is measured primarily by the volume of waste attributable to each PRP.[231]

When the EPA and the consenting parties reach an agreement, CERCLA rewards them with several benefits. The EPA signs a limited "covenant not to

228. CERCLA § 122(d)(1).

229. United States v. Cannons Engineering Corp., 899 F.2d 79 (1st Cir. 1990).

230. United States v. Cannons Engineering Corp., 899 F.2d 79, 87 (1st Cir. 1990).

231. United States v. Union Elec. Co., 934 F.Supp. 324, 329–30 (E.D.M. 1996), *aff'd*, 132 F.3d 422 (8th Cir. 1997).

sue" settling PRPs for future liability regarding the same site, under conditions set forth in § 122(f)(1). The covenant is subject to a "reopener" clause, however, for conditions not known at time of remediation completion or that endanger human health or the environment.[232] The EPA may provide contribution protection to settling PRPs under §§ 113(f)(2) and 122(h)(4), largely immunizing them from contribution actions filed by nonsettling PRPs. Another CERCLA provision, § 122(b)(1), permits the EPA to agree to pay from the Superfund all remediation costs attributable to "orphan shares,"—hazardous substances dumped on the site by unknown or bankrupt parties. These are called "mixed funding" settlements. However, these agreements are rare because the EPA prefers to preserve the use of its limited Superfund monies. As such, usually settling parties bare the cost of their pro rate percentage of the clean-up for the orphan shares.

Non-settlors, on the other hand, not only fail to receive these benefits, but also may be subject to costs sought by the government or other PRPs. CERCLA intends that non-settlors have no contribution rights against settlors regarding matters addressed in the settlement.

When the government reaches a settlement, it does not bear the risk that it settled for too little with one party, because under the Uniform Contribution Among Tortfeasors Act (UCATA), it may

232. CERCLA § 122(f)(6).

still pursue non-settlors for the remainder.[233] If a settlor brings a contribution action against non-settlors, under the Uniform Comparative Fault Act, the non-settlor's liability will only be reduced by the amount of the settlor's equitable share of the obligation, as determined by trial on liability.[234]

b.   De Minimis Settlements. Even before the EPA attempts to negotiate with major parties, it seeks to reach agreement with "de minimus" PRPs, those whose contribution to the site is minimal and for whom joint and several liability would be least fair. Section 122(g) encourages the EPA to engage in prompt "de minimis" settlements with PRPs whose involvement in the site is minimal, based on both the volume and toxicity of the hazardous wastes. Although the statute speaks of minimal contribution both with respect to quantity and toxicity,[235] the courts have generally permitted volume to be the sole determinant.[236]

Although the line between de minimis and non-de minimis is determined on a site-by-site basis, the rule-of-thumb is that any PRP who contributed less than 1% of total volume is a de minimis party.

233.   United States v. Cannons Engineering Corp., 899 F.2d 79, 92 (1st Cir. 1990) (when a party settles with the government, the non-settling party's liability is reduced only by the amount of the settlement).

234.   United States v. GenCorp, 935 F.Supp. 928, 932–35 (N.D. Ohio 1996); United States v. SCA Services of Indiana, 827 F.Supp. 526, 533–36 (N.D. Ind. 1993).

235.   CERCLA § 122(g)(1)(13).

236.   United States v. Cannons Engineering Corp., 899 F.2d 79, 88 (1st Cir. 1990).

Thus, any PRP who contributed 200 or fewer barrels to a 20,000 barrel site would probably be eligible for a de minimis settlement. However, the cutoff point has ranged from 0.7% to 10% of the total volume. In addition, a PRP will not qualify for a de minimis settlement unless its wastes are not significantly more toxic or hazardous than other substances found at the site.

There are several advantages to a de minimis settlement. As with major party settlements, de minimis settlements provide settling parties with government covenants not to sue,[237] and contribution protection from potential suits by other PRPs. [238] Unlike major party settlements, de minimis settlements, do *not* contain reopener clauses allowing the EPA to pursue settlors if conditions are discovered that were unknown at the time of settlement, giving them true finality on the matter. De minimis settlements also reduce the PRP's attorneys' fees and transaction costs, because such settlements are completed early in the negotiation process and can be effected administratively, without the need for entry as a consent decree.

There are certain risks for the EPA, however, for which the PRPs must pay. Risks occur because (1) the future response action has not been chosen; (2) the ultimate cost of remediation is uncertain; and (3) the solvency of remaining PRPs is unclear. To avoid any problems for the EPA resulting from these uncertainties, the EPA requires three condi-

237. CERCLA §§ 122(f) and (g)(2).

238. *Id.* §§ 113(f)(2) and 122(g)(4), and (h)(4).

tions to be met before it agrees to settlement. First, PRPs must provide the EPA will all information relevant to the site, as well as an assurance that they will be cooperative with respect to all response activities at the site, whether carried out by the EPA or other PRPs. Second, the EPA requires that the settlors pay an amount equal to their share of the clean-up costs. Third, in exchange for the ability to settle without normal reopeners, the EPA demands a "premium" payment in addition to the pro rata s

    c.   De Micromis Settlements. A de micromis settlement is a subcategory of the de minimis settlement discussed above. To qualify, a party's contribution to the hazardous waste at the contaminated site must be extraordinarily minor in terms of both volume and toxicity; the party must be responsible for less than 0.001% by volume of the waste. The de micromis settlement is a deal much like the de minimus settlement, except that the EPA normally does not demand a "premium" payment as part of the settlement amount. The de micromis settlor need only pay its anticipated share of the clean-up cost. For example, if the clean-up costs were $10 million, the party with a .001% share will pay only $100.

    d.   Brownfields. "Brownfields," as defined by the EPA, are "abandoned, idled, or under used industrial and commercial sites where expansion or redevelopment is complicated by real or perceived environmental contamination that can add cost, time or

uncertainty to a redevelopment project." Brownfields are often not on the NPL because they are
numerous and often not the most hazardous sites.
However, there are an estimated 400,000 contaminated brownfield sites in the United States that
could cost as much as $650 billion to clean up. But
because of CERCLA's strict, joint and several, and
retroactive liability scheme, potential developers of
these properties are reluctant to purchase them out
of fear that they will be subject to clean-up costs. As
a result, developers go to rural suburban sites
("greenfields") where there has been no contamination and no risk of CERCLA liability, while contaminated sites in urban areas sit idle and undeveloped.
In response to this unintended side-effect of CERC-
LA, in 1995, the EPA reformed CERCLA to encourage brownfields' redevelopment. This reform agen-
da has seven components:

1. *Landowners*—The EPA encourages greater
use of "comfort letters," which assure owners that
their properties will not be targets of CERCLA
enforcement actions if the owners engage in voluntary clean-ups.

2. *Prospective Purchasers*—The EPA uses "prospective purchaser agreements" that provide similar assurances to potential buyers of brownfields if
the purchaser agrees to perform a specified portion
of the clean-up.

3. *Coordination with States*—The brownfields
initiative encourages the EPA to work with states
and localities to clarify liability of prospective pur-

chasers, lenders, and property owners, and to coordinate federal-state-local enforcement priorities so
that brownfields redevelopment can take place.
Some EPA regions have entered into Memoran-
dums of Understanding (MOUs) with state environmental agencies. Under these MOUs, the EPA
promises not to take enforcement action at sites
where private parties have conducted clean-ups under the state's direction. In addition, most states
have adopted their own programs of liability protection for brownfields redevelopers.

4. *Delisting*—In order to remove the stigma of
being listed on the CERCLIS master inventory of
potential NPL sites, the EPA has delisted nearly
30,000 brownfields sites. A delisting confirms that
no further remedial action is planned at these sites.

5. *Future Land Use*—In order to expedite remedy selection for sites on the NPL, the EPA has
issued a directive permitting future land uses to be
considered when deciding upon appropriate exposure scenarios for the risk assessment of the site.

6. *Grants*—The EPA has agreed to fund economic redevelopment projects at brownfields sites.
Initially, it provided cities and states with grants of
up to $200,000 for brownfields pilot projects. In
1997, the Clinton Administration announced a
Brownfields National Partnership program that included $300 million in federal funds for brownfields
clean-ups, as well as the involvement of several
private organizations and federal agencies to redevelop 5,000 brownfields sites. In 2002, President

Bush signed the Small Business Liability Relief and Brownfields Revitalization Act, again increasing funding for brownfields, while making mining properties and petroleum sites, such as gas stations and underground storage tanks, eligible for the funds.[239]

7. *Tax Incentives*—As part of the Taxpayer Relief Act of 1997, Pub. L. No. 105–34, companies developing brownfields sites can deduct their clean-up costs.

3. *Private Cost-Recovery Actions*

When dealing with a Superfund site, there is rarely only one party involved. Typically, multiple parties were involved with the site over a long period of time. In cases where more than one private party has played a role in the contamination of a site, and there has been private expenditure of response costs (voluntary, or as a result of some government action), the party who has expended funds will initiate a cost-recovery action to recover some or all of the costs from other PRPs. Private parties would have incurred such costs in three ways: (1) the party may have complied with an administrative or judicial order (or consent decree) under § 106; (2) the party may have been forced to reimburse the costs of a government led clean-up after the government has brought a cost-recovery action under § 107(a)(4)(A); or (3) the party may have voluntarily cleaned up the site.

239. Laura Paskus, Brownfields Program Makes Cleanup Profitable, High Country News, Dec. 9, 2002, at 11.

CERCLA offers two ways for a private party to begin the cost-recovery process. Section 107(a)(4)(B) provides that a PRP shall be liable for "any other necessary costs or response" that have been "incurred by any other person." This provision is similar (but not identical) to governmental cost recovery under § 107(a)(4)(A) discussed above. Alternatively, section 113(f)(1) authorizes "any person" who is liable or potentially liable under § 107 "to seek contribution from any other person who is [similarly] liable or potentially liable under [§ 107(a)] during or following a civil action under [§§ 106 or 107]." Pursuant to § 122(3)(6), private party cost recovery claims do not need government approval unless the EPA initiated the RI/FS activities.

A private party who is not a PRP may bring a cost-recovery action under § 107(a)(4)(B) if four conditions are met:

(1) plaintiff is a "person,"

(2) defendant caused the plaintiff to incur response costs,

(3) plaintiff incurred "necessary costs of response," and

(4) the costs were "consistent with the national contingency plan."

a. *"Any Other Person"*. Section 107(a)(4)(B) makes a responsible party liable for response costs incurred by "any other person." Section 101(21) defines "person" broadly to include individuals, business organizations, and governmental entities.

Since § 107(a)(4)(A) already provides a cost-recovery action for the United States, states, and Indian tribes, a party able to bring a private cost-recovery action under § 107(a)(4)(B) includes anyone other than these three entities who fits the definition of person under § 101(21). At least one district court has added a further limitation on the class of private parties, by requiring that the plaintiff have a property interest in the contaminated site or is a PRP.[240] In accordance with this ruling, which has not been widely followed, a "good Samaritan" who voluntarily cleaned up a site would be unable to recover.

b. Causation. As discussed above, under CERCLA, a plaintiff need not directly link acts of a PRP to environmental harm. However, the plaintiff must have proof that a defendant caused the plaintiff to incur response costs.

c. "Necessary Costs of Response". Section 107(a)(4)(B) authorizes recovery of "necessary" response costs. To satisfy the "necessary" element, the plaintiff must establish that an actual and real threat to human health or the environment exists prior to initiating a response action.[241] Ordinarily, the plaintiff must plead at least one type of recover-

240. Pennsylvania Urban Develop. Corp. v. Golen, 708 F.Supp. 669 (E.D. Pa. 1989).

241. *See* Syms v. Olin Corp., 408 F.3d 95 (2d Cir. 2005) (physical maintenance including patching roadways, mowing grass, and plowing snow were not recoverable costs where landowner could not demonstrate that such maintenance was undertaken to facilitate clean-up).

able cost as part of its prima facie case under § 107. Additionally, courts have concluded that a response cost is only "necessary" if there is a nexus between the cost and the actual cleanup of the hazardous release.[242]

One important question has been whether attorneys' fees associated with bringing a cost-recovery action qualify as "necessary." In *Key Tronic Corp. v. United States*,[243] the Supreme Court held that CERCLA did not authorize such an award. Nor were non-litigation fees incurred in negotiating a consent decree with the EPA recoverable. The Court concluded that such expenses did not constitute necessary costs of response because the activities primarily served to protect the plaintiff's interests regarding its own liability for clean-up.

d. "Consistent with the National Contingency Plan". CERCLA makes consistency with the NCP a condition to a private cost recovery action. Consistency requires compliance with both procedural rules (*e.g.*, site investigations and public comment opportunities), and substantive requirements (*e.g.*, remedy selection and degree of clean-ups). As discussed above, when a governmental entity seeks cost reimbursement under § 107(a)(4)(A), it can only recover costs "not inconsistent with" the NCP. In actions under § 107(a)(4)(B), private parties can

242. Young v. United States, 394 F.3d 858, 864 (10th Cir. 2005) (where plaintiffs incurred costs by taking preliminary steps aimed at the discovery of hazardous wastes, their cost-recovery claim nevertheless failed because they took no additional action to actually clean up the site).

243. 511 U.S. 809 (1994).

only recover costs they incurred that were "consistent with" the NCP. Although these two standards sound similar, courts agree that the difference in language creates two differing elements that need to be proved in each plaintiff's prima facie case. As such, the PRP-*defendant* in a government led cost recovery action under § 107 bears the burden of showing that the government's costs are "not consistent with" the NCP. On the other hand, private *plaintiffs* seeking cost recovery from other PRPs must establish as an element of their prima facie case, that their incurred costs were "consistent with" the NCP.[244]

This burden can be substantial. Ordinarily, failure to comply with the NCP bars any recovery under a cost recovery action. However, the standard for compliance has been relaxed. Prior to the 1990 NCP, private parties were held to a "strict compliance" standard. Since the revised NCP in 1990, however, the EPA began to require only "substantial compliance" with procedural requirements,[245] and a "CERCLA-quality clean-up" under substantive standards.[246]

244. County Line Investment Co. v. Tinney, 933 F.2d 1508, 1512 (10th Cir. 1991); Tanglewood East Homeowners v. Charles–Thomas, Inc., 849 F.2d 1568, 1574–74 (5th Cir. 1988).

245. *See* 55 Fed. Reg. at 8793 (March 8, 1990) (EPA demands only "substantial compliance" because it recognizes that to provide a list of rigid requirements might defeat cost recovery for meritorious clean-up actions that experienced mere technical failure).

246. 40 C.F.R. § 300(c)(3)(I). *See* Young v. United States, 394 F.3d 858, 865 (10th Cir. 2005) (finding plaintiffs response actions

The issue of "consistency" with the NCP is typically a question of fact. Under that standard, the trial court's determination will be upheld unless clearly erroneous. Alternatively, other courts, including the Ninth Circuit, believe that "consistency" is a "mixed question" of law and fact.[247] Under that standard, the appellate court will review the overall determination *de novo,* but the factual findings of the decision will be upheld unless clearly erroneous.

4. *Cost-Recovery v. Contribution Actions*

The other way for a private party to shift some or all of the costs of a clean-up to other PRPs is through a private *contribution* action. Under § 113(f)(1), which was added by the 1986 SARA amendments, "any person may seek contribution from any other person who is liable or potentially liable under § 107(a) during or following any civil action under § 106 or § 107(a)." This section allows plaintiffs who already are or may be liable for clean-up costs to demand contribution from other PRPs. The requirement that a private party cannot seek contribution unless it is "during of following a civil action under § 106 or § 107(a)" was upheld by the Supreme Court in *Cooper Indus. v. Aviall Services.*[248] In *Cooper Indus.,* upon cleaning up four contaminated sites, Aviall sought contribution from

were inconsistent with the NCP where they failed to incur an expense for any—let alone CERCLA-quality—cleanup).

247. Louisiana–Pacific Corp. v. ASARCO Inc., 24 F.3d 1565 (9th Cir. 1994).

248. 543 U.S. 157, 125 S.Ct. 577 (2004).

Cooper, a PRP, under § 113(f)(1) without first filing a claim under § 107 (and where Cooper had not been compelled by the government to clean up the site under § 106). The Court looked at the natural language of the statute to hold that "contributions may only be sought subject to the specified conditions, namely, 'during or following' a specified civil action."[249]

The Supreme Court additionally has held that PRPs are limited by the provisions in § 113(f) in seeking cost recovery. As the Sixth Circuit explained in *Centerior Service Co. v. Acme Scrap Iron & Metal Corp.*,[250] "cost recovery actions by parties not responsible for site contaminations are joint and several cost recovery actions governed exclusively by § 107(a). Claims by PRPs, however, seeking costs from other PRPs are necessarily actions for contribution, and are therefore governed by ... § 113(f)."[251]

There are many similarities between a private cost recovery action under § 107 and a contribution action under § 113. For instance, the substantive elements and defenses are the same. In both types of recovery actions, liability depends on: (1) the plaintiff's proof that the defendant is a PRP; (2) the plaintiff's proof that there was a release or threat of

249. *Id.* at 583.

250. 153 F.3d 344 (6th Cir. 1998).

251. *See also* Morrison Enterprises v. McShares, 302 F.3d 1127 (10th Cir. 2002) (where plaintiff was a landowner and could not rely on § 107(b) defenses, it was a PRP under CERCLA, and therefore could only proceed with a contribution action under § 113(f)).

release of a hazardous substance from a facility that incurred response costs; and (3) the inability of the PRP-defendant to establish any of the statutory defenses. Additionally, under both, a plaintiff may seek a judicial determination that the defendants are liable in the future for some or all of the clean-up costs. Some courts, including the Fifth Circuit, have even combined the two actions; they test the merits of the claim for cost recovery against § 107, and allocate response costs between the plaintiff and the PRP-defendant under § 113.[252]

However, cost recovery and contribution actions are not identical. First, under § 107, liability is generally joint and several; the burden is on the defendants to prove that the injury is divisible, otherwise each defendant may be liable for the entire cost of clean-up. In theory, in cost recovery actions, a plaintiff could shift all of its response costs onto a defendant. In contrast, in actions seeking contribution under § 113, liability is several only; the PRP is liable for its equitable *share* of all response costs (not for the entire cost). In such an action, the burden is on the plaintiff to establish each defendant's equitable share of the response costs.[253] The plaintiff may only shift to the defendants that portion of its response costs that exceeds its own equitable share, and then only to a particular defendant in the amount of that defendant's pro

252. *See* Amoco Oil Co. v. Borden, Inc., 889 F.2d 664, 672–73 (5th Cir. 1989).

253. Adhesive Research Inc. v. American Inks & Coatings Corp., 931 F.Supp. 1231, 1244 n. 13 (M.D. Pa. 1996).

rata share. Second, the 1986 SARA amendments added a new six year statute of limitations for actions under § 107(a), but a three year period for § 113. Third, while courts have largely rejected non-statutory defenses in cost recovery actions, they sometimes permit equitable defenses, such as laches or unclean hands, in contribution claims.

5. *Apportionment of Liability*

CERCLA § 113(f)(1) provides only very general direction on the issue of apportioning costs among PRPs: "In resolving contribution claims, the court may allocate response costs among liable parties using such equitable factors as the court determines are appropriate." This language gives courts very broad latitude in adopting factors, weighing them, and balancing them among PRPs. Nevertheless, there are several recognized methods available to courts.

The commentary to the Restatement (Second) of Torts § 886A suggests a "pro rata" approach for contribution tortfeasors. Under this methodology, the calculation used by courts for determining a PRP's pro rata share is to take the total clean-up costs and simply divide by the number of present and solvent PRPs found to be jointly and severally liable. This method is favorable because of the ease of calculations, but has serious flaws because it may produce inequitable results if the PRPs have different degrees of responsibility for the status of the site.

Many courts have turned to the "Gore Factors" test, named after a failed amendment to CERCLA proposed by then-Congressman Al Gore:

- the parties' ability to distinguish their contribution;
- the quantity of the hazardous substance;
- the toxicity of the hazardous substance;
- the degree of involvement in generation, transportation, treatment, storage, or disposal of the hazardous substance;
- the degree of care exercised by the parties; and
- the degree of cooperation by the parties with government officials.[254]

Most courts relying on the Gore factors view the "volume" and "toxicity" of the material shipped to the site as the most useful basis for making the allocation decision. And, as between these two factors, volume is easier to measure.

Despite these methods, most courts have assumed that § 113(f)(1) permits "any factor," including "the state of mind of the parties, their economic status, any contracts between them bearing on the subject, any traditional equitable defenses as mitigating factors and any other factors deemed appropriate to balance the equities in the totality if the circumstances."[255] In *United States v. R.W. Mey-*

254. Control Data Corp. v. S.C.S.C. Corp., 53 F.3d 930 (8th Cir. 1995); Kerr–McGee Chemical Corp. v. Lefton Iron & Metal Co., 14 F.3d 321, 326 (7th Cir. 1994).

255. United States v. Davis, 31 F.Supp.2d 45 (D.R.I. 1998). *See also* Cadillac Fairview/California, Inc. v. Dow Chem. Co., 299

er,[256] the Sixth Circuit approved an apportionment decision based not only on the defendant site owner's physical contribution "but also its moral contribution as the owner of the site." Regardless of what factors the trial court uses, the appellate court will only reverse for "abuse of discretion."[257] One other approach used by courts following the Seventh Circuit in *Browning-Ferris Indus. of Illinois v. Ter Maat*,[258] is a pure fault based methodology. Courts allocate responsibility based not on the volume of pollutant, but on the toxicity of the hazardous substance, its harm to the environment, and the cost of cleaning it up. The court commented that "polluters differ in the blameworthiness of the decisions or omissions that led to the pollution, and blameworthiness is relevant to an equitable allocation of joint costs."

F.3d 1019 (9th Cir. 2002) (benefit to manufacturer was properly disregarded as allocation factor); United States v. Consolidation Coal Co., 345 F.3d 409 (6th Cir. 2003) (evidence that generators and transporters knew, or should have known, of presence of hazardous substance in industrial waste was a factor used to determine that that these parties were responsible for 60% of past and future response costs); Kalamazoo River Study Group v. Rockwell Int'l Corp., 355 F.3d 574 (6th Cir. 2004) (allocation of only small portion of investigation costs and no future remediation costs to second PRP was warranted where the PRPs use of hazardous waste was exceedingly minimal, the use had little impact on the site, and that contamination also resulted from other third parties).

256. 932 F.2d 568 (6th Cir. 1991).

257. *Id. See* Goodrich Corp. v. Town of Middlebury, 311 F.3d 154 (2d Cir. 2002) (no abuse of discretion where the court deferred to the special master's allocation recommendations).

258. 195 F.3d 953 (7th Cir. 1999).

Although courts have broad discretion in allocating CERCLA responsibility in contribution claims, these claims are usually settled by the parties themselves. In voluntary apportionment, a party's volumetric share of the hazardous substance contributed to the site is usually the determining factor for apportioning liability.

Oftentimes, the responsible parties will be insolvent, deceased, dissolved, or unable to be found. In such cases, the courts must divide the pro rata shares ("orphan" shares) of these parties among the solvent PRPs.[259] Courts take two approaches to this problem. First, under the traditional rule, PRPs are only liable for their equitable shares. As such, the party seeking contribution bears the risk of loss if a tortfeasor is insolvent.[260] Second, under § 2(d) of the Uniform Comparative Fault Act (UCFA), the court can apportion the orphan shares among all of the responsible, viable parties. Under the UCFA, for an orphan share of an indivisible harm for which joint and several liability was imposed, the solvent parties pick up the orphan shares

259. Sean T. McAllister, Unnecessarily Hesitant Good Samaritans: Conducting Voluntary Cleanups of Inactive and Abandoned Mines Without Incurring Liability, 33 ELR 10245 (Apr. 2003) (discussing the fear faced by "Good Samaritans"—government, non-profit, and corporate entities that seek to remediate abandoned or inactive mines that they do not own or for which they have no current legal responsibility—that they will obtain perpetual liability under CERCLA if their remediation efforts create a "release of a hazardous substance").

260. Restatement (Second) of Torts, § 886A.

in amounts corresponding to the solvent parties' relative equitable shares.[261]

G. Future of CERCLA

The Superfund tax expired in 1995, necessitating that CERCLA be reauthorized by the end of that year. However, Congress failed to reach agreement on reauthorization by 1995, so the tax expired and the Superfund program has depended ever since upon a series of constituting resolutions.[262] This dependence makes the future of CERCLA uncertain. Reauthorization would provide some predictability, but fundamental conflicts over the scope of private liability have paralyzed the legislative process. A main conflict is caused by supporters of industry, who propose to repeal retroactive liability, replace joint and several liability with some proportionate liability standard, and relax CERCLA cleanup standards. When and if reauthorization occurs, reform and amendment is likely to be in the following areas:

(1) *Polluter pays.* Congress must reexamine the "polluter pays" principle in CERCLA. This principle permits the EPA to require parties responsible for contributing to the contamination of a hazardous waste site to pay the costs of cleaning up the site, either initially, or by reimbursing the EPA for

261. *See, e.g.,* Charter Township of Oshtemo v. American Cyanamid Co., 898 F.Supp. 506 (W.D. Mich. 1995).

262. *See* Ann Klee & Ernie Rosenberg, The Moribund State of CERCLA Reauthorization, 13 Natural Resources & Environment 451 (1999).

its costs. Two important consequences of the "polluter pays" principle are that federal Superfund costs have been lowered (by minimizing federal clean-ups), but transaction costs associated with litigating assignment of liability have been increasing. In effect, CERCLA has shifted the transaction costs of deciding "who should pay" to private parties, and away from the federal government. This has occurred because under the statute's liability scheme, the EPA usually determines which private parties are responsible for the contamination of a hazardous waste site and then requires these parties *in gross* to pay for all the clean-up costs. Since CERCLA imposes joint and several liability, responsible parties seek compensation from other parties through contribution litigation, even though a party to such an action may have been only minimally involved in the site's contamination. These parties to a contribution action will vigorously litigate the liability issue, especially if their role has been minimal and their pockets are deep.

Superfund pits one firm against another. This creates an environmental conflict in which several players invest effort to avoid clean-up costs. The rules of the conflict set the underlying incentives that can either increase or decrease the transaction costs. In inquiring about the future of CERCLA, the following facts are worth keeping in mind as one considers methods to reduce the level of transaction costs in Superfund.

First, conflicts often involve fights between unevenly matched firms—a favorite and an underdog.

Economic literature has shown that if the underdog commits to its effort first, transaction costs are less than if the favorite moves first. The reason is that both players find it profitable when the underdog moves first because he reveals his relative lack of strength, thereby, allowing the favorite to respond efficiently. Since the underdog expects the favorite to react in proportion to his effort, he also reduces his effort. Consequently, overall transaction costs are lower, and both players and society gain from having the underdog move first. For Superfund, this implies that rules that allow smaller firms to move first may result in less transaction costs.

Second, the question of potential for reimbursement of legal fees in Superfund conflicts may be an issue. Currently, most major federal environmental laws allow for some reimbursement of private enforcement if the enforcer wins the case. The evidence suggests that private enforcement will increase in importance, and, thus, it is important to understand the efficiency impacts of reimbursement. Private enforcement actions have a very high probability of success if they reach the settlement stage, and success virtually guarantees recovery of attorneys' fees. Transaction costs will be influenced by how the reimbursement rules are defined in a Superfund conflict. If reimbursement is a based on a loser pays system, then either both parties will generate high transaction costs trying to win the case, or neither party will enter into the conflict for fear of spending more than the prize is worth.

The current CERCLA "polluter pays" liability system needs to be reformed to eliminate perverse incentives and high transaction costs. One suggested reform is a two-step approach. First, develop a tax-based system to fund clean-up of existing waste sites. The tax would allow existing hazardous waste sites to be cleaned up using the money generated from the tax, thereby eliminating the excessive transaction costs associated with apportioning clean-up costs. Second, a concurrent liability-based system could be used to address current and future pollution concerns, providing the incentive to reduce the benefits to private parties from releasing hazardous waste.[263]

There are, however, serious downsides to such reforms. A tax scheme would allow genuinely "bad guy" polluters, who caused the hazardous waste problem by recklessness and carelessness, to dilute their share of the financial responsibility for the clean-ups, since others—"good guy" firms or taxpayers generally—who had nothing to do with the contamination would also be liable for the tax. An environmental tax seems especially unlikely as a matter of political reality.

(2) *Clean-up levels.* Clean-ups under CERCLA traditionally have led to achieve a high degree of decontamination. Remedies that are permanent, and that permit virtually any land use on the site,

263. Thomas A. Rhodes and Jason F. Shogren, Current Issues in Superfund Amendment and Reauthorization: How is the Clinton Administration Handling Hazardous Waste?, 8 Duke Envtl. L. Pol'y Forum 245, 254–55 (1998).

have in the past been favored by the EPA. However, this has resulted in some extremely expensive cleanups, and the EPA has been criticized for allocating Superfund money to clean up sites that pose relatively small risks to human health and the environment. Future changes in CERCLA will most likely require the EPA to make a remedy selection based on the likely future land use and to allocate funds and enforcement priorities to those areas that pose the most serious and immediate threats.

(3) *Brownfields.* The Small Business Liability Relief and Brownfields Revitalization and Environmental Restoration Act of 2001 (BRERA) modifies CERCLA to encourage brownfields development by providing federal liability relief to prospective purchasers of brownfields properties and to persons who undertake cleanups of their properties under state law, and by providing funding to both state brownfields programs and to local governments who seek to return brownfields properties to productive use.

The act seeks to accomplish this goal in two ways. First, it creates a funding mechanism to assist state and local government efforts to redevelop specific brownfields sites and to aid the state in administering their voluntary clean-up programs. Next, it provides relief from liability under CERCLA for new purchasers of contaminated properties, property owners and others who conduct clean-ups under voluntary clean-up programs, as well as the owners of properties that are affected by contamination migrating from contiguous sites.

*

TABLE OF CASES

References are to Pages.

___

*

INDEX

References are to pages

ABATEMENT
Underground storage tanks, short-term abatement, 36

ACT OF GOD
CERCLA, statutory defense, 234

ACT OF WAR
CERCLA, statutory defense, 234–235

ADMINISTRATIVE ORDERS
EPA orders under CERCLA, 255–258

APPORTIONMENT
CERCLA, apportionment of liability, 277–280

ARRANGER LIABILITY
Comprehensive Environmental Response, Compensation, and Liability Act (CERCLA), this index

ATTORNEYS' FEES
CERCLA, proposal for reimbursement of legal fees, 283
RCRA, enforcement actions under, 120

BASEL CONVENTION
Transboundary movement of hazardous waste, 91–92

BROWNFIELDS
Comprehensive Environmental Response, Compensation, and Liability Act (CERCLA), this index

BURDEN OF PROOF
CERCLA, causal nexus between release and incurrence of response costs, 221

HAZARDOUS WASTE CLEAN–UP
Comprehensive Environmental Response, Compensation, and Liability Act (CERCLA), this index

HAZARDOUS WASTE DISPOSAL
Historical background, 1–10
Land Disposal Restrictions, this index
Resource Conservation and Recovery Act (RCRA), this index
State hazardous waste programs, 120–126
Underground Storage Tanks, this index

HISTORICAL BACKGROUND
Hazardous waste disposal, 1–10

HOLD HARMLESS AGREEMENTS
CERCLA liability, 246–247

IDENTIFICATION OF HAZARDOUS WASTE
Resource Conservation and Recovery Act (RCRA), this index

INDEMNIFICATION
CERCLA liability, 246–247

INDUSTRIAL WASTE
Resource Conservation and Recovery Act, 26

INJUNCTIONS
Resource Conservation and Recovery Act (RCRA), 115–117

INNOCENT LANDOWNERS
Comprehensive Environmental Response, Compensation, and Liability Act (CERCLA), this index

JOINT AND SEVERAL LIABILITY
CERCLA, 130, 180–182

JUDICIAL REVIEW
Comprehensive Environmental Response, Compensation, and Liability Act (CERCLA), this index

JURISDICTION
Federal jurisdiction, CERCLA limitations, 175–176

LAND CONTROL RESTRICTIONS
Subtitle C, Resource Conservation and Recovery Act (RCRA), 28

LAND DISPOSAL RESTRICTIONS
Resource Conservation and Recovery Act (RCRA), this index

RESOURCE CONSERVATION AND RECOVERY ACT (RCRA)
—Cont'd
Subtitle D. Solid waste, above
Subtitle I. Underground storage tanks, below
Subtitle structure, 24–25
Technology–based regulation, 22
Treatment, storage and disposal facility (TSDF) permits, 95–98
Treatment standards. Land disposal restrictions (LDRs), above
Trigger for corrective action, 99–100
Underground storage tanks (Subtitle I)
    Enforcement powers, 37
    Inventory by states, 36
    Leaking Underground Storage Tank Fund, 35
    Performance standards for new tanks, 35
    Reporting requirements, 36
    Short–term abatement, 36
Universal waste, special standards for, 68–69
Waste categories, 33
Waste management programs
      Generally, 24–37
    Hazardous waste (Subtitle C), 25–28
    Solid waste, nonhazardous (Subtitle D), 28–34
    Underground storage tanks (Subtitle I), 34–37
Waste minimization
    Statutory objective, 17
    Title D, 31

RETROACTIVITY
CERCLA liability, 130, 182–183

RISK ASSESSMENT AND MANAGEMENT
Generally, 7–9

SANITARY LANDFILLS
Federal regulations, 29–30

SECURED CREDITORS
CERCLA liability, secured creditors as potentially responsible
    parties, 186–187

SETTLEMENTS
Comprehensive Environmental Response, Compensation, and Liability Act (CERCLA), this index

SOLID WASTE
Hazardous Waste Disposal, this index
Resource Conservation and Recovery Act (RCRA), this index
Solid Waste Disposal Act of 1965, 13

†